Research and Documentation in the Electronic Age

Third Edition

Research and Documentation in the Electronic Age

Third Edition

Diana Hacker

Prince George's Community College

With research sources by

Barbara Fister

Gustavus Adolphus College

Bedford/St. Martin's   Boston ♦ New York

Acknowledgments

Boston Public Library screen shots. © 1997–2001 Boston Public Library. Reprinted by permission.

Carleton College Library screen shots. Images provided courtesy of Carleton College, Northfield, MN.

Columbia University Libraries. "Library Web" screen shot. © Columbia University Libraries. Reprinted by permission.

Google screen shot. © 2001 Google, Inc. Reprinted by permission.

Chan Lowe. "Yep, got my cell" cartoon. © Tribune Media Services. Inc. All Rights Reserved. Reprinted with permission.

Contents

Introduction

This inexpensive booklet supplements any of Diana Hacker's handbooks. It can be consulted for quick reference as you research and document sources across the curriculum. For advice about writing a research paper, consult *A Writer's Reference, The Bedford Handbook, Rules for Writers*, or *A Pocket Style Manual*, all by Diana Hacker.

Part I of this booklet offers guidelines on posing an appropriate research question and mapping out a search strategy. Part II gives general guidelines on finding and evaluating sources. Part III describes research practices across the curriculum and lists specialized library and Web resources in many disciplines. Part IV includes four documentation styles — MLA, *Chicago*, APA, and CBE — and ends with a list of style manuals. Documentation models are provided for both print and electronic sources. Part V is a glossary of library and Web terms.

This booklet is also available online at <http://www.bedfordstmartins.com/resdoc>.

PART I. RESEARCH QUESTIONS AND SEARCH STRATEGIES

"Research is formalized curiosity," writes novelist and anthropologist Zora Neale Hurston. "It is poking and prying with a purpose." All good research begins with a curious mind — a mind willing to pose challenging questions and then "poke" and "pry" in search of answers.

Your search strategies — whether you search your library's databases or catalog, explore the Web, or gather information in the field — will vary depending on the research questions you have posed.

Posing a research question

Working within the guidelines of your assignment, jot down a few questions that seem worth researching. Here, for example, are some preliminary questions jotted down by students enrolled in a variety of classes in different disciplines.

- Can a government-regulated rating system for television shows curb children's exposure to violent programming?

- Which geological formations are the safest repositories for nuclear waste?

- Will a ban on human cloning threaten important medical research?

- What was Marcus Garvey's contribution to the fight for racial equality?

- How can governments and zoos help preserve China's endangered panda?

- Why was amateur archaeologist Heinrich Schliemann such a controversial figure in his own time?

As you formulate possible questions, make sure that they are appropriate lines of inquiry for a research paper. Choose questions that are narrow (not too broad), challenging (not too bland), and grounded (not too speculative).

Choosing a narrow question

If your initial question is too broad, given the length of the paper you plan to write, look for ways to restrict your focus. Here, for example, is how some students narrowed their initial questions.

TOO BROAD

- What are the hazards of fad diets?
- What causes homelessness?

NARROWER

- What are the hazards of liquid diets?
- How has deinstitutionalization of the mentally ill contributed to the problem of homelessness?

Choosing a challenging question

Your research paper will be more interesting to both you and your audience if you base it on an intellectually challenging line of inquiry. Avoid bland questions that fail to provoke thought or engage readers in a debate.

TOO BLAND

- What is obsessive-compulsive disorder?
- How do lie detectors work?

CHALLENGING

- What treatments for obsessive-compulsive disorder show the most promise?
- How reliable are lie detectors?

You may well need to address a bland question in the course of answering a more challenging one. For example, if you were writing about promising treatments for obsessive-compulsive disorder, you would no doubt answer the question "What is obsessive-compulsive disorder?" at some point in your paper. It would be a mistake, however, to use the bland question as a focus for the whole paper.

Choosing a grounded question

Finally, you will want to make sure that your research question is grounded, not too speculative. Although speculative questions — such as those that address philosophical, ethical, or religious issues — are worth asking and may receive some attention in a research paper, they are inappropriate central questions. The central argument of a research paper should be grounded in facts; it should not be based entirely on beliefs.

TOO SPECULATIVE

- Do medical scientists have the right to experiment on animals?
- What is the difference between a just and an unjust law?

GROUNDED

- How have technical breakthroughs made medical experiments on animals increasingly unnecessary?
- Should we adjust our laws so that penalties for possession of powdered cocaine and crack cocaine are comparable?

Mapping out a search strategy

A search strategy is a systematic plan for tracking down sources. To create a search strategy appropriate for your research question, consult a reference librarian and perhaps take a look at your library's Web site, which will give you an overview of available resources.

Getting help

Reference librarians are information specialists who can save you time by steering you toward relevant and reliable sources. With the help of an expert, you can make the best use of electronic databases, Web search engines, and other reference tools.

When you ask a reference librarian for help, be prepared to answer a number of questions:

- What is your assignment?
- In which academic discipline are you writing?
- What is your tentative research question?
- How long will the paper be?
- How much time can you spend on the project?

It's a good idea to bring a copy of the assignment with you.

In addition to speaking with a reference librarian, you might log on to your library's Web site. Many libraries lead you to a wealth of information through their Web sites. On these sites, you will typically find links to the library's catalog and to a variety of databases and electronic sources. In addition, you may find links to other Web sites selected by librarians for their quality. While you will need to go to the library for some sources, you may be able to do much of your work from any computer that can connect to the campus network.

Many libraries provide reference help. Researchers can communicate with a librarian via the Internet (sometimes in real time) for help locating information. For example, students at Columbia University can go to their library's home page and click on Reference Help (see p. 6). In addition to helping you locate information, an online reference librarian may be able to link you to ask-an-expert services in a variety of subject areas.

Choosing an appropriate search strategy

There is no single search strategy that works for every topic. For some assignments, it may be appropriate to search for information in newspapers, magazines, and Web sites. For others, the best sources might be found in scholarly journals and books and specialized reference works. Still other assignments might ask you to do some field research — conducting interviews or surveys, for example.

When in doubt about the kinds of sources appropriate for your topic, check with your instructor or a reference librarian.

Refining keyword searches in databases and search engines

Although command terms and characters vary among electronic databases and Web search engines, some of the most commonly used functions are listed here.

— Use quotation marks around words that are part of a phrase: "Broadway musicals."

— Use AND to connect words that must appear in a document: Ireland AND peace. Some search engines require a plus sign instead: Ireland + peace.

— Use NOT in front of words that must not appear in a document: Titanic NOT movie. Some search engines require a minus sign (hyphen) instead: Titanic – movie.

— Use OR if only one of the terms must appear in a document: "mountain lion" OR cougar.

— Use an asterisk as a substitute for letters that might vary: "marine biolog*" (to find *marine biology* or *marine biologist,* for example).

— Use parentheses to group a search expression and combine it with another: (cigarettes OR tobacco OR smok*) AND lawsuits.

When full text is not available, the citation will give you enough information to track down an article. You will need to find out if the library owns the periodical in which the article appears and, if so, where it is kept. If the library does not own the periodical, it may be possible to request a photocopy of the article through interlibrary loan service.

How to search a database

To find articles on your topic in a database, you will conduct a keyword search. If the first keyword you try results in no matches, don't give up; experiment with other keywords and perhaps ask a librarian for help. If your keyword search results in too many matches, narrow your search. The most common way to narrow a search is to connect two search terms with AND: *cell phones AND driving* (see screens 1 and 2). This and other strategies for narrowing or broadening a search are included in the chart on page 9.

When to use a print index

If you want to search for articles published before the 1980s, you may need to turn to a print index. For example, if you are looking for a newspaper article written in the 1850s, you might consult the *New York Times Index*, an index that began coverage in 1851. To find older magazine articles, consult the *Readers' Guide to Periodical Literature* or *Poole's Index to Periodical Literature*.

DATABASE SCREEN 1: KEYWORD SEARCH

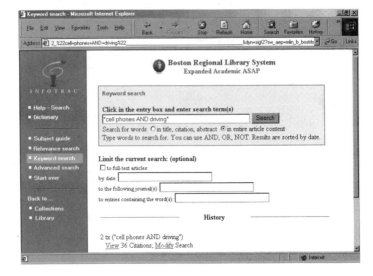

DATABASE SCREEN 2: RESULTS OF A KEYWORD SEARCH

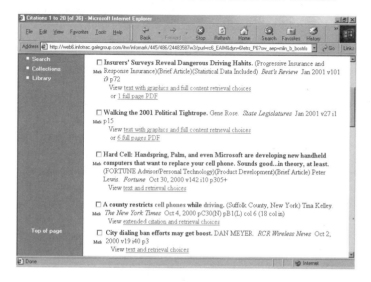

Finding books in the library's catalog

The books your library owns are listed in its computer catalog, along with other resources such as videos. You can search the catalog by author, title, or topic. Most of the time you will want to search by topic, especially at the beginning of a research project. The screens on pages 12 and 13 illustrate a search of a library catalog.

Most catalogs offer two different ways to search by topic:

- A *keyword* (or *word*) search matches words in the titles or subject headings of books. (It does not search the full text, as a periodical database or Web search engine does.)

- A *subject* search matches subject headings, words that librarians have used to describe the subjects of books.

Don't be surprised if your first search finds too few — or far too many — results. If you have too few results, experiment with other search terms or try broader concepts. If that doesn't work, ask a librarian for help or check the *Library of Congress Subject Headings*, a reference work that tells you which terms librarians have used to catalog books on a wide variety of topics. The *Library of Congress Subject Headings* is available in five print volumes usually placed near the catalog; it may also be available electronically through *Classification Plus.*

If a search gives you too many results, you will need to narrow your search. Many catalogs offer a "limit search" option that will help you narrow your topic. To limit your search, experiment with different additional terms to reduce the number of hits you receive. For example, a search for *apes* might turn up more than eighty hits, but a more spe-

COMPUTER CATALOG SCREEN 1: LIST OF BOOKS

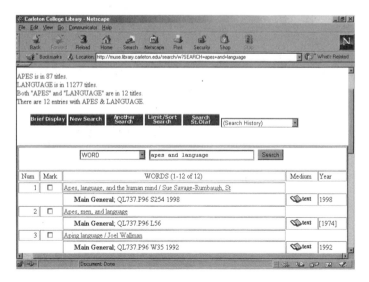

cific search for *apes and language* could significantly limit your results to twelve or fewer, as shown in screen 1.

Once you have narrowed your search to a list of relevant sources, you can display or print the complete record for each source, which indicates its bibliographic information (author, title, publication data) and a call number. Below is an example of a complete record for the first title from the list of books shown in screen 1. The call number, which appears in the horizontal bar, is the book's address on the library shelf. When you're retrieving a book from the shelf, take the time to scan other books in the area since they are likely to be on the same topic.

NOTE: The record for a book lists related subject headings. These headings are a good way to locate other books on your

COMPUTER CATALOG SCREEN 2:
COMPLETE RECORD FOR A BOOK

Author	Savage-Rumbaugh, E. Sue, 1946-	
Title	Apes, language, and the human mind / Sue Savage-Rumbaugh, Stuart G. Shanker, Talbot J. Taylor	
Publisher	New York : Oxford University Press, 1998	

LOCATION	CALL #	STATUS
Main General	QL737.P96 S254 1998	DUE 06-27-01

Descript.	x, 244 p. : ill. ; 24 cm
Subject	Bonobo -- Psychology
	Kanzi (Bonobo)
	Human-animal communication
	Language acquisition
	Neurolinguistics
Alt author	Shanker, Stuart
	Taylor, Talbot J
Bibliog.	Includes bibliographical references (p. 233-239) and index
ISBN	0195109864 (alk. paper)
LCCN	98014600

subject. For example, the record on page 13 lists the term *Human-animal communication* as an alternative to *apes and language*. Clicking on this term would provide additional books on the subject.

Finding a wide variety of sources on the Web

Especially for current topics, the Web is an excellent resource. For example, most government agencies post information on the Web, and federal and state governments use Web sites to communicate with citizens. The sites of many private organizations, such as the American Automobile Association and the Sierra Club, contain useful information about current issues. Even if your subject is not current, you may find the Web useful. Some historical primary sources are posted free on the Web: political speeches, treaties, classic literary texts, and so on.

Although the Web can be a rich source of information, some of which can't be found anywhere else, it lacks quality control. As you no doubt know, anyone can publish on the Web, so you will need to evaluate online sources with special care (see pp. 27–28).

This section describes the following Web resources: search engines, directories, archives, government and news sites, and Web and e-mail forums. For lists of both library and Web resources in a variety of academic disciplines, see Part III.

Search engines

Search engines take your search terms and seek matches among millions of Web pages. Some search engines go into more depth than others, but none can search the entire Web. Often it is a good idea to try more than one search engine, since each searches in its own way.

For current information about search engines, visit *Search Engine Watch* at <http://www.searchenginewatch

.com>. This site classifies search engines, evaluates them, and provides updates on new search features. Following are some popular search engines.

- *AltaVista* <http://www.altavista.com>
- *Ask Jeeves* <http://www.askjeeves.com>
- *Excite* <http://www.excite.com>
- *Google* <http://www.google.com>
- *HotBot* <http://www.hotbot.lycos.com>
- *Lycos* <http://www.lycos.com>
- *Metacrawler* <http://www.metacrawler.com>
- *NorthernLight* <http://www.northernlight.com>
- *Yahoo!* <http://www.yahoo.com>

In using a search engine, focus your search as narrowly as possible to prevent getting an impossible number of matches (or hits). You can sharpen your search by using many of the tips listed in the chart on page 9.

When searching the Web, you may have difficulty restricting the number of hits. For example, typing *cell phones* and *driving* into a search engine, you might retrieve thousands of matches. To narrow your search to a more manageable number, you might try *cell phones while driving* AND *accidents*. If your search still turns up an unmanageable number of hits, you can click on Advanced Search. On the Advanced Search screen, you could restrict your search to government-sponsored sites with URLs ending in .gov (see screen 1). The resulting list will be even briefer and may include promising sources for your paper.

Directories

Unlike search engines, which are powered by software known as *bots*, directories have a human touch. Directories are put together by information specialists who arrange sites by topic: education, health, public issues, and so on. Many search

SEARCH ENGINE SCREEN 1: ADVANCED SEARCH

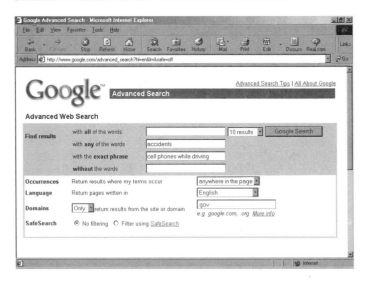

engines, such as *Google* and *Lycos*, offer a directory as an optional means of conducting a search.

Some directories are more selective and therefore more useful for scholarly research than the directories that typically accompany a search engine. For example, the directory for the *Internet Scout Project* was created with a research audience in mind; it includes annotations that are both descriptive and evaluative. The following list includes directories especially useful for scholarly research.

- *ArgusClearinghouse* <http://www.clearinghouse .net>
- *Infomine* <http://infomine.ucr.edu>
- *Internet Scout Project* <http://www.scout.cs.wisc .edu/archives/>

- *Librarian's Index to the Internet*   <http://www.lii .org>
- *World Wide Web Virtual Library*   <http://www.vlib .org>

Archives

Archives contain the texts of poems, books, speeches, political cartoons, and historically significant documents such as the Declaration of Independence and the Emancipation Proclamation. The materials in these sites are usually limited to older works because of copyright laws. The following online archives are impressive collections.

- *American Memory*   <http://memory.loc .gov>
- *Avalon Project*   <http://www.yale .edu/lawweb/ avalon/avalon .htm>
- *Electronic Text Center*   <http://etext.lib .virginia.edu>
- *Eurodocs*   <http://library .byu.edu/~rdh/eurodocs>
- *Internet History Sourcebooks*   <http://www .fordham .edu/halsall/index .html>
- *Online Books Page*   <http://digital. library.upenn.edu/ books/lists.html>

Government and news sites

For current topics, both government and news sites can prove useful. Many government agencies at every level provide online information. Government-maintained sites include resources such as legal texts, facts and statistics, government reports, and searchable reference databases. Here are just a few government sites (notice that the last one will lead you to others).

- *Census Bureau*   <http://www.census.gov>
- *Fedstats*   <http://www.fedstats.gov>
- *Thomas Legislative Information*   <http://thomas.loc .gov>

- *United Nations*   <http://www.un.org>
- *U.S. Federal Government Agencies Directory*   <http://www.lib.lsu.edu/gov/fedgov.html>

NOTE: You can access a state's Web site by putting the two-letter state abbreviation into a standard URL. For example, in the following URL, *ca* represents California: <http://www.state.ca.us>.

Many popular newsletters, magazines, and television networks offer up-to-date information on the Web. These online services often allow nonsubscribers to read current stories for free. Some allow users to log on as guests and search archives without cost, but to read actual articles users typically must pay a fee. The following are some news sites.

- *AJR NewsLink*   <http://ajr.newslink.org>
- *CNN*   <http://www.cnn.com>
- *Kidon Media-Link*   <http://www.kidon.com/media-link/index.html>
- *New York Times*   <http://www.nytimes.com>

Web and e-mail forums

The Web offers ways of communicating with experts and others who have an interest in your topic. You might join an online mailing list, for example, to send and receive e-mail messages relevant to your topic. Or you may wish to search a particular newsgroup's postings. Newsgroups resemble bulletin boards on which messages are posted and connected through "threads" as others respond. To find mailing lists and newsgroups, go to one of the following sites.

- *CataList*   <http://www.lsoft.com/catalist.html>
- *DejaNews*   <http://www.deja.com>
- *Directory of Scholarly and Professional E-Conferences* <http://ntht.com/KOVACS>

- *Liszt*   <http://www.liszt.com>

In addition to mailing lists and newsgroups, you might log on to real-time discussion forums such as MUDs, MOOs, or chats.

NOTE: Be aware that many of the people you contact will not be experts on your topic. Although you are more likely to find serious and worthwhile commentary in moderated mailing lists and scholarly discussion forums than in more free-wheeling newsgroups, it is difficult to guarantee the credibility of anyone you meet online.

Considering other search tools

In addition to articles, books, and Web sources, you may want to consult reference works such as encyclopedias and almanacs. Bibliographies (lists of works written on a topic) and citations in scholarly works are other useful tools.

Reference works

The reference section of the library holds both general and specialized encyclopedias, dictionaries, almanacs, atlases, and biographical references. Some are available in electronic format. Reference works provide information in easily digested nuggets; they often serve as a good overview of your subject. Check with a reference librarian to see which works are most appropriate to your topic.

NOTE: See Part III for descriptions of reference works and other resources likely to be useful in a variety of disciplines.

GENERAL REFERENCE WORKS   General reference works are good places to check facts and get basic information. Here are a few frequently used general references that you might want to turn to.

- *Encyclopedia Americana*
- *The New Encyclopaedia Britannica*
- *The Oxford English Dictionary*
- *World Almanac Book of Facts*
- *National Geographic Atlas of the World*
- *Webster's New Biographical Dictionary*

NOTE: Although general encyclopedias are often a good place to find background about your topic, you should rarely use them in your final paper. Many instructors expect you to rely on more specialized sources.

SPECIALIZED REFERENCE WORKS   Specialized reference works often go into a topic in depth, sometimes in the form of articles written by leading authorities. Many specialized works are available: *Encyclopedia of the Environment, Anchor Bible Dictionary, Almanac of American Politics, The Historical and Cultural Atlas of African Americans, Contemporary Artists*, and so on. Check with a reference librarian to see which works are available in your library.

Bibliographies and scholarly citations

Bibliographies are lists of works written on a particular topic. They include enough information about each work (author's name, title, and publication data) so that you can locate the book or article. Many bibliographies are annotated: They contain abstracts giving a brief overview of each work's contents. You can find book-length bibliographies by adding the term *bibliography* to a catalog search. For example, if you typed in the term *"Civil War" AND bibliography*, you could locate a book that listed and described publications about aspects of the Civil War.

Bibliographies in book form are usually housed in the reference collection. A reference librarian can tell you which would be most useful for your topic and perhaps point you to relevant bibliographies on the Web.

As you read scholarly books and articles on your topic, you will encounter citations to other scholarly works. A list of the works the author has cited usually appears at the end of an article or a book. These lists of sources are useful short-cuts: Often the author of the work has done some of your research for you. By scanning through these citations, you can quickly locate additional relevant sources on your topic.

Evaluating sources

With electronic search tools, you can often locate dozens or even hundreds of potential sources for your topic — far more than you will have time to read. Your challenge will be to home in on a reasonable number of quality sources, those truly worthy of your time and attention.

Later, once you have decided on some sources worth consulting, your challenge will be to read them with an open mind and a critical eye.

Select sources worth your attention

The previous sections showed you how to restrict the number of hits that come up in the library's book catalog, in databases, and in search engines. This section shows you how to scan through the lists of hits looking for those that seem most promising. It also gives you tips on previewing possible sources — without actually reading them — to see whether they are likely to live up to your expectations.

SCANNING LISTS OF HITS   As you scan through a list of hits, be alert for any clues indicating whether a source might be useful for your purposes. You will need to use somewhat different scanning strategies when looking at lists of hits from a book catalog, a database, or a Web search engine.

Book catalogs   The library's book catalog will usually give you a fairly short list of hits (see p. 12 for an example). A book's title and date of publication will often be your first clues about whether the book is worth consulting. If a title looks interesting, you can click on it for further information: its subject matter and its length, for example.

Databases   Most databases, such as *ProQuest* and *Lexis-Nexis,* list at least the following information, which can help you decide if a source is relevant, current, scholarly enough, and neither too short nor too long for your purposes.

- Title and brief description [How relevant?]
- Date [How current?]
- Name of periodical [How scholarly?]
- Length [How extensive in coverage?]

Web search engines   Anyone can publish on the Web, and unreliable sites often masquerade as legitimate sources of information. As you scan through a list of hits, look for the following clues about the probable relevance, currency, and reliability of a site — but be prepared to be disappointed, as the clues are by no means foolproof.

- Title, keywords, and lead-in text [How relevant?]
- A date [How current?]
- An indication of the site's sponsor or purpose [How reliable?]
- The URL, especially the domain name [How relevant? How reliable?]

Previewing sources   Once you have decided that a source looks promising, preview it quickly to see whether it lives up to its promise. If you can reject irrelevant or unreliable sources before actually reading them, you will save yourself time. Techniques for previewing a book or an article are relatively simple; strategies for investigating the likely worth of a Web site are more complicated.

Previewing a book   As you preview a book, keep in mind that even if the entire book is not worth your time, parts may prove useful. As you preview a book, try any or all of the following techniques.

- Glance through the table of contents, keeping your research question in mind.
- Skim the preface in search of a statement of the author's purposes.
- Using the index, look up a few words related to your topic.
- If a chapter looks useful, read its opening and closing paragraphs and skim any headings.
- Consider the author's style and approach. Does the style suggest enough intellectual depth — or is the book too specialized for your purposes? Does the author present ideas in an unbiased way?

Previewing an article   As with books, the techniques for previewing an article are fairly straightforward. Here are a few strategies for previewing an article.

- Consider the publication in which the article is printed. Is it a scholarly journal? A popular magazine? A newspaper with a national reputation?
- For a magazine or journal article, look for an abstract or a statement of purpose at the beginning; also look for a summary at the end.
- For a newspaper article, focus on the headline and the opening, known as the *lead.*
- Skim any headings and take a look at any visuals — charts, graphs, diagrams, or illustrations — that might indicate the article's focus and scope.

Previewing a Web site It is a fairly quick and easy job to track down numerous potentially useful sources on the Web, but evaluating those sources can require some detective work. Web sites can be put up by anyone, and their creators and purposes are not always readily apparent. In addition, there are no set standards for the design of Web sites, so you may need to do a fair amount of clicking and scrolling before locating clues about a site's reliability.

As you preview a Web site, check for relevance, reliability, and currency.

- Browse the home page. Do its contents and links seem relevant to your research question? What is the site trying to do: Sell a product? Promote an idea? Inform the public? Is the site's purpose consistent with your research?

- Look for the name of an author or Webmaster, and if possible assess his or her credibility. Often a site's author is named at the end of the home page. If you have landed on an internal page of the site and no author is evident, try linking to the home page.

- Check for a sponsor name, and consider possible motives the organization might have in sponsoring the site. Is the group likely to look at one side of an issue only?

- Find out when the site was created or last updated. Is it current enough for your purposes?

NOTE: If a site gives very little information about its creators or sponsors, be suspicious. Do not rely on such sites when conducting academic research.

Read with an open mind and a critical eye

As you begin reading the sources you have chosen, keep an open mind. Do not let your personal beliefs prevent you from listening to new ideas and opposing viewpoints. Your research question — not a snap judgment about the question — should guide your reading.

When you read critically, you are not necessarily judging an author's work harshly; you are simply examining its assumptions, assessing its evidence, and weighing its conclusions.

DISTINGUISHING BETWEEN PRIMARY AND SECONDARY RESOURCES   As you begin assessing evidence in a text, consider whether you are reading a primary or a secondary source. Primary sources are original documents such as letters, diaries, legislative bills, laboratory studies, field research reports, and eyewitness accounts. Secondary sources are commentaries on primary sources.

Although a primary source is not necessarily more reliable than a secondary source, it has the advantage of being a firsthand account. Naturally, you can better evaluate what a secondary source says if you have first read any primary sources it discusses.

BEING ALERT FOR SIGNS OF BIAS   Both in print and online, some sources are more objective than others. If you were exploring the conspiracy theories surrounding John F. Kennedy's assassination, for example, you wouldn't look to a supermarket tabloid, such as the National Enquirer, for answers. Even publications that are considered reputable can be editorially biased. For example, USA Today, National Review, and Ms. are all credible sources, but they are also likely to interpret events quite differently from one another. If you are uncertain about a periodical's special interests, check Magazines for Libraries. To check the reputation of a book, consult Book Review Digest. A reference librarian can help you locate these resources.

Like publishers, some authors are more objective than others. No authors are altogether objective, of course, since they are human beings with their own life experiences, val-

Evaluating all sources

CHECKING FOR SIGNS OF BIAS

— Does the author or publisher have political leanings or religious views that could affect objectivity?

— Is the author or publisher associated with a special-interest group, such as Greenpeace or the National Rifle Association, that might see only one side of an issue?

— How fairly does the author treat opposing views?

— Does the author's language show signs of bias?

ASSESSING AN ARGUMENT

— What is the author's central claim or thesis?

— How does the author support this claim — with relevant and sufficient evidence or with just a few anecdotes or emotional examples?

— Are statistics accurate? Have they been used fairly? (It is possible to "lie" with statistics by using them selectively or by omitting mathematical details.)

— Are any of the author's assumptions questionable?

— Does the author consider opposing arguments and refute them persuasively?

— Does the author fall prey to any logical fallacies?

ues, and beliefs. But if you have reason to believe that an author is particularly biased, you will want to assess his or her arguments with special care. For a list of questions worth asking, see the chart above.

ASSESSING THE AUTHOR'S ARGUMENT   In nearly all subjects worth writing about, there is some element of argument, so don't be surprised to encounter experts who disagree. When you find areas of disagreement, you will want to read your source's arguments with special care, testing them with your own critical intelligence. Questions such as those in the chart on page 26 can help you weigh the strengths and weaknesses of each author's argument.

Assess Web sources with special care

As you have no doubt discovered, Web sources can be deceptive. Sophisticated-looking sites can be full of dubious information, and the identities of those who created a site are often hidden, along with their motives for having created it. Even hate sites may be cleverly disguised to look legitimate. In contrast, sites with reliable information can stand up to careful scrutiny. For a checklist on evaluating Web sources, see below.

Evaluating Web sources

CAUTION: If the sponsorship and the authorship of a site are both unclear, be extremely suspicious of the site.

AUTHORSHIP

— Is there an author? You may need to do some clicking and scrolling to find the author's name. If you are on an internal page of a site, for example, you may need to go to the home page or click on an "about this site" link to learn the name of the author.

(continued on page 28)

Evaluating Web sources (continued)

— If there is an author, can you tell whether he or she is knowledgeable and credible? When the author's qualifications aren't listed on the site itself, look for links to a home page, which may provide evidence of the author's interests and expertise.

SPONSORSHIP

— Who, if anyone, sponsors the site? The sponsor of a site is often named and described on the home page.

— What does the domain name tell you? The domain name often specifies the type of group hosting the site: commercial (.com), educational (.edu), nonprofit (.org), governmental (.gov), military (.mil), or network (.net).

PURPOSE AND AUDIENCE

— Why was the site created: To argue a position? To sell a product? To inform readers?

— Who is the site's intended audience? If you do not fit the audience profile, is information on the site still relevant to your topic?

CURRENCY

— How current is the site? Check for the date of publication or the latest update.

— How current are the site's links? If many of the links no longer work, the site may be too dated for your purposes.

PART III. SPECIALIZED LIBRARY AND WEB RESOURCES

Researching in the Humanities

Research in the humanities generally involves interpretation of a text or a work of art within a historical and cultural context, frequently bringing to bear a particular type of analysis and often relying on establishing connections, attributing significance, and exploring contradictions or ambiguities. Scholars in the humanities typically use library resources in at least three ways:

- to obtain primary sources to be interpreted or analyzed
- to find secondary sources to put primary sources in a critical context
- to seek answers to specific questions that arise during research

Research in the humanities is often interdisciplinary, crossing boundaries between literature and history, philosophy and art, or music and religion. It also resists categorization and uses terminology that is less solid and agreed upon than in other fields. Researchers in the humanities are more likely to draw research material from texts and artifacts than from original data gathering and experimentation. Because of this they must be prepared to be

- flexible, both in search terminology and search strategy
- tolerant of multiple perspectives on the same object of study

- aware of the usefulness of citations given in texts that may provide leads to other materials and clarify connections among cited works

- willing to return to the library as new questions arise

Fortunately, there are many fine research tools to help. Those listed here are not available in every library, but they give you some ideas to start with. Always bear in mind, too, that librarians are a particularly user-friendly research tool. Plan to ask a librarian for recommended resources as you begin your research, and use the librarian's expertise as your research progresses and your questions grow more specific.

General resources in the humanities

DATABASES AND INDEXES IN THE HUMANITIES

Arts and Humanities Citation Index. Philadelphia: Institute for Scientific Information, 1978–. • An interdisciplinary index to articles in more than 1,000 periodicals that is searchable by author, keyword, and citation index. Providing citations and descriptive abstracts (no full-text articles), this index is available in print and electronic formats. It may be available as *AHSearch* or as part of the *Web of Science.*

Humanities Index. New York: Wilson, 1974–. • An interdisciplinary index to the most prominent English-language journals in the humanities, including art, music, history, and literature. Searchable by author or subject, the index includes many cross-references and subheadings that break large topics into components. This index provides citations only (no abstracts or full-text articles). It is available in print and electronic formats.

WEB RESOURCES IN THE HUMANITIES

Electronic Text Center, University of Virginia. <http:// etext.lib.virginia.edu> • A vast collection of electronic texts, in twelve languages. It is possible to search hundreds of texts at once by keyword and to download them to your computer. The site includes links to other electronic text collections on the Web. (Note that some texts are available only to University of Virginia students and staff.)

The Voice of the Shuttle: Web Page for Humanities Research. <http://vos.ucsb.edu>   •   A wide-ranging index to sites of interest to researchers in humanities disciplines: art, literature, philosophy, religion, and culture studies, with links to higher education and publishing sites. The site is maintained by Alan Liu, professor of English at the University of California, Santa Barbara.

REFERENCE BOOKS IN THE HUMANITIES

Dictionary of the History of Ideas: Studies of Selected Pivotal Ideas. Ed. Philip P. Wiener. 4 vols. New York: Scribner, 1973–74.   •   Covers topics in intellectual history, with lengthy, scholarly discussion of important ideas, primarily Western. It includes citations and some full texts of articles. Though dated, this work can provide solid overviews of key concepts. It is available in both print and electronic editions.

The Humanities: A Selective Guide to Information Sources. By Ron Blazek and Elizabeth Aversa. 4th ed. Englewood, Colo.: Libraries Unlimited, 2000.   •   A print guide to research tools in the humanities, including the arts, philosophy, religion, and language and literature. Critical annotations are provided for each source listed.

Art and architecture

DATABASES AND INDEXES IN ART AND ARCHITECTURE

ARTBibliographies Modern. Santa Barbara: ABC-Clio, 1974–.   •   An electronic index containing citations and descriptive abstracts of articles, books, catalogs, and essays on modern art (no full-text articles).

Art Index. New York: Wilson, 1930–.   •   An author and subject index to more than 400 art periodicals, covering all periods and media of art, including film and photography. The work is particularly helpful for locating reproductions in periodicals, for research studies, and for news of sales and exhibitions. The index offers citations only (no abstracts or full-text articles). It is available in print and electronic formats.

Bibliography of the History of Art (*BHA*). Santa Monica: John Paul Getty Trust, 1991–. • Comprehensive and up-to-date coverage of art in all periods and countries. Organized by author and subject, this index provides citations and descriptive abstracts of more than 4,000 books, articles, dissertations, and exhibit catalogs arranged in broad thematic categories (no full-text articles). Current volumes are available only in electronic format.

WEB RESOURCES IN ART AND ARCHITECTURE

The Art History Research Center. <http://www-fofa.concordia.ca/arth/AHRC/index.htm> • An index to international art history Web sites. Listings include newsgroups, mailing lists, library catalogs, article indexes, information on universities, and advice on citing resources, with links to libraries, biographical services, and other useful resources. The site is maintained by the Department of Art History at Concordia University, Montreal.

Art History Resources on the Web. <http://witcombe.bcpw. sbc.edu/ARTHLinks.html> • Provides links to hundreds of sites related to all periods of art history from prehistoric to twentieth century. Coverage includes non-European art, research resources in art history, museums and galleries, and three chronological categories for Western art. Many links are to artists' pages that provide biographical information and images. The site is maintained by Chris Witcombe, professor of art history at Sweet Briar College, Virginia.

INFOMINE. Scholarly Internet Resource Collections: Visual and Performing Arts. <http://infomine.ucr.edu/search/artssearch.phtml> • A catalog of select, annotated sites useful for research in art, literature, music, dance, theater, film, and photography. A search engine allows users to browse by title, keyword, or subject. The site was developed and is maintained by the library of the University of California, Riverside.

The Mother of All Art History Pages. <http://www-personal.umich .edu/~amidkiff/mother> • Provides links to a variety of sites related to art history, including research resources, image collections, museums, and art history departments. The site is hosted by the University of Michigan.

The PartheNet: Combined Internet Resources for Students of Art History. <http://home.mtholyoke.edu/~klconner/parthenet.html>

• A well-designed index of links to art history Web sites, organized in chronological order and by geographic region beginning with classical studies and ending with modernism.

World Wide Art Resources. <http://wwar.com>   •   Particularly strong in studio arts and the business side of the art professions.

WWW Virtual Library: Architecture. <http://www.clr.toronto.edu/VIRTUALLIB/arch.html>   •   Covers the history and practice of architecture, with links to a variety of sites of interest to students and practicing architects. Users can search for schools, firms, and jobs; portfolios; publications and software; conferences and mailing lists; and various types of architecture. The site is maintained by the Centre for Landscape Research at the University of Toronto.

WWW Virtual Library: ArchNet. <http://archnet.asu.edu>   •   A comprehensive guide to international archaeological Web pages. Links are organized by geographic regions, academic departments, museums, news, subjects within archaeology, and journals and publications. The site is searchable by keyword. It is hosted by the Archaeological Research Institute at Arizona State University.

WWW Virtual Library: Museums. <http://www.icom.org/vlmp>   •   An enormous directory of online museums and related resources on the Web, including galleries and archives. The online museums are good sources for visual images and basic information about works of art and exhibits. The site is hosted by the International Council of Museums, a nonprofit worldwide network of museum professionals, based in Paris.

REFERENCE BOOKS IN ART AND ARCHITECTURE

Contemporary Artists. Ed. Joanne Cerrito et al. 4th ed. Detroit: Gale Group, 1996.   •   Provides biographies of more than 800 current artists from around the world, including information on their work, lists of their exhibits, and bibliographies of sources for further research.

The Dictionary of Art. Ed. Jane Turner. 34 vols. New York: Grove's Dictionaries, 1996.   •   An exhaustive encyclopedia of world art containing scholarly articles on artists, movements, works, and subjects, with bibliographical references and an index. This work is available in print and electronic editions.

Encyclopedia of Aesthetics. Ed. Michael Kelly. 4 vols. New York: Oxford University Press, 1998. • Includes 600 substantial articles on philosophical concepts relating to art and aesthetics, including overviews of movements, major theorists, national and regional aesthetics, and subjects such as cyberspace, law and art, cultural property, politics and aesthetics, and the canon. Each article is followed by an up-to-date bibliography.

Encyclopedia of World Art. 16 vols. New York: McGraw-Hill, 1959–. • Offers thorough, scholarly articles on artists, movements, media, periods, national traditions, and so on. Each volume has text in the front and a section of plates in the back. There is an index to the entire set, and supplementary volumes present newer information.

Macmillan Encyclopedia of Architects. Ed. Adolf K. Placzek. 4 vols. New York: Free Press; London: Collier Macmillan, 1982. • Profiles more than 2,400 architects from all countries and periods, providing biographical and critical information and, in many cases, a bibliography for further research.

The Oxford Companion to Art. Ed. Harold Osborne. Oxford: Clarendon, 1970. • A handbook that provides articles, some brief and others several pages long, on topics in world art history, including artists, themes, media, and movements.

SPECIAL RESOURCES IN ART AND ARCHITECTURE

Many institutions have slide collections of art objects organized by period, country, or medium. Such collections can provide visual resources for study and presentations. However, many slide collections are maintained by the art department rather than the library and may have restricted circulation. To locate sources for slides, consult Norine Cashman's *Slide Buyer's Guide,* 6th ed. (Englewood, Colo.: Libraries Unlimited, 1990).

Classics

DATABASES AND INDEXES IN CLASSICS

L'Année philologique: bibliographie critique et analytique de l'antiquité Gréco-Latine. Paris: The Société Internationale de Bibliographie

Classique (SIBC), 1924/26–. • The most complete index available for classics, covering books and articles on all aspects of Greek and Latin cultures, including archaeology, literature, and philosophy. The index is international in scope and includes works in all languages. It offers citations only (no abstracts or full texts of articles). *L'Année philologique* is a print index, but it is available electronically as the *Database of Classical Bibliography.*

WEB RESOURCES IN CLASSICS

Argos. <http://argos.evansville.edu> • A search engine geared toward students, teachers, and scholars that searches only the contents of peer-reviewed ancient and medieval sites and the links included in them. The content is reviewed and managed by an editorial board of classics professors at institutions in the United States and abroad.

Classics and Mediterranean Archaeology. <http://rome.classics .lsa.umich.edu> • A searchable list of more than 600 links to resources in classics, with a focus on, but more inclusive than, archaeology. A lengthy table of contents reveals the breadth of this site: from texts, projects, journals, and bibliographies to field reports to newsgroups and mailing lists. The site is sponsored by the Department of Classical Studies at the University of Michigan.

Diotima: Materials for the Study of Women and Gender in the Ancient World. <http://www.stoa.org/diotima> • Includes primary sources from classical texts dealing with women as well as course materials, a searchable bibliography, and links to articles, books, databases, and visual images. The site is maintained by professors at the University of Kentucky and Southwest University, Louisiana.

Electronic Resources for Classicists: The Second Generation. <http:// www.tlg.uci.edu/~tlg/index/resources.html> • Offers a thorough list of sites of interest to classicists, including databases, collections of images, author-specific sites, classics departments, and electronic journals and discussion groups. The site is maintained by a professor at the University of California, Irvine.

The Internet Classics Archive. <http://classics.mit.edu> • An archive of more than 400 classical books, poems, and plays, in English translation, with links to other sites, great books, archaeology, mythology, trivia, and more. The site is hosted by the Massachusetts Institute of Technology.

Internet Resources for Classics. <http://sms-va.com/mdl-indx/
internet.htm> • An exhaustive list of links to Web resources in
the classics. Contents are indexed by topic, with extensive sublists.
Topics include classics, academic projects, organizations, mythology, and music. The site also provides a list of links to classics
search engines.

The Perseus Project. <http://www.perseus.tufts.edu> • A digital
library of resources for students researching the ancient world. Con-
structed and maintained by the Classics Department at Tufts University, this site focuses on ancient Greece and Rome and includes
information on everything from lexicons to images, maps, art, and
ancient texts and translations.

*University of Cambridge, Faculty of Classics: External Gateway to
Humanities Resources.* <http://www.classics.cam.ac.uk/faculty/
links.html> • Lists classics departments worldwide and provides
links to sources in literature, linguistics, history, and philosophy.
The site, hosted by the faculty of classics at the University of Cambridge, is well designed, continually updated, and full of useful links.

REFERENCE BOOKS IN CLASSICS

Ancient Writers: Greece and Rome. Ed. T. James Luce. 2 vols. New
York: Macmillan Library Reference, 1982. Offers lengthy critiques
and overviews of the works of classical writers. Each essay is written by an expert and followed by a selected bibliography of editions,
translations, commentaries, and criticism.

The Cambridge Ancient History. Ed. Alan Bowman et al. 13 vols.
Cambridge: Cambridge University Press, 1923– . • Covers the ancient world chronologically, with chapters written by experts in particular eras. Individual volumes have been revised periodically, and
there is a separate volume of plates for the first two volumes.

Civilization of the Ancient Mediterranean. Ed. Michael Grant and
Rachel Kitzinger. 3 vols. New York: Scribner, 1988. • Provides
lengthy articles on such topics as language and dialects, farming
and animal husbandry, myths and cosmologies, women, and building techniques. Each article is followed by a helpful bibliography.

Illustrated Encyclopaedia of the Classical World. Ed. Michael Avi
Yonah and Israel Shatzman. New York: Harper and Row,

1975. • Provides brief definitions and discussions of classical people, places, institutions, and culture. One of the work's strengths is the number of illustrations accompanying the entries.

Oxford Classical Dictionary. Ed. Simon Hornblower and Anthony Spawforth. 3rd ed. New York: Oxford University Press, 1996. • Provides concise and informative articles on people, places, events, works of art, and figures in mythology.

Oxford Companion to Classical Literature. Ed. M. C. Howatson. 2nd ed. New York: Oxford University Press, 1989. • A handy guide to writers and works from classical times, with concise discussions of the social and cultural context of the literature.

Oxford Encyclopedia of Archaeology in the Near East. Ed. Eric M. Meyers. 5 vols. New York: Oxford University Press, 1997. • Covers archaeological sites, regions, countries, and peoples in the Near East, from prehistoric times through the Crusades. The work also covers specific areas of archaeology, such as ethics and history and underwater archaeology.

The Oxford Guide to Classical Mythology in the Arts, 1300–1990s. Ed. Jane Davidson Reid. 2 vols. New York: Oxford University Press, 1993. • Lists examples of Western art from medieval to modern times that use figures and subjects from classical mythology as themes. Paintings, sculptures, musical compositions, ballets, and literary works are included.

Place-Names in Classical Mythology: Greece. By Robert E. Bell. Santa Barbara: ABC-CLIO, 1989. • Provides descriptions of places referred to in classical mythology and literature. The entries contain many references to literature in which the place is significant.

Princeton Encyclopedia of Classical Sites. Ed. Richard Stillwell et al. Princeton: Princeton University Press, 1976. • Offers descriptions of classical sites in Europe, North Africa, and the Middle East and includes references to relevant classical texts.

Literature and linguistics

DATABASES AND INDEXES IN LITERATURE AND LINGUISTICS

Contemporary Authors. Detroit: Gale Group, 1962–. • A full-text electronic database with bibliographic references for nearly 100,000 influential writers who were active prior to 1960. The database may be offered in your library in conjunction with *Contemporary Literary Criticism Select* and the *Dictionary of Literary Biography* databases. *Contemporary Authors* is also available in print form, with 196 volumes to date.

Contemporary Literary Criticism Select (*CLCS*). Detroit: Gale Group, 1973–. • A full-text electronic database of brief biographies of contemporary authors, with critical essays and excerpts from their work. Citations for original sources are included. The database may be offered at your library in conjunction with the *Dictionary of Literary Biography* and *Contemporary Authors* databases. *CLCS* is a handy place to become familiar with a modern writer's critical reception. It is also available in 146 print volumes to date, titled *Contemporary Literary Criticism*. When using the print volumes, consult the most recent cumulative index, which includes cross-references to other Gale biographical series.

Dictionary of Literary Biography (*DLB*). Detroit: Gale Group, 1978–. • A full-text database of lengthy biographies of authors with some criticism of their works. Though the *DLB* emphasizes American and British literary authors, it offers some coverage of writers from other countries and of journalists and historians. The database may be offered at your library in conjunction with the *Contemporary Authors* and *Contemporary Literary Criticism Select* databases. The *Dictionary of Literary Biography* is also available in print, in 245 volumes to date. The print volumes are arranged thematically, with a cumulative index in the last volume.

MLA International Bibliography of Books and Articles on the Modern Languages and Literatures. New York: Modern Language Association, 1921–. • The most important ongoing bibliographic index for literature and linguistics, by the Modern Language Association (<http://www.mla.org>). Since 1980, the print edition is published annually in two volumes. One volume is a subject index; the other provides citations arranged in four categories (national literatures, linguistics, general literature, and folklore). MLA lists works of all kinds — books, journal articles, articles in books, dissertations — in many languages. The index is also available in electronic format. Like the print edition, it offers citations (no abstracts or full-text articles).

WEB RESOURCES IN LITERATURE AND LINGUISTICS

American and English Literature Internet Resources. <http://library.scsu.ctstateu.edu/litbib.html> • This site, maintained by librarians at Southern Connecticut State University, is organized three main ways: by links to and about e-texts; by links to general literature resources; and by categories that become progressively more specific, moving from genre (poetry, fiction, science fiction, Native American literature) to authors.

Eserver.org. <http://english-www.hss.cmu.edu> • A site previously known as *The English Server*, maintained by graduate students and faculty at the University of Washington. *Eserver* provides many links to literature-related sites and publishes works such as essays and reviews. Its 42 collections offer diverse topics including criticism; cultural theory; gender, race, and Internet studies; and rhetoric. Most writings are shared publicly, but some are available to members only. Mailing lists and discussion groups are accessible, and users can submit their own work for possible inclusion on the site.

Ethnologue: Languages of the World. <http://www.sil.org/ethnologue/ethnologue.html> • A database of information on more than 6,700 languages, including dialects, numbers of speakers, locations, and linguistic affiliation. Users can find out where a language and its related dialects are spoken and where their origins are by clicking on words and word sounds. The site is maintained by SIL International, a nonprofit educational organization.

iLoveLanguages. <http://www.ilovelanguages.com> • A site formerly known as *The Human-Languages Page*. It is a comprehensive guide to language-related Internet resources with more than 2,000 links. Subject areas include languages and literature, institutions, and linguistic resources. They can be accessed in a variety of languages.

Internet Public Library Online Literary Criticism Collection. <http://www.ipl.org/ref/litcrit> • A collection of more than 4,000 links, selected for quality and organized by author, title, nationality, and period. Some links are to subscription databases that may not be available in your library, but most are freely accessible. The *Internet Public Library* (*IPL*) is a public service organization of the School of Information at the University of Michigan.

Linguistics Resources on the Internet. <http://www.sil.org/linguistics/topical.html> • Provides links for every aspect of linguistics, including grammar and syntax, second-language teaching, language rights, and glossaries of key terms. Users can also find information on conferences, computing resources, journals, and newsletters. The site is maintained by SIL International, a nonprofit educational organization.

A Literary Index: Internet Resources in Literature. <http://www.vanderbilt.edu/AnS/english/flackcj/LitIndex.html> • A selective index geared toward students and scholars that includes sections on conducting literary research, archives of e-texts, and information on books and presses, composition rhetoric and writing, and teaching literature. The site is well organized and provides background information on the resources it provides. Maintained by Chris Flack for the Department of English at Vanderbilt University.

Literary Resources on the Net. <http://andromeda.rutgers.edu/~jlynch/Lit> • A large, well-organized index to academic sites in English and American literature. It is organized topically, including sections on women's literature and feminism, ethnicity and nationality, and theory. Most links have brief annotations. The site is maintained by Jack Lynch, assistant professor in the English Department at Rutgers University.

The Online Books Page. <http://digital.library.upenn.edu/books> • Provides links to over 11,000 full-text books and journals in English. Maintained by John Ockerbloom of the University of Pennsylvania, the site is updated daily and offers searches by author, title, and subject as well as special exhibits on women writers, banned books, and prize winners.

Voice of the Shuttle: English Literature Main Page. <http://vos.ucsb.edu/shuttle/english.html> • An enormous, frequently updated site with links to sites in all of the humanities. The page for English literature is comprehensive and current. Users can access links on English and American literature and on specific periods to get information on both the literature and the culture of the period. The site is maintained by Alan Liu, professor of English at the University of California, Santa Barbara.

REFERENCE BOOKS IN LITERATURE AND LINGUISTICS

American Writers. 4 vols. New York: Scribner, 1979–87. With supplements. • Offers essays analyzing the life and work of major American writers, arranged chronologically with an alphabetical index. Scribner publishes a similar series for British, Latin American, and European writers. The work is available in electronic format, titled *Scribner Writers Series on CD-ROM.*

Bloomsbury Guide to Women's Literature. By Claire Buck. Upper Saddle River, New Jersey: Prentice-Hall, 1992. • A thorough compendium of information on women's literature from around the world, from early times to the present. This text provides concise and informative articles and includes lengthy regional surveys at the front of the book. Its coverage of non-Western women writers is particularly good.

Concise Oxford Dictionary of Literary Terms. By Chris Baldick. New York: Oxford University Press, 1990. • Defines and briefly discusses terms used in current critical theory.

Encyclopedia of World Literature in the Twentieth Century. Ed. Leonard Klein. 2nd ed. 5 vols. New York: Frederick Ungar, 1981–93. • Covers twentieth-century authors and movements and provides lengthy surveys of the modern literature of different countries.

International Encyclopedia of Linguistics. Ed. William Bright. 4 vols. New York: Oxford University Press, 1991. • Includes scholarly articles on all aspects of linguistics.

Literary Research Guide: A Guide to Reference Sources for the Study of Literatures in English and Related Topics. By James L. Harner. 3rd ed. New York: Modern Language Association, 1998. • A guide to tools and methods of literary scholarship, emphasizing English literature; includes annotated lists of reference sources.

The Oxford Companion to English Literature. Ed. Margaret Drabble. 5th ed. New York: Oxford University Press, 1985. • Brief descriptions of writers, literary works, schools and movements, and places of literary significance, arranged alphabetically. A number of *Oxford Companions* cover other national literatures and genres.

The Oxford English Dictionary. Ed. J. A. Simpson and E. S. C. Weiner. 2nd ed. 20 vols. Oxford: Clarendon, 1989. With supplements. • An invaluable source for understanding the various meanings of words and their changing definitions. The *OED* provides chronological examples showing how a word has been used throughout history and is unequaled in its depth of coverage. It is available in print and electronic editions.

Music

DATABASES AND INDEXES IN MUSIC

Music Index. Detroit: Information Coordinators, 1949–. • A subject and author index to more than 600 music periodicals. International in scope, it covers both musicology and performance journals. This index offers citations (no abstracts or full-text articles). It is available in print and electronic formats.

RILM Abstracts of Music Literature. New York: RILM, 1967–. • Offers abstracts of over 500 scholarly journal articles, books, dissertations, and other materials in the music field. This index includes citations — most with descriptive abstracts (no full-text articles). It is available in electronic format.

WEB RESOURCES IN MUSIC

The Classical Music Navigator. <http://www.wku.edu/~smithch/music/index2.htm> • Information on over 400 composers, with works listed by musical genre, a geographical roster, and an index of forms and styles. The site was created and is maintained by Charles H. Smith, associate professor of library public services at Western Kentucky University.

DW3: Classical Music Resources. <http://www.lib.duke.edu/music/resources/classical_index.html> • A comprehensive collection of classical music links, including over 2,000 well-organized links to noncommercial sites on composers and national and regional musical traditions; includes its own search engine. This site is maintained by the Duke University Music Library and Media Center.

Performance Practice Encyclopedia. <http://www.performancepractice.com> • An online continuation (from 1998 to the present) of the former print journal *Performance Practice Review* (1988–1997). Organized by topic (composer, instrument, musical term), this resource is geared toward music performance and music history.

The WWW Virtual Library: Music. <http://www.vl-music.com>
• A database of links that allows users to search by type of music
(including rap, rave, swing, and soul) and category (including genres,
instruments, composers, and festivals). A customized list of links is
generated based on the user's criteria. The site also includes a link
to a related site for classical music and is maintained by the *WWW
Virtual Library* <http://www.vlib.org>.

REFERENCE BOOKS IN MUSIC

Baker's Biographical Dictionary of Musicians. By Theodore Baker.
8th ed. New York: Schirmer, 1992.   •   Compact biographies of composers and performers with bibliographies of works by and about
them. This reference is good for a quick overview of a musician and
his or her impact.

Garland Encyclopedia of World Music. 10 vols. In progress. New York:
Garland, 1998–.   •   Covers the music of peoples of the world in
regional volumes that offer regional profiles, the social context of
music, and in-depth information on the musical traditions of specific nations and ethnic groups. The work includes musical examples
in accompanying CDs.

Music Reference and Research Materials. By Vincent Duckles. 5th
ed. rev. New York: Schirmer, 1997.   •   An annotated guide to the
literature of music, including histories, bibliographies, discographies,
and reference books. The book is arranged by type of source, with
subject, title, and author indexes.

New Grove Dictionary of Music and Musicians. Ed. Laura Macy. 2nd
ed. 29 vols. New York: Grove's Dictionaries, 2001.   •   An encyclopedia covering all aspects of music. The articles, written by scholars, are followed by very thorough bibliographies. Several more
specialized Grove encyclopedias cover topics such as jazz, musical
instruments, and opera. It is available in electronic format (by subscription to <www.grovemusic.com>).

New Oxford History of Music. 11 vols. to date. New York: Oxford
University Press, 1957–.   •   An excellent chronological exploration
of all aspects of music. Each volume covers a different musical
period.

The Oxford Dictionary of Music. By Michael Kennedy. 2nd ed. rev.
1994. Oxford: Oxford University Press, 1999.   •   Offers brief iden-

tifications of musical terms and musicians; a handy place to find dates and other facts.

Philosophy

DATABASES AND INDEXES IN PHILOSOPHY

Philosopher's Index. Bowling Green, Ohio: Philosophy Documentation Center, 1967–.   • Annotated index that lists major articles from anthologies and books in the field. Although the index itself does not provide articles, some libraries may offer the *Philosopher's Index* in combination with its periodical databases through searching and linking software (such as *Web SPIRS* and *SilverLink*). If so, full texts of some articles may be available. The index is available in print and electronic formats.

Routledge Encyclopedia of Philosophy Online. New York: Routledge, 1998.   • A full-text database of articles on philosophers and philosophical theories, with emphasis on developments in the past thirty years. It is also available in a print version, edited by Edward Craig and published in 10 volumes.

WEB RESOURCES IN PHILOSOPHY

Ethics Updates. <http://ethics.acusd.edu/index.html>   • Offers current popular and professional information about ethics, including ethical theory, and information on applied ethics topics such as animal rights and environmental ethics. The site is maintained by Lawrence M. Hinman of the University of San Diego.

Guide to Philosophy on the Internet. <http://www.earlham.edu/~peters/philinks.htm>   • A vast compilation of philosophy sites, carefully organized and frequently updated. The site has excellent sections on philosophers and topics in the field. The compiler, Peter Suber, a professor of philosophy at Earlham College, has marked recommended sites that are particularly helpful for accessing information quickly.

Hippias: Limited Area Search of Philosophy on the Internet. <http://hippias.evansville.edu>   • A selective peer-reviewed search engine that focuses exclusively on philosophy-oriented resources. The quality of Hippias is controlled by an editorial board of philosophy professors at a number of universities.

The Internet Encyclopedia of Philosophy. <http://www.utm.edu:80/research/iep> • A growing collection of articles on philosophers and their works as well as articles adapted from public domain sources. The site is edited by James Fieser of the University of Tennessee and Bradley Dowden of California State University, Sacramento. The content is edited by professors, philosophers, and authors who specialize in a given field.

Philosophy in Cyberspace. <http://www-personal.monash.edu.au/~dey/phil> • A cleanly designed list of philosophy sites annotated in detail. Organized into five sections — topics, texts, organizations, discussion forums, and miscellaneous — the site is notable for its selectivity and frequent updates. It is maintained by the Department of Philosophy at Monash University in Australia.

Stanford Encyclopedia of Philosophy. <http://plato.stanford.edu> • Offers authoritative articles that are updated to reflect changes in the field. Entries are kept current by experts in philosophy and reviewed by an editorial board.

REFERENCE BOOKS IN PHILOSOPHY

A Companion to Metaphysics. Ed. Jaegon Kim and Ernest Sosa. Oxford, England, and Cambridge, Mass.: Blackwell, 1995. • An encyclopedia covering philosophers and philosophical concepts in articles that range from one to five pages in length. Each article is followed by a brief bibliography.

Encyclopedia of Applied Ethics. Ed. Ruth Chadwick. 4 vols. San Diego: Academic Press, 1998. • Provides lengthy, scholarly discussions of the ethical aspects of current issues such as affirmative action, animal rights, and genetic screening as well as contemporary views on theories of humanism, hedonism, and utilitarianism.

Encyclopedia of Bioethics. Ed. Warren T. Reich. Rev. ed. 5 vols. New York: Macmillan, 1995. • Covers issues and controversies in bioethics in lengthy, scholarly articles, each accompanied by a current bibliography of key sources.

Encyclopedia of Philosophy. Ed. Paul Edwards. 8 vols. New York: Macmillan, 1967–. With supplement. • Offers articles on movements, concepts, and philosophers. A good starting place for research, this work is both scholarly and accessible.

The Oxford Dictionary of Philosophy. By Simon Blackburn. New York: Oxford University Press, 1994.   •   Offers succinct definitions of terms in philosophy, primarily Western, and biographical entries on individual philosophers.

Religion

DATABASES AND INDEXES IN RELIGION

Religion Index One: Periodicals. Chicago: American Theological Library Association, 1975–.   •   The most important index in the field of religion. Also known as the *ATLA Religion Database*, it provides bibliographic information, journal articles, book reviews, and essay collections from more than 1,000 publications. The index offers citations and bibliographies of each article (no descriptive abstracts or full-text articles). It is available in electronic format.

Religion Index Two: Multi-Author Works. Chicago: American Theological Library Association, 1975–.   •   *Two* indexes articles in essay collections, conference proceedings, and other publications by subject, author, and scriptural reference. Also known as the *ATLA Religion Database*, this index is a very useful companion to *Religion Index One.* It is available in electronic format (as part of the *ATLA Religion Database*).

WEB RESOURCES IN RELIGION

Bible Browser. <http://www.stg.brown.edu/webs/bible_browser /pbeasy.shtml>   •   A sophisticated search engine for the text of the Bible that offers a choice of three translations. It is maintained by the Brown University Scholarly Technology Group.

Boston University School of Theology: Religion and Philosophy Resources on the Internet. <http://www.bu.edu/sth/library /resources.html>   •   A clear, helpful point of entry to religious traditions, with useful links for academic research. The site is organized by major categories including general religion resources, Asian religions, Christianity, Islam, and Judaism.

Christian Classics Ethereal Library. <http://www.ccel.org> • A rich and comprehensive series of key Christian historical texts. Material is organized alphabetically by author, title, and type of text. *CCEL* is an online library at Calvin College.

Judaism and Jewish Resources. <http://shamash.org/trb /judaism.html> • A clearly organized abundance of Internet resources related to almost any aspect of Judaism and its history. The site includes annotated links on a variety of topics and links to museums, libraries, organizations, and centers for study. It is hosted by Shamash: The Jewish Network and Hebrew College, Boston.

Religion, Religions, Religious Studies. <http://www.clas.ufl.edu /users/gthursby/rel> • Offers selective, annotated links to religious traditions, including Afro-European and Asian, contemporary issues, religious studies programs, and research and teaching resources. It is maintained by an associate professor in the religion department at the University of Florida.

Religions and Scriptures. <http://www.wam.umd.edu/~stwright /rel> • Links and resources covering all of the major religions such as Christianity, Judaism, Buddhism, Islam, Jainism, Confucianism, Shintoism, and Baha'i faith. Links to at least one main text for almost all of the traditions can be found under individual categories. Well designed and easy to use, the site is hosted by the University of Maryland.

Sacred and Religious Texts. <http://davidwiley.com/religion .html> • A comprehensive site offering links to sacred texts from around the world. Visitors can link to either Old Testament Apocrypha or New Testament Apocryphal Gospels and visit Zen texts, Taoist texts, and Sikh texts, to name a few. The site is maintained by David Wiley, a professor at Utah State University.

REFERENCE BOOKS IN RELIGION

Anchor Bible Dictionary. Ed. David Noel Freedman et al. 6 vols. New York: Doubleday, 1992. • A definitive encyclopedia covering names, places, and events of the Bible as well as cultural history, social institutions, archaeological sites, and other topics of interest to biblical scholars. This work is available in electronic format as *Anchor Bible Dictionary on CD-ROM.*

Concise Encyclopedia of Islam. By Cyril Glasse. San Francisco: Harper and Row, 1989.   •   Provides definitions of and brief discussions on a wide variety of topics, with supplementary maps, chronology, charts, and bibliography.

Contemporary American Religion. Ed. Wade Clark Roof. 2 vols. New York: Macmillan Reference, 2000.   •   Five hundred articles that address the religious pluralism of the United States and provide contemporary analyses of practices, traditions, and trends.

Encyclopaedia Judaica. 16 vols. Jerusalem: Encyclopaedia Judaica; New York: Macmillan, 1971–72.   •   An excellent source of information on the Jewish culture and religion, offering in-depth, scholarly articles and ample illustrations. The work is available in electronic format.

Encyclopedia of Religion. 16 vols. New York: Macmillan, 1987.   •   Covers religions from around the world, including information about their ideas, histories, and cultures. The articles are written by experts in their fields and include excellent bibliographies. The work is available in electronic format.

Harper's Dictionary of Hinduism: Its Mythology, Folklore, Philosophy, Literature, and History. By Margaret Stutley and James Stutley. New York: Harper and Row, 1977.   •   Features short definitions and identifications of terms, figures, and texts important in Hinduism. Though the articles are not detailed, they are good for quick reference.

Mythologies. Ed. Yves Bonnefoy. 2 vols. Chicago: University of Chicago Press, 1991.   •   An encyclopedia surveying mythologies of the world, with articles on cosmology, cults, and myth traditions arranged in geographical sections. The articles are lengthy and scholarly, and they are accompanied by illustrations and thorough bibliographies.

Oxford Dictionary of the Christian Church. Ed. F. L. Cross. 3rd ed. New York: Oxford University Press, 1997.   •   A small compendium of a vast amount of information, with short, descriptive entries that run from Aaron to Zwingli. The entries provide very concise starting points for understanding and identifying people, concepts, events, places, and biblical references that are important in Christian church history.

Zen Dictionary. By Ernest Wood. Rutland, Vt.: Charles E. Tuttle, 1957.   • Offers brief explanations of concepts in Zen Buddhism.

Theater, dance, and film

DATABASES AND INDEXES IN THEATER, DANCE, AND FILM

Film Literature Index. Albany: Film and Television Documentation Center, SUNY Albany, 1975–.   • Includes articles about film, along with reviews and scholarly criticism. The index offers especially strong coverage of European film and includes sections on television and video.

WEB RESOURCES IN THEATER, DANCE, AND FILM

Artslynx International Dance Resources. <http://www.artslynx.org/dance>   • An index of links to dance organizations, competition sites, publications, research and scholarship, history resources, and libraries with an international scope. The site is maintained by Richard Finkelstein of the University of Colorado, Denver, and is sponsored by the Colorado Council on the Arts, Artslynx International Arts Resources, and the National Endowment for the Arts.

Brief Guide to Internet Resources in Theatre and Performance Studies. <http://www.stetson.edu/departments/csata/thr_guid.html>   • A comprehensive but discriminating guide to theater sites on the Internet: sites on actors and acting, stagecraft and technical theater, electronic journals, and arts management and nonprofit organizations. The site is maintained by Ken McCoy, assistant professor of communications studies and theater arts at Stetson University, Florida, who avoids including commercial organizations and thoroughly annotates all entries.

Cinema Sites. <http://www.cinema-sites.com>   • A directory of sites dealing with cinema and television, ranging from the academic to the entertaining. A good resource for information on the business side of the film industry, the site is maintained by David Augsburger, who works in television production.

The Internet Movie Database. <http://us.imdb.com>   • The largest and oldest Internet film site. The database includes information on more than 250,000 movies from the silents to the latest releases, offering for many of them information on the release, script, cast, reviews, and links to further information. The search engine allows searches by movie title, cast or crew member, year, genre, country, production company, or combinations. Updated daily, this site is an extraordinary resource, both in depth of coverage and organization.

Performing Arts Links. <http://www.theatrelibrary.org/links /index.html> • An international listing of materials relating to theater, dance, and film, arranged both topically and by country. Particularly strong in theater resources, it includes links to sites on puppetry, street theater, vaudeville, and other genres as well as to theater history, actors, and more. The site is maintained and frequently updated by Maria Teresa Iovinelli of the Burcardo Library and Theatre Collection in Rome.

Theatre History on the Web. <http://www.videoccasions-nw.com /history/jack.html> • Includes links of interest to the student, the researcher, and the dramaturg, organized by period and topic. The site is maintained by Jack Wolcott (retired) of the School of Drama at the University of Washington.

Theatre History Sites on the WWW. <http://www.win.net/~kudzu /history.html> • Focuses on historical information related to the theater, from classical, medieval, Elizabethan, later English, and illusionist theater to American theater. The site is maintained by P. Gerald Bangham, a theater historian and associate professor (retired) at Alcorn State University.

WWW Virtual Library: Theatre and Drama. <http://www .vl-theatre.com> • Offers links to electronic text archives, journals, newsgroups, theater images, and theater studies and provides a database of online plays, listed by author.

REFERENCE BOOKS IN THEATER, DANCE, AND FILM

Biographical Dictionary of Dance. By Barbara Naomi Cohen-Stratyner. New York: Schirmer, 1982. • An extensive collection of biographical sketches of both famous and lesser known choreographers and dancers representing various genres, from ballet to ballroom.

Cambridge Guide to World Theatre. Cambridge: Cambridge University Press, 1988. • Provides lengthy articles on national traditions, theatrical forms, and topics in international theater, with numerous illustrations.

A Dictionary of the Ballet. By George Buckley Laird Wilson. New York: Theatre Arts Books, 1974. • Covers dancers, ballets, ballet companies, and musical terms.

Dramatic Criticism Index: A Bibliography of Commentaries on Playwrights from Ibsen to the Avant-Garde. Ed. Paul F. Breed and Florence M. Sniderman. Detroit: Gale Group, 1972. • An index to criticism of plays, arranged by author, with subheadings for individual plays. Indexed sources range from scholarly analysis to substantial reviews in the popular press.

Encyclopedia of the Musical Theatre. By Kurt Ganzl. 2 vols. New York: Schirmer, 1994. • Surveys musical theater, providing detailed background on musicals and profiles of those involved with them.

European Drama Criticism, 1900–1975. By Helen H. Palmer. 2nd ed. Hamden, Conn.: Shoe String Press, 1977. • An index to books and articles containing criticism of plays by prominent European playwrights, arranged by author, with subheadings for titles of plays.

Film Encyclopedia. By Ephraim Katz. 4th ed. New York: HarperPerennial, 2001. • A reference of more than 1,500 pages offering 7,000 entries on terms, topics, and individuals related to the history of film. This work is available in electronic format.

Halliwell's Filmgoer's Companion: Everything You'd Ever Want to Know about Everyone in the Movies. By Leslie Halliwell. Ed. John Walker. 12th ed. New York: Hill and Wang, 1997. • Offers brief entries on major films, actors, directors, and producers as well as definitions of technical terms and subjects such as censorship. The book is useful for identifying films of a certain type, such as trial dramas.

International Encyclopedia of the Dance. 6 vols. New York: Oxford University Press, 1998. • The most exhaustive reference work on the dance, covering the historical evolution of dance in the countries of the world, analysis of dance techniques, theories of aesthetics, personalities, companies, and works.

McGraw-Hill Encyclopedia of World Drama. 2nd ed. 5 vols. New York: McGraw-Hill, 1984. • Contains articles on playwrights, periods of theatrical history, and notable figures in theater. Brief critical comments on plays are given under author entries. The work includes many photographs and plates of productions and an index to the entire set.

Modern Drama Scholarship and Criticism, 1981–1990: An International Bibliography. By Charles A. Carpenter. Toronto: University of Toronto Press, 1996.   •   An extensive bibliography of international sources in drama, arranged geographically, with subheadings by author; emphasizes scholarly criticism. An earlier publication covers criticism published between 1966 and 1980.

Oxford Companion to the Theatre. 4th ed. New York: Oxford University Press, 1983.   •   Includes brief entries on authors, theatrical terms, and periods in the history of theater.

World Encyclopedia of Contemporary Theatre. Ed. Don Rubin. 6 vols. London: Routledge, 2000.   •   An authoritative, up-to-date guide to current theater, with a global perspective and thorough coverage by country.

Researching History

Research in history involves developing an understanding of the past through the examination and interpretation of evidence. Evidence may exist in the form of texts, physical remains of historic sites, recorded data, pictures, maps, artifacts, and so on. The historian's job is to find evidence, analyze its content and biases, corroborate it with other evidence, and use the evidence to develop an interpretation of past events that has some importance for the present. Historians use libraries to

- locate primary sources (firsthand information like diaries, letters, and original documents) for evidence
- find secondary sources, historians' interpretations and analyses of historical evidence
- verify factual material as inconsistencies arise

Doing historical research is a little like excavating an archaeological site. It requires patience, insight, and imagination as well as diligence and the right tools. As you find and examine primary sources, you need to imagine them in their original context and understand how your present-day point of view may distort your interpretation of them. You need to recognize not only your own biases but the biases that shaped primary materials in their own period. You need to brush away the layers of interpretation that time has imposed on them and imaginatively re-create the complexities of the environment in which they were created. Students doing historical research should be prepared to

- survey historians' interpretations of the past while recognizing how their purposes or backgrounds might influence their interpretations
- understand the context in which primary sources were generated

- identify conflicting evidence and locate factual and interpretive information that can help resolve or illuminate those differences

Many bibliographies can help you identify primary and secondary sources related to a particular topic or historical period. Be sure to examine bibliographies and footnotes in secondary sources as you find them, since they will often lead you to primary sources. Finally, innumerable encyclopedias, dictionaries, handbooks, and chronologies can provide you with information to round out your interpretations and ground them in fact. Consult a librarian to find out what the reference shelves offer for your topic and whether the library has any special collections of microfilm, archives, manuscripts, or other primary sources especially suited to historical research.

General resources in history

DATABASES AND INDEXES IN HISTORY

Humanities Index. New York: Wilson, 1974–.   • An interdisciplinary bibliographic index to more than 400 of the most prominent journals in the humanities, including art, music, history, and literature. Searchable by author or topic, this index offers citations only (no abstracts or full texts of articles). It is available in print and in electronic format.

WEB RESOURCES IN HISTORY

Bedford/St. Martin's Links to History Resources. <http://www.bedfordstmartins.com/history/links>   • Provides annotated links and online maps relevant to general history and U.S. history. U.S. categories include regional, gender, Native American, African American, Revolutionary, Civil War, and twentieth-century history.

Historical Text Archive. <http://historicaltextarchive.com>   • Offers more than 3,000 links to materials by country and region (with the United States receiving the strongest coverage) and by topic such as Native American, African American, movie history, and genealogy. Resources include both primary and secondary sources.

WWW Virtual Library: History Central Catalog. <http://www.ukans.edu/history/VL>   •   The premier meta-site for history, organized into research methods and materials, eras and epochs, historical topics, countries and regions, and world history.

REFERENCE BOOKS IN HISTORY

American Historical Association Guide to Historical Literature. Ed. Mary Beth Norton and Pamela Gerardi. 3rd ed. 2 vols. New York: Oxford University Press, 1995.   •   Offers 27,000 citations of important historical literature, arranged in 48 sections covering theory, international history, and regional history. An indispensable guide, this work has been recently updated to include current trends in historical research.

Dictionary of Historical Terms. Ed. Chris Cook and Susanne Jaffe. 2nd ed. New York: Random House Value Publishing, 1998.   •   Covers a wide variety of terms related to historical events, places, and institutions in a remarkably small package. This is a good place for quick identification of terms used in the field.

Encyclopedia of Historians and Historical Writing. 2 vols. London: Fitzroy Dearborn, 1998.   •   Provides information on historians, on regions and periods, and on topics in the field such as history of religion, women's and gender history, and art history.

World history

DATABASES AND INDEXES IN WORLD HISTORY

Historical Abstracts. Santa Barbara: ABC-CLIO, 1955–.   •   Provides citations and descriptive abstracts of articles and other materials from over 2,000 journals published on world history — from 1450 to the present (no full texts of articles). The work excludes North America, which is covered in the index *America: History and Life.* It is available in print and electronic formats.

WEB RESOURCES IN WORLD HISTORY

ABZU: Guide to Resources for the Study of the Ancient Near East. <http://www.oi.uchicago.edu/OI/DEPT/RA/ABZU/ABZU.HTML>   •   Links to thousands of sites in history, with indexes organized by author, publication, and topic. Resources include primary and secondary sources, information on archaeological digs, book and film sources, and book reviews. This is a truly exhaustive list from the Research Archives of the Oriental Institute at the University of Chicago.

The Labyrinth: Resources for Medieval Studies. <http:// labyrinth.georgetown.edu> • An enormous network of medieval studies resources on the Internet, sponsored by Georgetown University. Both primary and secondary sources are included. Links are annotated, and users can perform a search within the site by category, type of material, or keyword.

REFERENCE BOOKS IN WORLD HISTORY

The Blackwell Companion to the Enlightenment. Ed. Roy Porter et al. Oxford and Cambridge, Mass: Blackwell, 1991. • Offers brief articles, generally with bibliographies, on topics, themes, major figures, and ideas of the Enlightenment.

Cambridge History of Africa. 8 vols. Cambridge: Cambridge University Press, 1982–. • Covers African history chronologically in some depth. Use the table of contents and indexes for access. Other *Cambridge History* works cover many countries and continents.

Civilization of the Ancient Mediterranean. Ed. Michael Grant. 3 vols. New York: Scribner, 1988. • Provides lengthy articles that introduce many facets of the classical world. Each article is followed by a helpful bibliography.

Civilizations of the Ancient Near East. Ed. Jack M. Sasson. 4 vols. New York: Scribner, 1995. • A collection of essays on the culture and history of Egypt, Syro-Palestine, Mesopotamia, and Anatolia. The work includes some coverage of Arabian, northeast African, and Aegean cultures as well as extensive bibliographies.

Companion Encyclopedia of the History of Medicine. Ed. W. F. Bynum and Ray Porter. 2 vols. New York: Routledge, 1994. • Includes essays on body systems and how they have been perceived through time, theories of illness (including the history of specific diseases and their treatments), clinical history, and medicine in society and culture.

Dictionary of the Middle Ages. Ed. Joseph R. Strayer. 13 vols. New York: Scribner, 1982–89. • An encyclopedia covering people, events, ideas, movements, texts, and cultural features of the medieval world. Articles are often illustrated with period artwork and are followed by bibliographies of primary and secondary sources.

Encyclopedia of Asian History. Ed. Robin Lewis and Ainslie Embree. 4 vols. New York: Macmillan Library Reference, 1988. • Discusses people, places, events, and topics in detailed and well-documented essays covering central Asia, southern Asia, and the Far East.

Encyclopedia of the Holocaust. Ed. Israel Gutman. 5 vols. New York: Macmillan Library Reference, 1996. • Offers lengthy articles on people, places, events, and concepts related to the Holocaust, each followed by a selective bibliography.

Encyclopedia of the Renaissance. Ed. Paul F. Grendler. 6 vols. New York: Scribner, 1999. Offers nearly 1,200 substantial articles covering topics related to the culture and history of the period.

Encyclopedia of the Vietnam War: A Political, Social, and Military History. Ed. Spencer C. Tucker. Santa Barbara: ABC-CLIO, 1998. 3 vols. Includes 900 entries, with biographies of prominent figures, coverage of military events, and protests against the war. The third volume offers a wealth of primary source documents in English and English translation.

New Cambridge Modern History. 14 vols. Cambridge: Cambridge University Press, 1957–79. • Covers world history from 1493 to 1945, chronologically and by topic, providing detailed and lengthy narrative surveys of the times. Similar works published by Cambridge University Press cover ancient and medieval history.

The Oxford Companion to World War II. Ed. I. C. B. Dear and M. R. D. Foot. New York: Oxford University Press, 1995. • Offers fairly substantial summary articles on topics, people, places, and events related to World War II; includes a chronology and maps.

The Oxford Encyclopedia of the Reformation. Ed. Hans J. Hillerbrand. 4 vols. New York: Oxford University Press, 1996. • Covers people, places, events, documents, and ideas related to the Reformation in lengthy, scholarly articles. Each reflects current research and interpretation and is followed by a selective bibliography.

Times Atlas of World History. Ed. Geoffrey Barraclough and Geoffrey Parker. 4th ed. New York: Hammond, 1993. • Offers more than 600 maps showing historical periods and movements such as the spread of world religions, the industrial revolution, and European expansion overseas. The maps are supplemented by explanations and discussions of each period.

The Timetables of History: A Horizontal Linkage of People and Events. By Bernard Grun. 3rd ed., rev. New York: Simon and Schuster, 1991. • Provides chronological tables that cover, for a given year, worldwide politics, religion, the arts, and science. This work provides an interdisciplinary and global picture of a period.

American history

DATABASES AND INDEXES IN AMERICAN HISTORY

America: History and Life. Santa Barbara: ABC-CLIO, 1964–. • Provides citations and descriptive abstracts of articles from more than 1,800 varied publications on U.S. and Canadian history and culture (no full-text articles). Searchable by keyword, author, subject, and source, the index offers in-depth coverage of specialist publications in North American history and allows for interdisciplinary examinations of American culture. It is available in print and electronic formats.

WEB RESOURCES IN AMERICAN HISTORY

American Women's History: A Research Guide. <http://frank.mtsu.edu/~kmiddlet/history/women.html> • Offers clearly organized information on more than 1,000 resources in print and online, with over 700 links. It was created and is kept current by Ken Middleton, a reference librarian at Middle Tennessee State University.

WWW Virtual Library: United States History. <http://www.ukans.edu/history/VL/USA/index.html> • Organized by period and topic, the Virtual Library includes a rich set of research tools and links to journals, documents, timelines, and more. It is maintained by Lynn Nelson, a history professor at the University of Kansas.

REFERENCE BOOKS IN AMERICAN HISTORY

The ABC-CLIO Companion to Women's Progress in America. By Elizabeth Knappman-Frost. Santa Barbara: ABC-CLIO, 1994. • Offers brief articles on American women who are notable for contributions to women's progress and covers related topics and organizations. A chronology and bibliography are included.

American National Biography. By the American Council of Learned Societies. Ed. John Arthur Garraty and Mark C. Carnes. 24 vols. New York: Oxford University Press, 1999.   •   Includes biographical sketches of Americans whose lives, because of achievement, fame, or influence, are historically significant. Only people who died before 1996 are featured. Each sketch is followed by a critical bibliography.

Black Women in America: An Historical Encyclopedia. Ed. Darlene Clark Hine et al. 2 vols. Bloomington: Indiana University Press, 1994.   •   A scholarly compilation of biographical and topical articles covering key issues and the lives of African American women, celebrated and unknown, through history.

Dictionary of American History. Rev. ed. 7 vols. New York: Scribner, 1976. With supplements.   •   An encyclopedia of terms, places, and concepts in U.S. history. For biographical information, consult the *American National Biography* (Oxford University Press, 1999).

Encyclopedia of American Economic History: Studies of the Principal Movements and Ideas. Ed. Glenn Porter. 3 vols. New York: Scribner, 1980.   •   Offers surveys of economic history — chronological, social, and institutional — that provide valuable summaries of such topics as taxation, slavery, antitrust, and social mobility.

Encyclopedia of American Social History. Ed. Mary Clayton et al. 3 vols. New York: Scribner, 1993.   •   Fills in the gaps left by conventional political-biographical history sources. The set presents lengthy and well-documented articles covering topics such as religion, class, gender, race, popular culture, regionalism, and everyday life in the United States from pre-Columbian to modern times.

Encyclopedia of the Confederacy. Ed. Richard N. Current. 4 vols. New York: Simon and Schuster, 1993.   •   Covers Confederate society, culture, and politics as well as events and people in the Civil War–era South. The articles are arranged alphabetically.

Encyclopedia of the North American Colonies. Ed. Jacob Ernest Cook. 3 vols. New York: Scribner, 1993.   •   A collection of lengthy essays covering government and law, economic life, labor, social issues, families, the arts, education, and religion, arranged thematically. The third volume contains a thorough index.

Encyclopedia of the United States in the Twentieth Century. Ed. Stanley I. Kutler. 4 vols. New York: Scribner, 1996.   •   An ambitious survey of U.S. cultural, social, and intellectual history in broad articles arranged topically. Each essay is followed by a thorough bibliography.

United States History: A Selective Guide to Information Sources. By Ron Blazek and Anna Perrault. Englewood, Colo.: Libraries Unlimited, 1994.   •   A selective and descriptive guide to research materials in U.S. history, including electronic resources.

Primary sources

There is no simple, foolproof way to find primary sources for historical research; rather, locating such sources tends to be an intuitive and creative process involving guesswork and blind alleys. Potentially useful materials can be found in journals, memoirs, letters, magazines, newspapers, and official documents published during the time you are interested in. Try searching the library catalog, adding the search term *sources* or *documents* to your keyword or using the names of prominent figures as authors. Primary documents may also be available in your library or on the Internet, through the following sources.

DATABASES AND INDEXES: THE POPULAR PRESS

American Periodicals Series, 1741–1900. 2,770 reels. Ann Arbor: University Microfilms International, 1946–79.   •   A large collection of articles from journals published from colonial times through the nineteenth century. This database identifies journals focused on specific topics and offers full-text articles. It is available on microfilm and in electronic format.

The Civil War: A Newspaper Perspective. Accessible Archives.   •   Offers selected full-text articles in plain-text format from more than 2,500 issues of newspapers representing both southern and northern perspectives for the years 1860–1865. The database includes eyewitness accounts, hundreds of maps, official reports of battles, and advertisements from the period. It is available in electronic format.

Harper's Weekly: Civil War and Reconstruction. Norfolk, Va.: HarpWeek, 1990–.   •   An electronic edition of a popular, illustrated publication covering the years 1857–1916. Images of the pages have been digitally scanned to retain the original appearance — illustrations and full text. It is available in electronic format as *HarpWeek: The Civil War Era.*

New York Times Index. New York: New York Times, 1851–.   •   A valuable print source for finding newspaper coverage on a particular historical topic. Topics are grouped under broad subjects, with individual stories listed chronologically. Each index citation provides the date, section, page, and column of a story. Even without reading the stories themselves, users can get detailed chronologies of events from this index. It is available on microfilm and in electronic format as the *Historical Index to the* New York Times.

The Official Index to the Times. London: Times Publishing.   •   An excellent source for news on British life and world affairs of the nineteenth and twentieth centuries, covering 1790 to 1980. It offers citations for articles from the *London Times* (no full-text articles) and is available in print and electronic formats. The electronic index is searchable by keyword, headline, date, and page number.

Poole's Index to Periodical Literature, 1802–1881. 6 vols. Boston: Houghton Mifflin, 1892. With supplement covering 1882–1906.   •   Provides citations to American and English periodicals, books, newspapers, and government documents of the nineteenth century. An electronic edition is also available, with 3.8 million citations and enhanced indexing.

Readers' Guide to Periodical Literature. New York: Wilson, 1890–.   •   A good source for popular reactions to events, literary topics, and popular culture of the twentieth century. This index is organized by author and subject and offers bibliographic citations and abstracts. It is available in print and electronic formats; the electronic version includes some full-text articles.

INTERNET RESOURCES: PRIMARY DOCUMENTS

American Memory: Historical Collections for the National Digital Library. <http://memory.loc.gov>   •   A rich source of electronic reproductions of texts, images, and film from the collections of the Library of Congress. Materials that can be downloaded include a motion picture from as early as 1897, sound recordings from World War I and the 1920 election, and more than 300 pamphlets written by African Americans between Reconstruction and World War I.

The Avalon Project at the Yale Law School: Documents in Law, History, and Diplomacy. <http://www.yale.edu/lawweb/avalon/avalon.htm> • A collection of primary source (full-text) documents particularly rich in legal and diplomatic history. Organized by period and topic and searchable by keyword, this collection is well edited and high quality. Documents include internal links to materials referenced in the text.

EuroDocs: Primary Historical Documents from Western Europe. <http://www.lib.byu.edu/~rdh/eurodocs> • A wealth of primary source material from 22 countries (plus Vatican City). Sites are sorted by country and listed chronologically. Available sources include letters, facsimiles of paintings and photographs, journals, and official documents.

Internet History Sourcebooks Project. <http://www.fordham.edu/halsall/index.html> • A large collection of online texts and primary documents for the study of history. Three major sourcebooks cover ancient, medieval, and modern history; other collections are focused on history of science, African history, Islamic history, women's history, and more. Edited by Paul Halsall at Fordham University, this is a rich and very well organized collection of primary documents

INTERNET RESOURCES: GOVERNMENT DOCUMENTS

Foreign Relations of the United States: Diplomatic Papers. <http://www.state.gov/www/about_state/history/frusonline.html> • Provides collected correspondence, memoranda, treaties, presidential messages, and other documents related to U.S. foreign policy, arranged chronologically and by region. Online volumes cover the years from Truman's through Johnson's administrations. For earlier documents, see the print collection, *Foreign Relations of the United States: Diplomatic Papers* (Washington, D.C.: Government Printing Office, 1861–).

Public Papers of the Presidents of the United States. <http:// www.access.gpo.gov/su_docs/help/hints/ppapers.html> • A repository of proclamations, speeches, statements, photographs, and other presidential papers. Currently available online are documents from the Clinton administration. For earlier materials, from Hoover onward, see the print or microfiche version of *Public Papers of the Presidents of the United States* (Washington, D.C.: Office of the Federal Register, 1957–).

REPRINT SERIES

American Culture Series II (ACSII). 643 reels. Ann Arbor: University Microfilms International, 1941–74. • A 35mm microfilm series that reproduces 5,600 American books and pamphlets published between 1493 and 1875. The materials are organized by 12 disciplines and are available on microfilm only. Series I spans 1493–1806; the larger Series II expands the pre-1806 material and extends to 1875.

American Women's Diaries. 90 reels. New Canaan, Conn.: Readex, 1980–. • A microfilm collection that reproduces the diaries of women who lived and traveled in the western, southern, and eastern United States. Available on microfilm only.

Early English Books, 1475–1640. 2,034 reels. Ann Arbor: University Microfilms International, 1938–67. *Early English Books, 1641–1700.* 2,396 reels. Ann Arbor: University Microfilms International, 1961–. • A vast collection of books from the first texts printed in England to the Restoration. Full texts are available in 35mm microfilm and in electronic format as *Early English Books Online (EEBO)*; check your library's online databases and indexes.

Early English Text Society Series. 287 vols. London: Early English Text Society and IDC Publisher, 1864–. • A long-running scholarly series that republishes Old English and Middle English texts not available elsewhere in good editions. Available on microcard or microfiche. Parts of the series are now published in print for the Early English Text Society by the Oxford University Press.

March of America Facsimile Series. 103 vols. Ann Arbor: University Microfilms International, 1966. • A reprint series of original editions of early English accounts of travel to the New World. Available in print only.

ORAL HISTORIES AND LOCAL HISTORY COLLECTIONS

You may want to undertake an oral history project or track down oral histories that others have compiled. You can consult the *Oral History Index* (Westport, Conn.: Meckler, 1990) or the *Directory of Oral History Collections* (Phoenix: Oryx Press, 1988). Or you can simply search your library's catalog using the term *oral history* or adding the term *oral history* to your keyword. Also consider getting primary sources from a county or state historical society's collections or even from the archives of your own college or university. You may find yourself working with material no one else has analyzed before.

Researching in the Social Sciences

Social scientists interpret and analyze human behavior, generally using empirical methods of research. Though original data gathering and analysis are central to social sciences research, researchers also use library and Internet resources to

- obtain raw data for model building or analysis
- locate information about a particular model, theory, or methodology to be used in a research project
- review the literature to place new research in context

Subjects of study in the social sciences sometimes cross disciplines and evade the systems of subject headings — whether the Library of Congress Subject Headings (LCSH) or another system — of the best indexes and abstracts. Further, new theories often emerge too quickly for references and guides to keep up. Because of this, the researcher should be prepared to

- systematically identify useful search terms in indexes and abstracts and work from most recent to older sources
- follow leads given in citations — often the most efficient way to trace theoretical connections
- sort research materials into schools of thought, identifying the key works relevant to a particular problem or question

A review of the relevant literature in a social sciences research project not only should identify what research has been done but should compare and contrast the available information, evaluating its significance.

Each of the social sciences has a well-developed set of research tools to help you find relevant material, whether numerical data or research reports. The tools listed here will give you ideas for beginning your research. Consult a librarian for help in locating available information.

General resources in the social sciences

DATABASES AND INDEXES IN THE SOCIAL SCIENCES

American Statistics Index. Washington, D.C.: Congressional Information Service, 1974–. • A useful index to statistics that appear within government publications. Providing bibliographic citations and abstracts, it is available in print and electronic formats. The online version, titled *Statistical Masterfile* or *Statistical Universe,* contains some links to full texts of articles. It is searchable by keyword, subject, author, title, agency, or year.

Social Sciences Citation Index. Philadelphia: Institute for Scientific Information, 1956–. • An index to more than 1,700 journals in the social sciences. Searchable by author or keyword, the index gives bibliographic citations, 60 percent of which include descriptive abstracts. It is available in print and electronic formats. The online version may be offered as part of the *Web of Science,* and it may include links to some full-text articles.

Social Sciences Index. New York: Wilson, 1974–. • An interdisciplinary index to key journals in the social sciences, including anthropology, psychology, sociology, economics, and political science. Searchable by author and subject, this index offers citations and abstracts; it is available in print and electronic formats. The electronic version covers from 1983 to the present. Your library may also offer the *Social Sciences Index/Full Text,* which includes citations, abstracts, and the full texts of articles from 1989 to the present.

WEB RESOURCES IN THE SOCIAL SCIENCES

FedStats. <http://www.fedstats.gov> • A well-organized, searchable portal for statistical information available through U.S. government agency sites.

Internet Crossroads in the Social Sciences. <http://dpls.dacc .wisc.edu/internet.html> • A thorough guide to information and data sources available on the Internet, created by staff at the University of Wisconsin (Madison) Data and Program Library Service.

Searchable by keyword, the site includes links to government and nongovernment sites concerned with domestic and international economics and labor, health, education, geography and history, politics, sociology, and demography. Each link is accompanied by a description and explanation.

SOSIG: Social Sciences Information Gateway. <http://scout18.cs.wisc.edu/sosig_mirror> • A selective catalog of thousands of Web sites in the social sciences, hosted by the Internet Scout Project at the University of Wisconsin, Madison. Users can browse by topic and region or search by keyword. Each entry has been reviewed and is annotated. The compilers, an international group, avoid including lists of links but focus instead on sites that can provide information directly. This site is frequently updated and rigorously maintained.

U.S. Census Bureau. <http://www.census.gov> • Offers access to an astounding amount of demographic, social, and economic data. The search engine allows for pinpointing relevant statistical tables and reports. The site is updated almost daily with newly released reports on such subjects as fathers as care providers, children without health care, and trade statistics. Many of the tables can be downloaded in portable document format (pdf).

REFERENCE BOOKS IN THE SOCIAL SCIENCES

The Gallup Poll. Wilmington, Del.: Scholarly Resources, 1972–. • An annual print compilation of opinion poll statistics gathered by the Gallup organization. Covers 1935 to the present. Current and archived polls from 1997 to the present are available in electronic format at the Gallup Web site <http://www.gallup.com/poll/releases/pr01610.asp>.

Historical Statistics of the United States, Colonial Times to 1970. 2 vols. Washington, D.C.: Government Printing Office, 1975. • These volumes, which include a subject index, offer vital statistics, economic figures, and social data for the United States over time. The work is available in print and electronic formats. This information is not updated — for more recent figures, consult the *Statistical Abstract of the United States.*

International Historical Statistics, 1750–1993: Europe. By B. R. Mitchell. New York: Grove's Dictionaries, 1998. • Offers time-series data for countries, including figures on population, agriculture, the economy, transport and communications, and education. Other volumes by the same author cover other regions of the world. The work is available in print format only.

Social Science Encyclopedia. Ed. Paul Kegan. 2nd ed. London: Routledge, 1996. • Offers short articles defining concepts in the social sciences, with bibliographies of key references; available in print format only.

Sources of Information in the Social Sciences: A Guide to the Literature. By William H. Webb et al. 3rd ed. Chicago: American Library Association, 1986. • An annotated guide to research sources in the social sciences; a good place to find key works as well as reference tools. The work is available in print format only.

Statistical Abstract of the United States. Washington, D.C.: Government Printing Office, 1879–. • Perhaps the single most useful collection of statistical information available in a small package. It includes hundreds of tables of figures on areas such as population, economics, and social factors, with references to the original sources. An index to the tables provides easy access. Statistical abstracts from 1995 to the present are available online at <http://www.census.gov/prod/www/statistical=abstract=us.html>.

Statistical Abstract of the World. Ed. Marlita A. Reddy. 4th ed. Detroit: Gale Group, 1998. • Presents data on over 180 countries, covering geography, demographics, education, science and technology, government and law, and economics. Sources for all data are noted, and an appendix lists and describes sources, offering important leads to additional data. The work is available in print format only.

The U.N. Demographic Yearbook. New York: United Nations, 1948–. *Statistical Yearbook.* New York: United Nations, 1948–. • Annual compilations of demographic, economic, and social statistics from around the world. Some years include a special thematic or historical focus. Available in print and electronic formats.

Anthropology

DATABASES AND INDEXES IN ANTHROPOLOGY

Abstracts in Anthropology. Farmingdale, N.Y.: Baywood, 1970–. • Offers descriptive abstracts of articles from journals and books and includes conference proceedings in cultural and physical anthropology, archaeology, and linguistics; available in print only.

Human Relations Area Files (HRAF) Collection of Ethnography • A huge collection of anthropological data — including books, articles, and field reports — arranged into 300 cultural groups. Within each group, information is categorized by subject, such as food production, interpersonal relations, and religion. Because the organization is the same under each culture, it is easy to make cross-cultural comparisons. Material from 1993 can be accessed electronically; the *HRAF* database provides the full texts of articles and is searchable by keyword. Material published before 1993 is available on microfiche as *Human Relations Area Files* (New Haven: Human Relations Area Files Press, 1949–) and is organized by the classification systems found in the *Outline of World Cultures* (*OWC*), 6th ed., rev. (New Haven: Human Relations Area Files Press, 1983) and *Outline of Cultural Materials* (*OCM*), 5th ed., rev. (New Haven: Human Relations Area Files Press, 1982).

WEB RESOURCES IN ANTHROPOLOGY

Anthromorphemics. <http://www.anth.ucsb.edu/glossary/index2.html> • A well-designed, searchable glossary of terms used in the field, covering cultural and physical anthropology and archaeology. The site is maintained by the Anthropology Department at the University of California, Santa Barbara.

Anthropology Resources on the Internet. <http://home.worldnet.fr/clist/Anthro/index.html> • A lengthy list of sites of interest, originally selected and maintained by anthropologist Allen Lutins and currently maintained by archaeologist Bernard-Olivier Clist. Though the presentation is simple and unadorned, the site is well organized and frequently updated. Many of the links have brief explanatory annotations. Coverage includes cultural and physical anthropology, archaeology, linguistics, organizations, field schools, electronic discussion groups and publications, and guides to resources.

AnthroTECH. WWW Virtual Library: Anthropology. <http://anthrotech.com/resources> • A comprehensive list of Web resources related to the field, with sections on linguistic anthropology, applied anthropology, archaeology, and biophysical anthropology and links to discussion forums, journals, organizations, and more. Well-organized and regularly updated, it includes explanatory annotations for each link. *AnthroTECH*, both the site and the company, were created by Eliot Lee, an applied anthropologist and graduate of Northern Arizona University.

Native American Sites. <http://www.nativeculture.com/lisamitten/indians.html> • Includes links to native nations, organizations, tribal colleges, languages, the mascot issue, native media, individuals in the arts, native businesses, and natives in the military. It serves as the home page for the American Indian Library Association, an affiliate of the American Library Association. The site is maintained by Lisa Mitten, formerly a research librarian at the University of Pittsburgh.

WWW Virtual Library: ArchNet. <http://archnet.uconn.edu> • Covers topics by region as well as academic department, publication, and museum. Well-organized and deep in content, this site also features attractive layout and graphics. It is maintained by the Archaeological Research Institute at Arizona State University.

REFERENCE BOOKS IN ANTHROPOLOGY

Atlas of World Cultures: A Geographic Guide to Ethnographic Literature. By David H. Price. Newbury Park, Calif.: Sage, 1989. • Places bibliographic information about cultures in a geographic context. Forty maps are used to locate 3,500 cultural groups, for which bibliographies are provided.

Cambridge Encyclopedia of Human Evolution. Ed. Steve Jones et al. Cambridge: Cambridge University Press, 1995. • Surveys human evolution in thematic chapters.

Dictionary of Anthropology. By Charlotte Seymour-Smith. Boston: G. K. Hall, 1986. • Defines terms used in the field and offers a selective bibliography. Physical anthropology is not covered, nor are archaeology, linguistics, or related fields.

Dictionary of Concepts in Cultural Anthropology. By Robert H. Winthrop. New York: Greenwood, 1991. • Defines key concepts, explores the evolution of each concept, and leads the researcher to key sources. This work is especially useful for tracking the significance and influence of an idea in the field.

Encyclopedia of Cultural Anthropology. Ed. David Levinson and Melvin Ember. 4 vols. New York: Holt, 1996. • Offers 340 lengthy articles written by specialists on approaches, methods, concepts, and topics related to cultural anthropology. Articles are followed by up-to-date bibliographies of key research.

Encyclopedia of World Cultures. Ed. David Levinson. 10 vols. Boston: G. K. Hall, 1991–. • Covers more than 1,500 cultural groups, alphabetically arranged within regions. Entries summarize information on the distribution, belief systems, kinship structures, and history of the groups and provide selective bibliographies. The encyclopedia is based on information in the *Human Relations Area Files.* This work is available in electronic format (CD-ROM).

Worldmark Encyclopedia of Cultures and Daily Life. Ed. Timothy L. Gall. 4 vols. Detroit: Gale Group, 1998. • Covers the cultural and social lives of ethnic groups throughout the world. Each entry includes traditions, contemporary living conditions, food, language, and religious expression of over 500 peoples. Available in print only.

Business and economics

DATABASES AND INDEXES IN BUSINESS AND ECONOMICS

Accounting and Tax Index. Ann Arbor: University Microfilms, 1992–. • Supersedes the *Accountant's Index Supplement, 1920–1992.* A detailed index of more than 1,000 articles on taxation and accounting, conference papers, reports, and books. The index, updated annually, provides bibliographic citations only (no abstracts or full-text articles). It is available in print and electronic formats. (While the index itself does not offer full texts of articles, some articles licensed by your library may be available online through *ProQuest.*)

EconLit. Nashville: American Economic Association, 1969–. • An electronic bibliographic index of economic literature. This index provides citations (some with descriptive abstracts of articles) of scholarly economic journals.

Gale Group Business and Company Resource Center. Detroit: Gale Group, 2001–. • An online, full-text database of business magazine articles, company histories, rankings, and industry information.

Lexis/Nexis Academic Universe. Dayton, Ohio: Lexis-Nexis, 1998–.
• A full-text database containing more than one billion articles
and other documents from specialized business and legal sources,
including the *New York Times* and the *Economist.*

National Economic, Social, and Environmental Data Book (NESE).
Washington, D.C.: Department of Commerce, 1991–.   • A CD-ROM
database of documents from 19 federal agencies, on topics such as
domestic markets, small business, the costs of environmental regulation, and social factors related to business. The database offers
access to print publications including the *Economic Report of the
President* and Census Bureau publications such as *U.S. Industrial
Outlook.* Providing full texts of over 65,000 documents, including
tables, reports, and articles from periodicals, it is searchable by
source, topic, or government program.

National Trade Data Bank (NTDB). Washington, D.C.: Department
of Commerce, 1990–.   •   A CD-ROM database of STAT-USA, the
statistical service of the U.S. Department of Commerce. It includes
enormous amounts of data on international trade, economics, and
other topics. Check your library's online databases and indexes.

WEB RESOURCES IN BUSINESS AND ECONOMICS

Current Industrial Reports. <http://www.census.gov/ftp/pub/cir
/www> • Quarterly data from the Census Bureau on a variety of
industries. Reports are in pdf format and organized by subject, industry, title, or document number.

Economic Report of the President. < http://www.access.gpo.gov/eop>
• Sponsored by the Executive Office of the President and located
at the Web site of the U.S. Government Printing Office, the report
explains the rationale for the budget submitted to Congress. Of particular interest are the tables that cover income, production, and
employment in time series. The report is available in pdf format
(1995 to the present).

Economic Statistics Briefing Room. <http://www.whitehouse.gov/
fsbr/esbr.html> • A White House Web page that offers quick access to the most current economic indicators collected by various
government agencies on topics including production, employment,
income, prices, and transportation.

Hoover's Online: The Business Network. <http://www.hoovers.com>
• Bills itself as "the Web's most comprehensive source of business information." This site offers company and industry information and articles, facts and figures on money management, career development, and news.

NetEc. <http://netec.wustl.edu/NetEc.html> • An international project that lists and describes information of interest to academics and economists. It has sections on printed working papers, electronic working papers, home pages on economics, computer programs of use to economists, and a vast, well-organized resource guide to economics Internet sites. The site is hosted by the Department of Economics at Washington University in St. Louis.

Ohio State's Virtual Finance Library. <http://www.cob.ohio-state
.edu/dept/fin/overview.htm> • Well-organized links on banks, exchanges, and market news, with pages for various audiences: students, researchers, executives, and educators.

Securities and Exchange Commission: EDGAR Database of Corporate Information. <http://www.sec.gov/edgarhp.htm> • Provides information about publicly held corporations, which are required by federal law to file reports on their activities with the Securities and Exchange Commission. Most reports filed from 1994 to the present are publicly available through EDGAR (Electronic Data Gathering, Analysis, and Retrieval System) on this site. The information about each company includes financial status, chief officers, stock information, company history, pending litigation that might have an economic impact on the company, and more.

Vibes: Virtual International Business and Economic Sources. <http://libweb.uncc.edu/ref-bus/vibehome.htm> • Provides over 1,600 links to sites related to international business and economics. Links include free full-text files of recent articles, reports, and statistical tables. They are organized by topics such as international trade law, patents, emerging markets, and regional and national sites. The site is maintained by Jeanie Welch, business librarian at the University of North Carolina, Charlotte.

WWW Virtual Library: Resources for Economists on the Internet. <http://rfe.wustl.edu/EconFAQ.html> • A guide to economics resources, with annotated links to more than 700 sites chiefly related to economics, but some related to general scholarly interest. The site is compiled and updated by Bill Goffe of the Department of Economics at SUNY, Oswego.

REFERENCE BOOKS IN BUSINESS AND ECONOMICS

Blackwell Encyclopedic Dictionary of Business Ethics. Ed. Patricia Werhane and R. Edward Freeman. Cambridge, Mass.: Blackwell, 1997.   •   Offers substantial entries written by experts in the fields of business ethics on such topics as equal opportunity, corporate crime, participatory management, environmental risk, business ethics in different cultures, and electronic surveillance. Entries include bibliographies. This work is part of the series *The Blackwell Encyclopedia of Management* (available in print only).

Encyclopedia of Political Economy. Ed. Philip Anthony O'Hara. 2 vols. London: Routledge, 1999.   •   Provides analyses of topics related to money and finance, labor, family and gender, political ideologies, development, theoretical schools, and methodology.

New Palgrave: A Dictionary of Economics. Ed. John Eatwell et al. 4 vols. London: Macmillan Reference; New York: Stockton Press, 1987.   •   A revision of the classic *Palgrave's Dictionary of Political Economy,* offering lengthy, scholarly analyses of economic theories and theorists. The work includes excellent bibliographies.

New Palgrave Dictionary of Economics and the Law. Ed. Peter Newman et al. 3 vols. London: Macmillan Reference; New York: Stockton, 1998.   •   Offers in-depth coverage of such topics as antitrust, cartels, contracts, civil procedure, theories of economics with legal import, taxation, securities regulation, and property rights.

New Palgrave Dictionary of Money and Finance. Ed. Peter Newman et al. 3 vols. London: Macmillan Reference; New York: Stockton, 1992.   •   Defines financial terms and provides detailed discussions of concepts related to monetary economics, finance, and banking.

Communications

DATABASES AND INDEXES IN COMMUNICATIONS

CommSearch: Index to Journals in Communication Studies. Falls Church, Va.: Speech Communication Association, 1974–.   •   A database of bibliographic citations, descriptive abstracts, and the full text of some articles. It provides the tables of contents for the major speech and communications journals and is searchable by title, author, and keyword. The print version of this source, *Index to Journals in Communication Studies,* is often called the Matlon, after its first editor, Ronald J. Matlon.

Communication Abstracts. Beverly Hills: Sage, 1978–. • Provides bibliographical citations and descriptive abstracts of articles (no full texts) from more than 150 journals, books, and research reports, arranged in broad topic categories and indexed by subject and author. This index is available in print (1978–) and electronic formats. The electronic database *EBSCO* provides coverage from 1996 to the present; FirstSearch provides coverage starting in 1998.

Speech Index: An Index to Collections of World Famous Orations and Speeches for Various Occasions. 4th ed. Metuchen, N.J.: Scarecrow, 1966–. With supplements through 1980. • A print index to speeches included in more than 250 anthologies.

We Shall Be Heard: An Index to Speeches by American Women, 1978–1985. By Beverley Manning. Metuchen, N.J.: Scarecrow, 1988. • An author and a subject index to speeches by American women, with bibliographic information for published sources that include those speeches; available in print format only.

WEB RESOURCES IN COMMUNICATIONS

The American Communication Association (ACA). <http://www.americancomm.org> • Provides a wealth of communications links organized by fields within the discipline. Resources include writers' tools and electronic information sources, access to synchronous and asynchronous discussions, information on communications law, and news from the association. The ACA is a nonprofit professional organization of researchers, teachers, and businesspeople.

First Amendment Handbook. <http://www.rcfp.org/handbook/viewpage.cgi> • Provides detailed analyses of constitutional law issues as they relate to the practice of journalism. Sections cover access to courts, places and people, the Freedom of Information

Act, confidentiality, surreptitious recording, libel, invasion of privacy, prior restraint, and copyright. This site was created and is maintained by the Reporters Committee for the Freedom of the Press, a nonprofit organization that provides free legal help to journalists and news organizations.

The Freedom Forum Online. <http://www.freedomforum.org> • A wealth of information in communications. The main categories are Newseum (an interactive museum of news), First Amendment (news, analysis, and commentary on the First Amendment), Newsroom Diversity (aimed at recruiting people of color for careers in journalism), and International Media Issues (news, analysis, and commentary on global media issues). The Freedom Forum is a nonpartisan international foundation dedicated to free expression.

Kidon Media-Link. <http://www.kidon.com/media-link> • A directory of international newspapers and news sources on the Internet. Based in the Netherlands, this site is searchable by region and country or by language, type of media, title, or city. The site provides radio and television as well as print news sources, with depth of coverage. *Kidon Media-Link* is an independent site that originated from a list of sources compiled by a political science student at the University of Amsterdam, Kees van der Griendt, who is now a Web designer.

MCS: The Media and Communication Studies Site. <http://www.aber.ac.uk/media> • A rich meta-index of sites relevant to a wide range of areas within communications studies, including theory, nonverbal communication, culture studies, advertising, and the news media. The site is maintained by a media theory professor in Britain.

Telecom Information Resources on the Internet. <http://china.si.umich.edu/telecom/telecom-info.html> • An online directory of more than 8,000 links providing information related to the technical, economic, public policy, and social aspects of telecommunications. The site includes 26 categories (presented as a table of contents), including Telecom News and Headlines, Global Information Infrastructure, and Research Labs, Testbeds, and Projects. The site is maintained by Jeffrey Macke Mason, a professor at the University of Michigan.

Telecoms Virtual Library. <http://www.analysys.com/vlib> • Provides more than 8,000 links accessed by a subject index in telecommunications that covers a broad array of topics and subtopics, including communications, teleworking, telemedicine, and economic and legal issues. The site is sponsored by Analysys, an international corporation that provides industry research and consulting services.

REFERENCE BOOKS IN COMMUNICATIONS

ABC-CLIO Companion to the Media in America. By Daniel Webster Hollis. Santa Barbara: ABC-CLIO, 1995. • Covers important developments in mass media and significant media organizations and people in concise articles. This work is part of the ABC-CLIO series *American History Companions* and is available in print form only.

American Voices: Significant Speeches from American History, 1640–1945. Ed. James Andrews and David Zarefsky. New York: Longman, 1991. • A chronologically arranged anthology of major speeches of historical and oratorical significance.

Biographical Dictionary of American Journalism. Ed. Joseph P. McKerns. New York: Greenwood, 1989. • Provides lengthy biographical sketches of major journalists, each followed by a list of sources.

History of the Mass Media in the United States: An Encyclopedia. Ed. Margaret A. Blancard. Chicago: Fitzroy Dearborn Publishers, 2000. • Covers all forms of mass media from 1690 to 1990, offering short articles on technological, legal, economic, and political developments as well as major organizations and institutions.

International Encyclopedia of Communications. Ed. Erik Barnouw et al. 4 vols. New York: Oxford University Press, 1989. • A multidisciplinary compilation of essays on communications, ranging from animal communications to dance as a means of communication to communications theory. Each essay is followed by a selected bibliography.

Museum of Broadcast Communications Encyclopedia of Television. Ed. Horace Newcomb et al. 3 vols. Chicago: Fitzroy Dearborn, 2000. • Covers genres, programs, people, organizations, and topics related to television history. Information on television programs includes cast, producers, programming history, and bibliographies.

Education

DATABASES AND INDEXES IN EDUCATION

Education Index with Full Text (also known as *Education Abstracts, Full Text*). New York: Wilson, 1994–. • An author-subject database to over 300 current, specialized periodicals (many full texts of articles available). The print version of the work, *Education Index*, covers 1929 to the present.

ERIC. Washington, D.C.: Educational Resources Information Center, 1966–. • Provides descriptive abstracts to articles in over 700 periodicals, as well as to hundreds of thousands of research reports, conference papers, curriculum guides, and other materials that are not formally published. *ERIC*, an invaluable tool for educators, is sponsored by the U.S. Department of Education. It may be delivered at your library through *EBSCO* or *SilverPlatter*.

WEB RESOURCES IN EDUCATION

AskERIC. < http://ericir.syr.edu> • Provides free access to the *ERIC* database as well as sections on lesson plans, a "toolbox" of resources for teachers through the Web, a calendar for educators, and more. *ERIC* is sponsored by the U.S. Department of Education.

ENC Online: Eisenhower National Clearinghouse. <http:// www.enc.org> • A Web site maintained at Ohio State University by the Eisenhower National Clearinghouse for Mathematics and Science Education, offering links to math and science curriculum materials on the Web, ideas for teachers, information on innovative reforms in the curriculum, and a sophisticated search engine.

The Gateway to Educational Materials. <http://thegateway.org> • A directory of selective educational sites. The site also offers powerful searching by grade level as well as topic. Search results lead to lesson plans, curriculum units, and other Web materials for educators. The site is sponsored by ERIC, a project of the U.S. Department of Education.

U.S. Department of Education. <http://www.ed.gov> • Offers quick links to the most frequently visited pages at the Department of Education, including statistical and financial information sources. The site provides a useful search engine.

REFERENCE BOOKS IN EDUCATION

Encyclopedia of American Education. Ed. Harlow G. Unger. 3 vols. New York: Facts on File, 1996. • Offers about 2,500 brief articles on a wide variety of topics, including administration, pedagogy, history, reform, civil rights, minority education, and women's education.

Encyclopedia of Early Childhood Education. Ed. Leslie R. Williams and Doris P. Fromberg. New York: Garland, 1992. • Offers articles on historical, political, economic, sociocultural, intellectual, and educational influences on early childhood education.

Encyclopedia of Educational Research. Ed. Marvin C. Alkin. 6th ed. 4 vols. New York: Macmillan, 1992. • Provides surveys of research in the field, ranging from class size to critical thinking, each followed by bibliographies for further research.

Philosophy of Education: An Encyclopedia. Ed. J. J. Chambliss. New York: Garland, 1998. • Offers substantial analyses covering various philosophers and their contributions, philosophical topics such as behaviorism, critical thinking, and epistemology, and concepts such as *school* and *truth* from a philosophical angle.

World Education Encyclopedia. Ed. George Kurian. New York: Facts on File, 1988. • Provides overviews of education at all levels throughout the world and some discussion of administration and financing and the state of the profession.

Ethnic and area studies

DATABASES AND INDEXES IN ETHNIC AND AREA STUDIES

Bibliography of Asian Studies. Ann Arbor: Association for Asian Studies, 1971–. • An electronic index to European-language scholarly publications in Asian studies. Organized by country, with subdivisions by topic, the index provides more than 410,000 bibliographic citations (no abstracts or full-text articles). This work is also available in print format (1956–).

Ethnic NewsWatch. Stamford, Conn.: Softline, 1985–. • An electronic full-text database specializing in publications published by ethnic communities in the United States and often left out of most full-text databases. This work includes many publications in Spanish.

HAPI: Hispanic American Periodical Index. Los Angeles: UCLA Latin American Center, 1970–. • An electronic index to articles in over 400 scholarly journals published in Latin America or covering topics relevant to Latin America and Latin Americans living in North America. This work is also available in print format.

WEB RESOURCES IN ETHNIC AND AREA STUDIES

Africa: South of the Sahara. < http://www-sul.stanford.edu/depts /ssrg/africa/guide.html> • Selected Web sites organized by country and region and by topic. The site is edited and maintained for the African Studies Association by Karen Fung, deputy curator of the Africa collection at the Hoover Library at Stanford University.

AFRO American Almanac. <http://www.toptags.com/aama> • An educational resource that provides over 900 pages of historical documents, biographies, commentaries, and speeches related to the African American experience from slavery through the civil rights movement. The site is edited and maintained by Donald E. Jones II, an instructor with the U.S. Air Force, and Dr. Jack Powell.

Asian American Studies Resources. <http://sun3.lib.uci.edu /~dtsang/aas2.htm> • A no-frills list of links to bibliographies, publications, research institutes, movements, gay Asian resources, and more. This list was compiled by Daniel C. Tsang, Asian American studies bibliographer at the University of California, Irvine.

Center for World Indigenous Studies (CWIS). <http://www.cwis.org> • A rich site for information on various indigenous peoples and the issues of political and cultural identity and nationhood. Of particular note is the Fourth World Documentation Project, which provides full-text documents related to communities in Africa, the Americas, Asia, Europe, and the Pacific as well as relevant international and multilateral documents. CWIS is a nonprofit international research and educational organization.

CLNet: Building Chicana/o Latina/o Communities through Networking. <http://latino.sscnet.ucla.edu> • Information on Chicano/ Chicana and Latino/Latina issues and cultures, including statistics, a community resource directory, excellent information on cultures and traditions, a museum, electronic publications, and library resources. The site is based at UCLA but cosponsored by many organizations throughout the country.

Latin American Network Information Center. (LANIC). <http://lanic.utexas.edu> • A site sponsored by the University of Texas Institute of Latin American Studies that provides information on Latin America. The site contains country-specific links, links by topic, and assorted links to libraries, institutes, and conferences. The site is thorough, deep, clearly organized, and frequently updated.

Library of Congress HLAS Online: Handbook of Latin American Studies. <http://lcweb2.loc.gov/hlas> • A Web-accessible version of a selective, annotated bibliography of scholarly works on Latin America, published from 1935 to the present. This is an excellent source of research information for any topic in Latin American studies, including Hispanic populations in the United States. The site can be searched by keyword or subject heading in English, Spanish, or Portuguese.

NativeWeb. <http://www.nativeweb.org> • A rich site for information on native peoples, particularly strong for North American indigenous peoples, but global in scope; includes cultural, historical, educational, and current affairs information. The site is hosted by NativeWeb, a nonprofit international educational organization.

WWW Virtual Library: Asian Studies. <http://coombs.anu.edu.au/WWWVL-AsianStudies.html> • Covers information on all regions of Asia and the Middle East. This site is comprehensive, frequently updated, and highly organized by an alphabetical index and a hierarchical topical index. It was edited by T. Matthew Ciolek of Australian National University in conjunction with a team of more than 40 subject specialists.

WWW Virtual Library: Migration and Ethnic Relations. <http://www.ercomer.org/wwwvl> • A thorough list of international resources sponsored by the European Research Centre on Migration and Ethnic Relations at Utrecht University, the Netherlands. Most of the entries are annotated and can be viewed by section or in a complete list without annotations.

REFERENCE BOOKS IN ETHNIC AND AREA STUDIES

Africana: The Encyclopedia of the African and African American Experience. New York: Basic Civitas, 1999.   •   A one-volume trove of information, lavishly illustrated. Edited by the distinguished scholars Kwame Anthony Appiah and Henry Louis Gates Jr. This work is available in print and on CD-ROM.

American Immigrant Cultures: Builders of a Nation. Ed. David Levinson and Melvin Ember. 2 vols. New York: Macmillan Library Reference, 1997.   •   Offers in-depth profiles of immigrant communities in the United States, including their defining features, patterns of cultural variation, immigration history, demographics, and cultural characteristics.

Atlas of the North American Indian. By Carl Waldman. New York: Facts on File, 1985.   •   Offers maps on tribal locations, reservations, sites of cultural and archaeological importance, and other significant places; includes related text and bibliographies.

Dictionary of Native American Mythology. By Sam D. Gill and Irene F. Sullivan. Santa Barbara: ABC-CLIO, 1992.   •   Provides quick access to information about individuals, events, and topics in Native American mythology, from all tribes and periods; includes a bibliography.

Encyclopedia of African American Civil Rights: From Emancipation to the Present. Ed. Charles D. Lowery and John F. Marszalek. New York: Greenwood, 1992.   •   A one-volume dictionary of terms, events, and prominent people related to the civil rights movement.

Encyclopedia of African-American Culture and History. Ed. Jack Salzman, Cornel West, and David L. Smith. 5 vols. New York: Macmillan Library Reference, 1996.   •   Offers extensive articles on people, institutions, events, issues, and themes related to African Americans; includes many illustrations and up-to-date bibliographies.

Encyclopedia of Africa South of the Sahara. Ed. John Izard Middleton. 4 vols. New York: Scribner, 1997.   •   Covers countries, ethnic groups, and topics in nearly 900 substantial articles.

Encyclopedia of Contemporary French Culture. Ed. Alex Hughes and Keith Reader. London: Routledge, 1998.   •   Short articles on a wealth of topics, covering French and Francophone culture from

1945 to the present. Other volumes cover contemporary German, Spanish, and Italian cultures.

Encyclopedia of Latin American History and Culture. Ed. Barbara A. Tenenbaum and Georgette M. Dorn. 5 vols. New York: Scribner, 1996. Covers a wide variety of topics in over 5,000 articles that together constitute an overview of current knowledge about the region. There are entries by country and by topic (such as slavery, art, Asians in Latin America) as well as biographical entries.

Encyclopedia of Multicultural America. Ed. Julie Galens et al. 2 vols. Detroit: Gale Group, 1999. • Offers more than 100 substantial essays on ethnic groups in the United States, covering origins, circumstances of arrival, family, community, culture, economy, politics, and significant contributions. Each essay ends with a bibliography and contacts for further research.

Encyclopedia of the Modern Middle East. Ed. Reeva S. Simon et al. 4 vols. New York: Macmillan Library Reference, 1996. • Covers political, historical, social, economic, and cultural topics in substantial, well-documented articles.

Gale Encyclopedia of Native American Tribes. 4 vols. Detroit: Gale Group, 1998. • Offers information on the history and current status of nearly 400 tribes, with historical background, past and current location, religious beliefs, language, means of subsistence, healing practices, customs, oral literature, and current issues facing the tribe.

Handbook of Hispanic Culture in the United States. 4 vols. Houston: Arte Publico, 1993. • A survey of art, history, sociology, and anthropology of Hispanic Americans. Chapters within each volume are arranged by topic, and articles are lengthy and well illustrated.

Handbook of North American Indians. 15 vols. Washington, D.C.: Smithsonian Institution, 1978–. • A multivolume set that offers scholarly essays on the history, social situation, politics, religion, economics, and tribal traditions of Native American groups. The work covers aboriginal cultures in North America by region and topics such as white-Indian relations, the arts, and languages.

The Historical and Cultural Atlas of African Americans. By Molefi K. Asante and Mark T. Mattson. New York: Macmillan, 1991. • A geographically oriented overview of African American life, experiences, and traditions. Included are maps representing African origins, the slave trade, the Civil War, current social and economic status, and other topics.

Oxford Encyclopedia of the Modern Islamic World. 4 vols. New York: Oxford University Press, 1995. • Covers Islamic peoples, movements, and issues throughout the world.

Geography

DATABASES AND INDEXES IN GEOGRAPHY

Geobase. Barking, Essex: Elsevier, 1989–. • An electronic index to books and articles relevant to human and physical geography. This work provides bibliographical citations and descriptive abstracts of more than 2,000 books and reports and more than 3,000 articles. The print version of this index, Geographical Abstracts, is issued monthly and provides an annual subject, author, and regional index.

The Online Geographical Bibliography. <http://geobib.lib.uwm.edu>. Milwaukee: American Geographical Society, 1938–. • An electronic index to current journal articles, books, and maps in the field of geography from the American Geographical Society collection. This work, which provides bibliographic citations (no abstracts or full-text articles), covers topics such as biogeography, climatology, human geography, hydrology, and physical geography as well as regional geography. The print version of this index — titled Current Geographical Publications: Additions to the Research Catalogue of the American Geographical Society — is issued ten times a year.

WEB RESOURCES IN GEOGRAPHY

INFOMINE. Scholarly Internet Resources Collections: Maps and Geographical Information Systems (GIS). <http://infomine.ucr.edu/cgi -bin/search?maps> • A searchable directory of Web sites containing maps and mapmaking programs, satellite images, photographs, and text and image databases; all entries at the site are annotated. The site is edited and supported by the library of the University of California, Riverside.

Perry Castañeda Library Map Collection. <http://www.lib.utexas
.edu/maps/index.html> • An excellent and frequently updated
list of over 2,400 online maps in digital form. The site is maintained
by the General Libraries at the University of Texas at Austin and is
available through the UT Library Online.

U.S. Census Bureau: U.S. Gazetteer. <http://www.census.gov/cgi
-bin/gazetteer> • A database of basic information on locations
in the United States, including links to maps and census data. The
database is searchable by place name, state, and zip code.

REFERENCE BOOKS IN GEOGRAPHY

Columbia Gazetteer of the World. Ed. Saul B. Cohen. 3 vols. New
York: Columbia University Press, 1998. • Provides the exact location of places and geographical features around the world and
gives a very brief definition or description. The most complete gazetteer available, it has been recently updated to reflect new and
changed place names.

Dictionary of Concepts in Human Geography. Ed. Robert P. Larkin
and Gary L. Peters. Westport, Conn.: Greenwood, 1983. Covers the
development of theories in the field, with excellent references to key
publications.

Dictionary of Human Geography. Ed. Ron Jonson et al. New York
and Oxford: Blackwell, 2000. • Defines and discusses terms, topics, and concepts in human geography. Brief bibliographies follow
many of the entries.

Encyclopedic Dictionary of Physical Geography. Ed. Andrew Goudie
et al. New York and Oxford: Blackwell, 1999. • Defines and discusses terms and concepts in physical geography and includes brief,
selective bibliographies.

SPECIAL RESOURCES IN GEOGRAPHY

Maps and atlases are basic tools for the geographer. Atlases, because of their size, are often shelved in special bookcases; maps
may be housed in a special collection of their own. Think in terms
not only of the familiar sort of world atlas, such as the *Atlas of the
World,* 8th ed. (New York: Oxford University Press, 2000), but also

of atlases that provide information on population, trade, history, water resources, and so on.

Law

DATABASES AND INDEXES ON LAW

Index to Legal Periodicals and Books. New York: Wilson, 1994–. • Electronic index to legal journals, law reviews and books, government publications, institutions, and bar associations. This work, which offers bibliographic citations (no abstracts or full-text materials), is searchable by topic and by legal citation. Also available in print, including an earlier version started in 1908, which concentrates on journal articles.

Lexis/Nexis Universe. Dayton, Ohio: Lexis-Nexis, 1998–. • This collection of databases includes an extensive legal section. The law review database offers the full texts of detailed articles analyzing legal issues — over a billion documents from 8,700 news and business sources and 4,800 legal sources. The database also covers statutes and case law and includes a feature called the "Get a Case" section, in which a court decision can be found by party name or citation.

WEB RESOURCES ON LAW

Findlaw. <http: www.findlaw.com> • Billed as "the leading web portal focused on law and government." In addition to being an excellent full-text database of Supreme Court decisions, the site links to federal and state case and statutory law. *Findlaw* also provides a law dictionary, a legal subject index, and the "LawCrawler" limited search engine. *Findlaw* began in 1995 as a resource compiled for the Northern California Law Librarians.

Legal Information Institute, Cornell University Law School. <http:// www.law.cornell.edu> • A directory to legal information on the Web, including texts of case law and statutes for state, federal, and international jurisdictions. The site — organized alphabetically by topic — also provides links to court opinions and directories to law organizations and journals.

National Archives and Records Administration: Code of Federal Regulations. <http://www.access.gpo.gov/nara/cfr/index.html>

• Provides access to federal and executive government documents. This site is searchable by keyword, title, or citation information.

The Oyez Project: U.S. Supreme Court Multimedia Database. <http://oyez.nwu.edu> • An electronic database of constitutional law cases of note, with audio files of the oral arguments of many landmark Supreme Court cases. The site is edited and maintained by Jerry Goldman, a political scientist at Northwestern University.

U.S. Code. <http://www4.law.cornell.edu/uscode> • Online text of federal statutes. The site is searchable by topic, title, by popular name of an act (such as "Hatch Act,") by a specific section, or by a phrase anywhere in the code. It is part of the Legal Information Institute at the Cornell University Law School.

U.S. Supreme Court Opinions. <http://www.findlaw.com/casecode /supreme.html> • Searchable full-text opinions of Supreme Court decisions from 1893, available at *Findlaw* with hyperlinked citations. Though other Web sites offer versions of these texts, this site is particularly well designed. Search by citation, party name, or full text. Full-text searches give the option of retrieving the portion of the decision that uses the search terms or the entire text.

REFERENCE BOOKS ON LAW

Black's Law Dictionary. Ed. Bryan A. Garner and Henry Campbell Black. 7th ed. St. Paul: West, 1999. • Offers brief, technical definitions of legal terms.

Encyclopedia of the American Constitution. Ed. Leonard Williams Levy et al. 2nd ed. 6 vols. New York: Macmillan Library Reference, 2000. • Covers essential topics and landmark cases related to constitutional law.

Encyclopedia of the American Judicial System. Ed. Robert J. Janosik. 3 vols. New York: Macmillan Library Reference, 1987. • Offers substantial articles covering the workings of the court and its effects on society.

Historic U.S. Court Cases, 1690–1990: An Encyclopedia. John W. Johnson. New York: Routledge, 2001. • Essays on major cases that have had an impact on American law and society, with sections on civil liberties, minority rights, women, and economics.

West's Encyclopedia of American Law. 12 vols. St. Paul: Gale Group, West Group, 1998. • Covers legal issues clearly in articles written for a general audience.

Political science

DATABASES AND INDEXES IN POLITICAL SCIENCE

Congressional Universe. Bethesda: LexisNexis Academic & Library Solutions, 1970– (with Congressional Indexes from 1789 to 1972). • The most comprehensive database of information on the U.S. Congress. *Congressional Universe* provides bibliographic citations, descriptive abstracts, and the full texts of documents including bills, laws (with legislative histories), committee reports, the *Congressional Record* and more.

Monthly Catalog of United States Government Publications. Washington, D.C.: Government Printing Office, 1895–. • An index to publications from federal agencies and Congress, arranged by issuing body and indexed by author, title, subject, and series or report number. This work includes bibliographic citations (no descriptive abstracts or full-text documents). Available online at <http://www.gpo.gov>.

PAIS International. New York: Public Affairs Information Service, 1972–. • An electronic index to books, articles, and government documents on public affairs — including politics, social issues, and economics. International in scope, this work provides bibliographic citations with descriptive abstracts (no full-text articles), combining the *Public Affairs Information Service* (1915–90), a long-running publication that is a good resource for historical analysis of politics, and *PAIS Foreign Language Index* (1972–90). The print version of this work is *PAIS International in Print.*

WEB RESOURCES IN POLITICAL SCIENCE

Foreign Affairs Online. <http://www.people.virginia.edu/~rjb3v/rjb.html> • A meta-index to sites related to international law, international relations, and U.S. foreign policy. Well organized and annotated, this site is hosted by the Department of Information Technology and Communication at the University of Virginia.

Governments on the WWW. <http://www.gksoft.com/govt/en> • A clearly organized directory of governmental institutions and political parties from around the world. The site is edited and maintained by Gunnar Anzinger of the Technische Universität, Munich, Germany.

Infonation. <http://www.un.org/Pubs/CyberSchoolBus/infonation /e_infonation.htm> • A database of current statistics for United Nations member states. This site allows users to compare the statistics of up to seven countries at a time, providing quick reference to authoritative comparative statistics. This site is hosted and maintained by the United Nations.

Library of Congress Country Studies. <http://lcweb2.loc.gov/frd /cs/cshome.html> • Online editions of book-length country profiles produced for U.S. diplomats. This site includes substantial information on each nation's culture, history, economy, and political system. It is searchable by topic and country. Be sure to note publication dates for the most current information; some volumes are more than ten years old and may include outdated materials.

National Political Index. <http://www.politicalindex.com> • Provides access to sites related to participation in politics; an eclectic gathering of sources of political information including news, events, humor, state and local parties, and candidates. The index links to more than 3,500 Web sites with political ties, including 200 political science departments, 50 political think tanks, and 600 political activist groups. The National Political Index is a nonpartisan, nonprofit organization.

National Security Archive. <http://www.gwu.edu/~nsarchiv> • The Web site of a project that has collected the world's largest nongovernmental archive of declassified documents, many of them covering controversial issues and obtained through the Freedom of Information Act. Though many documents are not accessible through the Web site, there are collections of papers called *briefing books* on a variety of foreign affairs topics. The National Security Archive is an independent nongovernmental research institute and library at George Washington University.

THOMAS: Legislative Information on the Internet. <http:// thomas.loc.gov> • A site maintained by the Library of Congress that provides in-depth information on the U.S. Congress. Users can search the site by bill number or keyword to learn about the legislative process, find a state's members of Congress, and access a comprehensive database on current and past legislation. The site also provides a full-text search of the *Congressional Record*, a daily record of activity in Congress, and committee information.

United Nations. <http://www.un.org>   •   Offers news releases, virtual tours, documents, and basic information about the United Nations and its bodies. Three different search engines explore a large database and list of links. The site includes a wealth of reports, statistical data, and other information on human rights, international law, peacekeeping missions, and other topics.

United States Department of State. <http://www.state.gov>   •   Includes many full-text documents of interest, with particularly rich resources in the Countries and Regions and International Topics and Issues areas of the site.

University of Michigan Documents Center: Political Science Resources. <http://www.lib.umich.edu/libhome/Documents.center /polisci.html>   •   An enormous series of links related to political science and political theory. Links are annotated, and sponsoring institutions of listed sites are named.

WWW Virtual Library: Political Science Virtual Library. <http:// spirit.lib.uconn.edu/PoliSci/polisci.htm>   •   An enormous but simply organized site that provides an exhaustive list of links to political science resources on the Web. The site is maintained by Thomas Hartley of the Department of Political Science at the University of Connecticut and is part of the *WWW Virtual Library* <http:// www.vlib.org>.

WWW Virtual Library: U.S. Federal Government Agencies. <http:// www.lib.lsu.edu/gov/fedgov.html>   •   A well-organized and constantly updated guide to U.S. federal government information on the Web, organized by branch of government and agency. The site is maintained by the Louisiana State University Libraries and is part of the *WWW Virtual Library* <http://www.vlib.org>.

REFERENCE BOOKS IN POLITICAL SCIENCE

Almanac of American Politics. Ed. Michael Barone and Richard E. Cohen. Washington, D.C.: National Journal, 1972–.   •   Summarizes the state of American politics at both national and state levels, giving voting results on key issues and state-by-state analyses of political concerns. The almanac is updated every two years.

America Votes. Ed. Richard M. Scammon. Washington, D.C.: Congressional Quarterly, 1956–. • A biennial summary of state and national election returns; useful for historical as well as current information.

Congressional Quarterly Almanac. Washington, D.C.: Congressional Quarterly, 1945–. • An annual summation of U.S. politics that analyzes key issues, important legislation, voting records of congressional representatives, and major Supreme Court decisions.

Congressional Quarterly's Guide to Congress. 5th ed. Washington, D.C.: Congressional Quarterly, 1999. • Provides detailed histories and discussions of congressional processes and issues. Similar guides put out by the same publisher cover the presidency, the Supreme Court, and U.S. elections.

Congressional Quarterly Weekly Report. Washington, D.C.: Congressional Quarterly, 1967–. • A weekly magazine covering events in Washington; includes a detailed index every six months. Another weekly magazine that provides similar coverage is the *National Journal.*

The Encyclopedia of Political Thought. Ed. Janet Coleman et al. Oxford: Blackwell, 1991. • Offers concise but thorough discussions of political concepts and theories, including definitions of terms such as *consent, power, exploitation,* and *just war.* This work also provides historical contexts for ideas and the names of individuals associated with specific political ideas.

Encyclopedia of U.S. Foreign Relations. Ed. Bruce W. Jentleson and Thomas G. Paterson. 4 vols. New York: Oxford University Press, 1997. • Includes over 1,000 articles covering historical events, relations with countries, biographical sketches of leaders associated with foreign policy, treaties, doctrines, and key concepts. This work, published under the auspices of the Council on Foreign Relations, also provides chronologies and comparative country data.

International Encyclopedia of Public Policy and Administration. Ed. Jay M. Shafrirz. 4 vols. Boulder: Westview, 1998. • Covers topics in public administration such as regional development, emergency management, budget reform, cost of living adjustments, and more.

This work, with its global scope and interdisciplinary coverage, provides broad perspectives. It also includes coverage of principles, theories, legal concepts, and management topics as well as definitions of terms — such as *groupthink* and *muddling through* — used in the field of public policy.

Political Handbook of the World. Ed. Arthur S. Banks and Thomas C. Muller. Binghamton, N.Y.: CSA Publications, 1927–. • Covers countries of the world, giving basic background information, discussions of political parties and structures, and analyses of current political trends. The work is updated annually.

United States Government Manual. Washington, D.C.: Government Printing Office, 1973–. • Outlines the organization of federal government agencies, providing organizational charts, contact names and addresses, and descriptions of agencies' missions.

Psychology

DATABASES AND INDEXES IN PSYCHOLOGY

PsycInfo (or *PsycLit*). Washington, D.C.: American Psychological Association, 1927–. • An electronic index covering books, book chapters, and journal articles from more than 1,300 journals in psychology and related fields. The index, updated monthly, provides bibliographic citations and descriptive abstracts of articles, technical reports, and books and book chapters. A list of the subject descriptors used by the compilers of the abstracts helps a researcher determine effective search terms. The print version of this index is titled *Psychological Abstracts.*

WEB RESOURCES IN PSYCHOLOGY

APA PsycNet: American Psychological Association. <http://www.apa.org> • The site for the American Psychological Association, providing information on the science and practice of psychology as well as information on APA journals and other relevant publications.

CyberPsychLink.   <http://cctr.umkc.edu/user/dmartin/psych2.html> • A comprehensive directory to psychology sites on the Web. This site provides links to databases, archives, reference materials, and catalogs. The links are simply and clearly annotated, and the site is easy to navigate.

Internet Mental Health. <http://www.mentalhealth.com /main.html> • Provides detailed information on 54 mental disorders and 72 of the most commonly prescribed medications, along with the full texts of articles and pamphlets useful to researchers in psychology. Internet links are organized by mental health issues and disorders. *Internet Mental Health* is a free online encyclopedia and magazine created by Canadian psychiatrist Phillip Long.

Psych Central: Dr. John Grohol's Mental Health Page. <http:// psychcentral.com> • Offers articles, essays, live chats, and a vast directory of mental health and psychology resources online. Although the site emphasizes consumer information rather than academic information, it provides a well-organized, annotated list of current Web resources. The site is edited by John Grohol, a Boston-based author and researcher who has contributed to a number of well-known publications and Web sites in psychology.

Psychcrawler. <http://www.psychcrawler.com> • Provides access to sites of interest to the researcher in psychology. Though the number of sites searched is limited and very selective, the search engine allows for highly focused searches. *Psychcrawler* is a product of the American Psychological Association.

PsychWeb. <http://www.psywww.com> • A guide to Web resources, including scholarly resources, sport psychology, and self-help resources. The site was created and is maintained by Dr. Russell A. Dewey of Georgia Southern University.

The Social Psychology Network. <http://www.socialpsychology.org> • An exhaustive list of more than 5,000 links to resources in psychology. This site is searchable, and menus are available under both social psychology and general psychology. It is maintained by Scott Plous of Wesleyan University.

WWW Virtual Library: Psychology. <http://www.clas.ufl.edu/users /gthursby/psi> • A selective but vast list of links on many aspects of the field, including school psychology, psychology of religion, and mental health. The site is edited by Dr. Gene R. Thursby of the College of Liberal Arts and Sciences at the University of Florida and is part of the *WWW Virtual Library* <http://www.vlib.org>.

REFERENCE BOOKS IN PSYCHOLOGY

Blackwell Dictionary of Cognitive Psychology. Ed. Andrew W. Ellis et al. Oxford: Blackwell, 1994.   •   Contains substantial surveys of major topics in cognition and provides selective bibliographies.

Companion Encyclopedia of Psychology. Ed. Andrew M. Colman. 2 vols. London: Routledge, 1994.   •   Offers survey articles of major topics in psychology, including perception, learning, biological aspects of behavior, developmental psychology, abnormal psychology, and research methods. Each article is written at a fairly technical level and includes a selected bibliography and references.

The Corsini Encyclopedia of Psychology and Behavioral Science. Ed. W. Edward Craighead and Charles B. Nemeroff. 3rd ed. 4 vols. New York: Wiley, 2000.   •   Defines and discusses terms, theories, methodology, and issues in psychological practice and offers brief biographies of important psychologists.

Diagnostic and Statistical Manual of Mental Disorders (DSM-IV). 4th ed., rev. Washington, D.C.: American Psychiatric Association, 2000.   •   Classifies and describes mental disorders and includes diagrams to aid in the diagnosis of mental disorders as well as a glossary of technical terms.

Encyclopedia of Human Behavior. Ed. V. S. Ramachandran. 4 vols. San Diego: Academic Press, 1994.   •   Offers articles on a wide variety of topics from such specifics as left- or right-handedness and blushing to broader concepts such as interpersonal communications and intelligence. Each article provides an overview of the current state of knowledge about a topic and provides references to research.

Encyclopedia of Human Intelligence. Ed. Robert J. Sternberg. 2 vols. New York: Macmillan, 1994.   •   A collection of more than 250 articles on various aspects of intelligence, including reasoning, problem solving, aphasia, and measurement.

Encyclopedia of Mental Health. Ed. Howard S. Friedman et al. 3 vols. San Diego: Academic Press, 1998.   •   Includes substantial articles on major disciplines in the field, research areas, and topics of public interest. Designed for both students and health professionals, this work provides current and thorough coverage of mental disorders, treatments, personality traits, and psychological aspects of such topics as television viewing, parenting, and homelessness.

Encyclopedia of Psychology. Ed. Alan E. Kazdin. 8 vols. Washington, D.C.: American Psychological Association, 2000. • An up-to-date and thorough treatment of psychology topics including methodology, findings, advances in research, and applications.

Mental Measurements Yearbook. Lincoln: Buros Institute of Mental Measurements, 1938–. • An essential reference work for those interested in psychological tests. This work surveys and reviews tests of aptitude, education, achievement, and personality and includes bibliographies of related research. It is available in electronic format (through SilverPlatter). The electronic version includes the full texts of articles from 1983 through the present.

Sociology

DATABASES AND INDEXES IN SOCIOLOGY

Population Index on the Web. Princeton: Office of Population Research, 1935–. • An electronic index to books, articles, government publications, charts, tables, and conference proceedings containing demographic research. The index provides bibliographic citations and descriptive abstracts and is searchable by author, subject, region, or text within citations and abstracts. This work also includes topical articles, charts, and tables. The *Population Index* is also available in print and is updated quarterly.

SocioFile. San Diego: Sociological Abstracts, 1974–. • The most important index in sociology, covering approximately 2,000 journals from 55 countries. This electronic index (available through SilverPlatter) provides bibliographic citations and descriptive abstracts and is searchable by author and subject. The print version of this index is titled *Sociological Abstracts*, with coverage from 1952 to the present.

WEB RESOURCES IN SOCIOLOGY

The George Warren Brown School of Social Work: Social Work and Social Services Web Sites. <http://gwbweb.wustl.edu/websites .html> • Features links for the practicing social worker, organized alphabetically and thematically, covering topics such as families, health care, poverty, crisis intervention, and types of therapy. The site is frequently updated and is maintained by Violet E. Horvath as a service of the George Warren Brown School of Social Work at Washington University, St. Louis.

Julian Dierkes's Comprehensive Guide to Sociology Online. <http://www.sociolog.com>   •   Offers links to information on topics in the field and research institutes. The site is regularly updated and maintained by Julian Dierkes of the Japan Research Center at the University of Cambridge.

A Sociological Tour through Cyberspace. <http://www.trinity.edu/~mkearl/index.html>   •   Provides links of interest to sociologists, including theory, data resources, methodology, advice for writing research papers, and coverage of topics in the field. Each section begins with a brief essay on the practice of sociology. The site is clearly organized and provides up-to-date links. It is edited and maintained by Michael C. Kearl, sociology professor at Trinity University.

The SocioWeb: Independent Guide to Sociological Resources on the Internet. <http://www.sonic.net/~markbl/socioweb>   •   Features links to sites on major sociologists, theories, and research data. This site is updated frequently and includes a search engine and a sociology-focused chat room. It is edited and maintained by Mark Blair, a sociology graduate of Sonoma State University.

WWW Virtual Library: Demography and Population Studies. <http://demography.anu.edu.au/VirtualLibrary>   •   Lists more than 150 worldwide population resources online, including institutes, government resources, and organizations. The site, organized topically and alphabetically, is frequently updated and maintained by Diana Crow, a programmer for the Demography Program of Australian National University.

REFERENCE BOOKS IN SOCIOLOGY

Encyclopedia of Crime and Justice. Ed. Joshua Dressler. 2nd ed. 4 vols. New York: Gale Group, 2001.   •   Provides overviews of key topics in the field of criminal justice, with useful bibliographies. For additional information on law enforcement practices, see the *Encyclopedia of Police Science*, edited by William G. Bailey, 2nd ed., rev., (New York: Garland, 1998).

Encyclopedia of Social Work. Ed. Richard L. Edwards et al. 19th ed. 3 vols. Washington, D.C.: National Association of Social Workers Press, 1995. With supplements.   •   Offers substantial articles, with bibliographies, on subjects such as foster care for children, adolescence, and public health services as well as short biographies of important figures in the field.

Encyclopedia of Sociology. Ed. Edgar G. Montgomery et al. 4 vols. New York: Macmillan Library Reference, 2000.   •   Provides scholarly discussions of such topics as class and race, ethnicity, economic sociology, and social structure. The articles are written by specialists and include excellent bibliographies.

Women's studies

DATABASES AND INDEXES IN WOMEN'S STUDIES

Contemporary Women's Issues. New York: Gale Group, 1992–.
•   An electronic database providing access to 1,500 journals, newsletters, reports, and fact sheets from the United States and abroad. The database provides bibliographic citations, descriptive abstracts, and the full texts of most documents. It is updated monthly. (No print version is available.)

Women Studies Abstracts. Rush, N.Y.: Rush Publishing, 1972–.
•   An electronic index providing bibliographic citations and descriptive abstracts of books, articles, and other publications. Also available in print, the index is published quarterly and includes an annual subject index.

WEB RESOURCES IN WOMEN'S STUDIES

Diotima: Materials for the Study of Women and Gender in the Ancient World. <http://www.stoa.org/diotima>   •   Includes primary sources from classical texts dealing with women as well as course materials, a searchable bibliography, and links to articles, books, databases, and visual images. The site is edited and maintained by professors at the University of Kentucky and Southwest University.

The Electra Pages: Directory of Women's Organizations. <http://electrapages.com>   •   A feminist database maintained by the Women's Information Exchange, a group of 9,000 feminist organizations. The site provides extensive links to e-zines and Web sites on women's music, feminist activism, lesbian studies, women of color, and global feminism.

Feminist Majority Foundation Online. <http://www.feminist.org> • A research, information, and political action site sponsored by the Feminist Majority Foundation. The site includes information on women's issues, organized by date, and provides extensive links to sites on violence against women, women and work, women's health, reproductive rights, and global feminism.

Institute for Women's Policy Research. <http://www.iwpr.org> • Links to information on violence, employment and economic change, democracy and society, poverty and welfare, the family and work, and health-care policy. The Institute for Women's Policy Research is a nonprofit organization that conducts scientific research for use by women's organizations.

Medieval Feminist Index: Scholarship on Women, Sexuality, and Gender. <http://www.haverford.edu/library/reference/mschaus/mfi/mfi.html> • Provides an index (not including abstracts or full texts of articles) to more than 2,500 articles, reviews, and essays on women, sexuality, and gender in the Middle Ages. Searchable by author, title, or subject, the site also links to other sites on women and medieval studies and to libraries with strong holdings in medieval studies. The site was created by a group of scholars and librarians and is edited by Margaret Schaus, a librarian at Haverford College.

National Women's History Project. <http://www.nwhp.org/index.html> • A well-designed site that provides information about the diversity of women and women's contributions to history. The National Women's History Project is a nonprofit educational organization.

Selected Women and Gender Resources on the World Wide Web. <http://www.library.wisc.edu/libraries/WomensStudies/others.htm> • A well-organized directory of research links to women's studies resources, women's organizations, university departments, and libraries as well as to journals and books on the Web. Follow the link to the *Women's Studies Librarian* page to find lists of recommended books in a wide range of women's studies topics. The site is edited and maintained by the Office of the Women's Studies Librarian at the University of Wisconsin.

WomensNet. <http://www.igc.org/igc/gateway/wnindex.html>
• A network of current developments, news, and issues in women's studies, this site is particularly strong in covering international news and controversies. The site is updated regularly and is part of the IGC Internet, the Web portal for the Institute for Global Communication, a nonprofit organization.

WWW Virtual Library: Women and Gender Studies Web Sites. <http //libraries.mit.edu/humanities/WomensStudies/wscd.html> • A directory of women's and gender studies resources organized by topic and selected by specialists in the field. The site is edited and maintained by the Women's Studies Section of the Association of College and Research Libraries; it is part of the *WWW Virtual Library* <http://www.vlib.org>.

REFERENCE BOOKS IN WOMEN'S STUDIES

The ABC-CLIO Companion to Women's Progress in America. By Elizabeth Knappman-Frost and Sarah Kunan. Santa Barbara: ABC-CLIO, 1994. • Covers notable American women as well as topics and organizations that have been significant in women's quest for equality.

The Dictionary of Feminist Theory. By Maggie Humm. 2nd ed. Columbus: Ohio State University Press, 1995. • Covers theoretical issues in feminism and is particularly useful for putting them in historical context. The work is also helpful for pinpointing primary documents related to feminist theory.

From Suffrage to the Senate: An Encyclopedia of American Women in Politics. By Suzanne O'Dea Schenken. 2 vols. Santa Barbara: ABC-CLIO, 1999. • Coverage includes political leaders, issues and movements, organizations, and court cases.

Notable American Women, 1607–1950: A Biographical Dictionary. Ed. Edward T. James et al. 3 vols. Cambridge: Harvard University Press, 1974. With supplements and related series books. • Provides lengthy and thorough biographies of women, followed by useful bibliographies. A supplement, *Notable American Women: The Modern Period*, published in 1983, profiles women who died between 1951 and 1975.

Women in the Third World: An Encyclopedia of Contemporary Issues. Ed. Edith H. Altbach and Nelly P. Stromquist. New York: Garland,

1998. • Offers substantial overviews of topics related to women in the developing world, including theoretical issues, political and legal contexts, sex-role ideologies, demographics, economics, and the environment. It also provides regional surveys.

Women in World History: A Biographical Encyclopedia. Ed. Anne Commire and Deborah Klezmer. 7 vols. to date. New York: Gale Group, 1999. • Contains biographies of historically significant women from all walks of life from all countries. When complete, this will be the largest compilation of biographical material on the world's women.

The Women's Chronology: A Year-by-Year Record, from Prehistory to the Present. By James Trager. New York: Henry Holt, 1994. • Provides brief descriptive entries related to women through history. Entries are arranged chronologically and are marked with symbols indicating the topic area in which they fall.

Women's Studies: A Guide to Information Sources. By Sarah Carter. Jefferson, N.C.: McFarland, 1990. • An annotated list of more than 1,000 reference books and other resources on women, organized in broad topic areas.

Women's Studies Encyclopedia. Ed. Helen Tierney. 3 vols., rev. and expanded. New York: Greenwood, 1999. • Provides lengthy articles on women's involvement in a wide variety of fields. The first volume treats the sciences; the second deals with literature, the arts, and learning; and the third covers history, philosophy, and religion. This work is available in electronic format.

For other biographical sources on women, consult *Native American Women: A Biographical Dictionary,* edited by Gretchen M. Bataille and Laurie Lisa, 2nd ed. (New York: Taylor and Francis, 2001); *European Immigrant Women in the United States: A Biographical Dictionary,* edited by Judy Barrett Litoff and Judith McDonald (New York: Garland, 1994); and African American Women: A Biographical Dictionary, edited by Dorothy C. Salem (New York: Garland, 1993).

Researching in the Sciences

Research in the sciences generally involves recognizing a scientific problem to be solved, setting up an experiment designed to yield useful data, and interpreting the data in the context of other scientific knowledge. Researchers use library resources to

- keep up with current thinking in the field so they can recognize a question worth asking
- review what is known about a given phenomenon so they can place new knowledge in context
- locate specific information they need to successfully carry out an experiment or project

The large volume of scientific literature being produced can be daunting at first. However, a number of resources are available to help you find what is relevant to your research, and most of the resources are searchable online. When planning to search for scientific materials, be prepared to

- choose your search terms carefully so that they match those used by your index or database
- work from the most recent publications to earlier ones, sorting out schools of thought and lines of inquiry as you go
- know when to stop, bearing in mind that a literature review can't cover everything ever published on a topic but is a selection of the most important and relevant research

The resources listed here will give you an idea of where to start. Consult a librarian to determine which resources are best for your research and whether they are available in electronic format.

General resources in the sciences

DATABASES AND INDEXES IN THE SCIENCES

American Men and Women of Science Online. New York: Bowker, 1989–. • An electronic database providing biographical information about living scientists. This database, searchable by name or discipline, provides profiles of more than 119,000 scientists and engineers in 10 disciplines and 190 subdisciplines. This work is also available in a print version, *American Men and Women of Science*, a publication that began in 1906 as *American Men of Science.*

General Science Index. New York: Wilson, 1984–. • An electronic index designed for the nonspecialist and covering about 190 major research publications and popular science magazines. The index offers bibliographic citations. To access descriptive abstracts, see the *General Science Abstracts* database; for the full texts of selected publications, see the *General Science Full Text* database (both databases are also published by Wilson). The *General Science Index* is also available in print, with coverage beginning in 1978.

The Web of Science. Philadelphia: Institute for Scientific Information, 1961–. • An interdisciplinary index to more than 8,000 scholarly journals. The index, updated weekly, provides bibliographic citations and descriptive abstracts (no full-text articles). It allows users to find out who has cited a particular work (in the bibliographies of other publications), an efficient way to trace the importance of a piece of research. This index is available in print as the *Science Citation Index*, with coverage beginning in 1961.

WEB RESOURCES IN THE SCIENCES

Academic Press Dictionary of Science and Technology. <http://www.harcourt.com/dictionary> • An online technical dictionary that concisely defines more than 130,000 terms.

EurekAlert. <http://www.eurekalert.org> • A regularly updated source for information about research advances in science, medicine, health, and technology. The site includes links to other science sites, access to databases, and a searchable archive of news releases. Content for the site is screened by an advisory committee of journalists and public information specialists. The site is maintained by the American Association for the Advancement of Science, the world's largest general science organization.

REFERENCE BOOKS IN THE SCIENCES

Breakthroughs: A Chronology of Great Achievements in Science and Mathematics, 1200–1930. By Claire L. Parkinson. Boston: G. K. Hall, 1985. • Organized by year, a handy guide to the historical period and context of major discoveries in science and mathematics.

Dictionary of Scientific Biography. 14 vols. New York: Macmillan Library Reference, 1970–2000. With supplements. • Profiles scientists from early to modern times, considering both their lives and technical aspects of their work. Each biography is followed by a bibliography of primary and secondary sources.

McGraw-Hill Dictionary of Scientific and Technical Terms. 8th ed. 20 vols. New York: McGraw-Hill, 1997. • Offers concise, up-to-date definitions of technical terms beyond those found in a standard dictionary.

McGraw-Hill Encyclopedia of Science and Technology. 8th ed. New York: McGraw-Hill, 1997. • A specialized encyclopedia covering scientific topics in detail. Technical discussions are fully illustrated with charts, diagrams, and photographs. This work is available in electronic format as *The McGraw-Hill Multimedia Encyclopedia of Science and Technology,* release 2.0.

Biology

DATABASES AND INDEXES IN BIOLOGY

Biological and Agricultural Index Plus. New York: Wilson, 1983–. • An electronic index to more than 290 journals in biology and agriculture, covering topics in botany, zoology, microbiology, genetics, and biochemistry. This index provides biological citations, descriptive abstracts, and links to the full texts of articles from 45 of the journals indexed (through Wilson Web only). The work is also available in print format, Biological and Agricultural Index, with coverage beginning in 1964.

BIOSIS. Philadelphia: Biosis, 1980–. • The most complete index to biological literature with over 5 million records. The index provides bibliographic citations and descriptive abstracts. It is organized by subject, author, keyword, genus and species, biosystem, and concept. The index is updated quarterly. It is published semimonthly and cumulative indexes are published twice a year. The print version of this work, *Biological Abstracts*, provides coverage beginning in 1926.

WEB RESOURCES IN BIOLOGY

BioChemLinks.com. < http://www.biochemlinks.com> • A portal to excellent resources in biology, biochemistry, and chemistry, with links to full-text science news sources. The links are organized by subject — general chemistry, organic chemistry, biochemistry, biotechnology, and the teaching of science — and geared toward science education and the nonspecialist. The site is the product of Schmidel & Wojciki, editorial Web developers of a number of science sites. Dyann Schmidel has also taught graduate and undergraduate courses in chemistry, biochemistry, and biotechnology.

BioLinks. <http://www.biolinks.com> • A search engine for a select database of Web sites in biology that avoids irrelevant or nonscientific search results. Results are listed in specific categories, such as databases, journals, and companies. Most, but not all, search results are annotated. This site has links to related areas and is updated regularly. The sponsor of this site, Bioview.com, is an employment resource for the field of biotechnology that also provides industry news.

National Center for Biotechnology Information. <http:// www.ncbi.nlm.nih.gov> • A federal government site that focuses on biological and medical research. The site provides access to biotechnology databases and educational resources.

The Tree of Life. <http://phylogeny.arizona.edu/tree/phylogeny .html> • An enormous and expanding Web site of more than 1,300 schematic trees that map out biological relationships and provide information about organisms as well as detailed bibliographies. The site contains an internal search function to help users find information as well as a glossary of terms and an introduction to phylogenetic biology. It is edited by 347 subject specialists from universities, museums, and research institutions and is maintained by David Maddison at the Department of Entomology at the University of Arizona.

The University of Michigan Museum of Zoology's Animal Diversity Web. <http://animaldiversity.ummz.umich.edu> • Provides detailed information on animals: mammals, birds, amphibians, reptiles, sharks, bony fishes, mollusks, arthropods, and echinoderms. A sophisticated search mechanism allows users to search the site by keyword and within search fields, including conservation status, reproductive habits, physical description, and geographic range. Each animal is classified by phylum, order, class, and family, and detailed descriptions are provided on everything from physical characteristics, behavior, and habitat to "economic benefits for humans." Bibliographies are included as well.

WWW Virtual Library: Bio Sciences. <http://vlib.org /Biosciences.html> • An index to the many virtual library pages relating to biology, with links to biodiversity and ecology, biotechnology, botany, cell biology, and medicine. The site is part of the *WWW Virtual Library* <http://www.vlib.org>.

REFERENCE BOOKS IN BIOLOGY

Encyclopedia of Human Biology. Ed. Renato Dulbecco. 2nd ed. 9 vols. San Diego: Academic Press, 1997. • Offers substantial articles on topics in human biology, ranging from behavior, biochemistry, genetics, and psychology to medical research. The final volume includes an index to the set.

Encyclopedia of Microbiology. Ed. Joshua Lederberg. 2nd ed. 4 vols. San Diego: Academic Press, 2000. • Covers topics in microbiology, reviewing research in such areas as bacteriophages, anaerobic respiration, and AIDS. The articles, written for the informed nonspecialist, are substantial and include bibliographies.

Fieldbook of Natural History. Ed. E. L. Palmer and G. A. Parker. 2nd ed. New York: McGraw-Hill, 1995. • A handy compilation of information on the natural world, devoted chiefly to the description of plants and animals with some information on their environment and behavior; arranged by topic with an alphabetical index.

Grzimek's Animal Life Encyclopedia. Ed. Bernhard Grzimek. 13 vols. New York: Van Nostrand Reinhold, 1977. • A survey of animals, organized by taxonomic class, in several volumes; discusses species' distribution, behavior, and appearance and includes numerous color plates.

Oxford Companion to Animal Behavior. New York: Oxford University Press, 1982. • Offers short articles, arranged alphabetically, covering topics in ethnology, defining terms and discussing theories and discoveries in the field.

Walker's Mammals of the World. By Ronald M. Nowak. 6th ed. 2 vols. Baltimore: Johns Hopkins University Press, 1999. • Describes the appearance, habitat, behavior, and biology of every genus of living mammal; arranged taxonomically.

Chemistry

DATABASES AND INDEXES IN CHEMISTRY

Beilstein Abstracts Database. <http://www.chemweb.com> • An electronic database of publications about organic compounds, providing bibliographic citations and descriptive abstracts (no full-text articles). Access to the site is free but registration is required. The print version of this work is *Beilstein's Handbook for Organic Chemistry*, 25 vols. (New York: Springer-Verlag New York 1918–40, with periodic updates). For information about inorganic compounds, see *Gmelin's Handbuch der Anorganischen Chemie* (Berlin: Springer, 1921).

Chemical Abstracts Service. Columbus, Ohio: American Chemical Society, 1967–. • A comprehensive electronic index to chemistry, providing bibliographic citations and descriptive abstracts to publications. The index is searchable by publication title, subject, chemical structure, formula, and more. The print version of this work is titled *Chemical Abstracts* and provides coverage beginning in 1907.

CRC Handbook of Chemistry and Physics, Online. Ed. David R. Lide. Boca Raton: CRC Press, 1999–. • A compilation of formulas, numeric data, tables, lists, and charts of interest to scientists. The electronic database, searchable by keyword and subject, provides the full texts of these materials. The print version of this work, the *CRC Handbook of Chemistry and Physics*, provides coverage beginning in 1913; it is updated annually.

e-Eros. Ed. Lewo A. Pacquette. 8 vols. New York: Wiley, 1995. • An electronic full-text database of over 48,000 reactions and 3,500 of the most frequently consulted reagents. Search options include keywords, reagent name, and author. The print version of this work is the *Encyclopedia of Reagents for Organic Synthesis*. When using the print version, consult volume 8 for a subject index, a formula index, a reagent structural class index, and a reagent function index.

Kirk-Othmer Encyclopedia of Chemical Technology, Electronic Version. New York: Wiley, 1991–. • An online encyclopedia (in some libraries part of the *Wiley InterScience* databases) providing in-depth articles on chemical properties, manufacturing, and technology, and organized alphabetically by subject, with an advanced search option. (Users can sign in as a guest at <http://jws-edck .interscience.wiley.com:8095> to obtain abstracts of articles; however, to obtain full texts, the library must subscribe to Wiley.) The print version of this work is titled *Kirk-Othmer Encyclopedia of Chemical Technology*, 4th ed., 25 vols. (New York: Wiley, 1991–).

WEB RESOURCES IN CHEMISTRY

BioChemLinks.com. <http://schmidel.com/bionet.cfm> • A portal to excellent resources in biology, biochemistry, and chemistry, with links to full-text science news sources. The links are organized by subject — general chemistry, organic chemistry, biochemistry, biotechnology, and the teaching of science — and geared toward science education and the nonspecialist. The site is the product of Schmidel & Wojciki, editorial Web developers of a number of science sites. Dyann Schmidel has also taught graduate and undergraduate courses in chemistry, biochemistry, and biotechnology.

Chemicool Periodic Table. <http://www.chemicool.com /index.html> • A chart linked to basic information about each element in the periodic table, including states, conductivity, abundance, and reactions. The site is edited and maintained by David Hsu of the Massachusetts Institute of Technology.

Molecule of the Month. <http://www.bris.ac.uk/Depts/Chemistry /MOTM/motm.htm> • A site that provides detailed graphic and textual information on molecules, from mustard gas to aspirin. This site is part of the *Links for Chemists* of the *WWW Virtual Library*; it is maintained by Paul May of the School of Chemistry at the University of Bristol.

WWW Virtual Library: Links for Chemists. <http://www.liv.ac.uk /Chemistry/Links/links.html> • A well-organized directory of more than 8,400 chemistry links. The site is maintained by the Department of Chemistry at the University of Liverpool. It is part of the *WWW Virtual Library* <http://www.vlib.org>.

REFERENCE BOOKS IN CHEMISTRY

Macmillan Encyclopedia of Chemistry. Ed. Joseph J. Lagowski. 4 vols. New York: Macmillan Library Reference, 1997. • A wide range of brief articles on research and practical concepts in chemistry, including key ideas in the field, individual chemists and their contributions, and common chemical substances.

Merck Index: An Encyclopedia of Chemicals, Drugs, and Biologicals. Ed. Susan Budavari et al. 12th ed. Whitehouse Station, N.J.: Merck, 1996. • Contains about 10,000 entries on chemicals, including many pharmaceuticals, as well as chemical formulas, properties, uses, and references to literature. This work is also available in electronic format.

General resources in engineering

DATABASES AND INDEXES IN ENGINEERING (GENERAL)

Applied Science and Technology Abstracts. New York: Wilson, 1983– (abstracts begin 1993). • Covers more than 400 core scientific and technical journals and important trade and industrial publications in engineering, mathematics, computer technology, the environment, and natural science. This database — available in print and electronic formats and updated monthly — provides bibliographic citations and descriptive abstracts (no full-text articles).

Some libraries may subscribe to *Applied Science and Technology Index*, which is available in electronic or print format. Note that *Applied Science and Technology Index* provides bibliographic citations only.

EI Engineering Village 2: *Compendex*. Hoboken: Engineering Information, 1970–. • The most comprehensive electronic index covering all engineering disciplines with over five million bibliographic citations and descriptive abstracts (no full texts) of journal articles, technical reports, and conference papers and proceedings. *Compendex* is searchable by author, author affiliation, journal or conference title, keyword, and subject heading; searches can be limited by publication year, engineering discipline, and publication type. *Compendex* is also available in print form as *Engineering Index*; the CD-ROM version is titled *Compendex Plus*.

In addition to providing access to *Compendex, EI Engineering Village 2* allows subscribers to search more than 10,000 evaluated Web site abstracts, patents, industry specifications and standards, as well as the popular *CRC Handbooks.*

Ingenta. <http://www.ingenta.com> • A large database of research articles covering many subject areas within the disciplines of engineering and technology. Subscribers to the print journal can access full-text articles.

MatWeb: The Online Materials Information Resources. <http://www.matweb.com> • A database of over 18,000 documents on topics including thermoplastics, thermosets, ferrous metals, non-ferrous metals, and ceramics.

PubScience. <http://pubsci.osti.gov> • A database of peer-reviewed journal literature on the physical sciences, engineering, and other disciplines. *PubScience* is part of the Web site of the Office of Scientific and Technical Information at the U.S. Department of Energy. The full texts of articles are available online to subscribing libraries.

WEB RESOURCES IN ENGINEERING (GENERAL)

Edinburgh Engineering Virtual Library. <http://www.eevl.ac.uk> • Provides reviews of and access to quality sites on engineering topics such as bioengineering and manufacturing and to online scholarly and trade journals. The site is maintained by the Heriot-Watt University Library, Edinburgh, and is part of the *WWW Virtual Library* <www.vlib.org>.

ICE Internet Connections for Engineering. <http://www.englib.cornell.edu/ice> • A useful resource for engineers, researchers, engineering students, and faculty. The site is maintained by the Engineering Library at Cornell University.

REFERENCE BOOKS IN ENGINEERING (GENERAL)

McGraw-Hill Dictionary of Engineering. Ed. Sybil Parker. New York: McGraw-Hill, 1997. • Covers all fields of engineering including building construction.

Standard Handbook of Engineering Calculations. Ed. Tyler G. Hicks. 1 vol. New York: McGraw-Hill, 1995.   •   A classic compendium of step-by-step calculations for solving the most frequently encountered engineering problems in many engineering disciplines.

Van Nostrand's Scientific Encyclopedia. Ed. Douglas M. Considine and Glenn D. Considine. 9th ed. New York: Wiley, 2001.   •   Provides up-to-date and accessible coverage of almost every topic in science and technology.

Chemical engineering

DATABASES AND INDEXES IN CHEMICAL ENGINEERING

Chemical Abstracts. Columbus, Ohio: American Chemical Society, 1907–.   •   The largest and most current collection of chemical engineering information. *Chemical Abstracts* includes bibliographic citations and descriptive abstracts of journal articles and patents. Available in electronic format, from 1967 to the present, this index is updated weekly. The electronic version is titled *Chemical Abstracts* or *Chemical Abstracts/SciFinder Scholar.*

WEB RESOURCES IN CHEMICAL ENGINEERING

Chemfinder. <http://chemfinder.cambridgesoft.com>   •   A chemical database and Web search engine that makes it easy to locate common types of chemicals including physical property data and two-dimensional chemical structures. *Chemfinder* may be searched by category or keyword. The site is hosted by the CambridgeSoft Corporation, a producer of an Internet browser and of chemistry CAD software.

Chemical Engineers Resources Page. <http://www.cheresources .com/onlinecalc.shtml>   •   An online calculator for chemical engineers. The site is maintained by a chemical engineer at West Virginia University.

WWW Virtual Library: Chemical Engineering. <http:// www.che.ufl.edu/WWW-CHE/index.html>   •   Provides access to resources for chemical and process engineering and is conveniently divided into a helpful list of subtopics. The site is maintained by the Chemical Engineering Department at the University of Florida and is part of the *WWW Virtual Library* <www.vlib.org>.

REFERENCE BOOKS IN CHEMICAL ENGINEERING

Concise Encyclopedia of Chemical Technology. Ed. Jacqueline I. Kroschwitz. 4th ed. New York: Wiley, 1999.   •   A single-volume condensation of the premier 27-volume *Kirk-Othmer Encyclopedia of Chemical Technology* (4th ed., 1998). It includes all topics from the full set and is suitable for university chemical engineering and chemistry students.

Perry's Chemical Engineers' Handbook. New York: McGraw-Hill, 1997.   •   A classic reference book that covers all aspects of chemical engineering, including chemical and physical property data and fundamentals of chemical engineering.

Civil engineering

INDEXES AND DATABASES IN CIVIL ENGINEERING

ASCE Civil Engineering Database, 1975–. <http://www.pubs .asce.org/cedbsrch.html>   •   A resource from the American Society of Civil Engineers providing bibliographic citations and descriptive abstracts (no full texts) of documents published by the society since 1975. It covers journals, conference proceedings, books, standards, manuals, magazines, and newsletters.

The Environmental Protection Agency Envirofacts: Data Warehouse and Applications. <http://www.epa.gov/enviro/index_java.html>   •   A point of access to selected U.S. Environmental Protection Agency environmental data. It includes maps that can be printed.

National Service Center for Environmental Publications. <http:// www.epa.gov/ncepihom>   •   Access to over 6,000 full-text EPA documents available free of charge in print and multimedia formats.

TRIS Online. <http://www.ntl.bts.gov>   •   A comprehensive searchable database of articles produced and maintained by the Transportation Research Board and the National Academy of Sciences.

U.S. Department of Energy Information Bridge. <http://www.osti.gov /bridge>   •   Provides free access to full-text research and development reports in physics, energy technologies, engineering, computer and information science, renewable energy, and other topics. Documents can be viewed or downloaded.

WEB RESOURCES IN CIVIL ENGINEERING

United States Environmental Protection Agency. <http://www.epa.gov> • A searchable Web site with information about all the activities and publications of the EPA.

WWW Virtual Library: Civil Engineering. <http://www.ce.gatech.edu/WWW-CE/home.html> • Access to civil engineering sites organized into commercial, educational, organizational, and journalistic groups. The site is hosted by the Civil Engineering Department at the Georgia Institute of Technology and is part of the *WWW Virtual Library* <www.vlib.org>.

REFERENCE BOOKS IN CIVIL ENGINEERING

Encyclopedia of Environmental Science and Engineering. Ed. James R. Pfafflin and Edward N. Ziegler. Newark, N.J.: Gordon and Breach, 1998. • Provides information on the major aspects of environmental science and engineering.

Structural Engineering Handbook. Ed. Edwin H. Gaylord, Charles N. Gaylord, and James E. Stallmeyer. New York: McGraw-Hill, 1996. • Covers a variety of engineering structures including bridges and buried conduits.

Electrical and electronics engineering

DATABASES AND INDEXES IN ELECTRICAL AND ELECTRONICS ENGINEERING

ACM Digital Library, 1985–. <www.acm.org/dl> • Provides bibliographic citations, descriptive abstracts, and full-text articles from most periodicals and conference proceedings of the Association for Computing Machinery and affiliated societies. Access to full texts is available by subscription only, but visitors can search the citations and abstracts.

INSPEC. Edison, N.J.: Institution of Electrical Engineers, 1967–. • The leading electronic index to the world's scientific and technical literature in physics, electrical engineering, electronics, communications, control engineering, computers and computing, and information technology. *INSPEC* provides bibliographic citations and descriptive abstracts to over 7 million articles, books, reports, and dissertations. While full-text articles are not available online, it is possible to request full-text documents through *Infotrieve, INSPEC*'s document delivery service.

WEB RESOURCES IN ELECTRICAL AND ELECTRONICS ENGINEERING

Chip Center. <http://www.chipcenter.com> • Provides electrical and electronics resources organized by function, including chip lists, chip printouts, and lists of chip manufacturers. *Chip Center* is a network that provides editorial content and e-commerce for electrical engineers. It is owned by Arrow Electronics.

Institute of Electrical and Electronic Engineers. <http://ieeexplore .ieee.org/lpdocs/epic03> • An index to the contents of the publications of the Institute of Electrical and Electronics Engineers, including transactions, journals, magazines, and conference proceedings since 1988, and all current IEEE standards. Access to full-text articles is available by subscription to *IEEE Explore.*

WWW Virtual Library: Electrical and Electronics Engineering. <http: //webdiee.cem.itesm.mx/wwwvlee> • Provides access to selected resources in electrical and electronics engineering. The site is organized into topics: academic research and institutions, information resources, journals, products and services, and standards. It is hosted by the Department of Electrical and Electronics Engineering at Monterrey Tech (Tecnológico de Monterrey), state of Mexico campus, and is part of the *WWW Virtual Library* <www.vlib.org>.

REFERENCE BOOKS IN ELECTRICAL AND ELECTRONICS ENGINEERING

The Electronics Handbook. Ed. Jerry Whitaker. Boca Raton: CRC, 1996. • Covers theory and principles governing electronic devices and systems.

Mechanical engineering

DATABASES AND INDEXES IN MECHANICAL ENGINEERING

Applied Mechanics Reviews. New York: American Society of Mechanical Engineers, 1948–. • A bimonthly abstracting journal that covers mechanics and related subjects. This index provides bibliographic citations and descriptive abstracts of articles from 500 international research journals. The electronic format is titled *AMR Online Database* and covers 1989 to the present.

WEB RESOURCES IN MECHANICAL ENGINEERING

American Society of Mechanical Engineers. <http://www.asme.org> • An informative site about the profession of mechanical engineering. The site provides access to abstracts and tables of contents to all journals published by ASME International. Access to the full-text articles of all online journals is available to subscribers to the print version.

Edinburgh Engineering Virtual Library: Mechanical Engineering. <http://www.eevl.ac.uk/mech_eng.html> • Provides access to resources in mechanical engineering and related industries. The site is searchable through a useful subject guide or by keyword. It is edited and maintained by a team of specialists from universities and institutions in the U.K. and is hosted by Heriot-Watt University. The site is part of the *WWW Virtual Library* <www.vlib.org>.

REFERENCE BOOKS IN MECHANICAL ENGINEERING

Mark's Standard Handbook for Mechanical Engineers. 10th ed. New York: McGraw-Hill, 1996. • A widely used reference with an excellent index and many diagrams, drawings, graphs, and charts.

Mechanical Engineers' Handbook. Ed. Myer Kutz. 2nd ed. New York: Wiley, 1998. • Covers fundamental topics and emerging issues in mechanical engineering.

Environmental sciences

DATABASES AND INDEXES IN ENVIRONMENTAL SCIENCES

Enviroline. Bethesda: Cambridge Scientific Abstracts, 1975–. • This electronic index provides bibliographic citations and descriptive abstracts (no full text) of papers and reports, as well as journal articles from 800 periodicals in the field of environmental science. This work, international in scope, is updated monthly. The print version is titled *Environmental Abstracts.*

WEB RESOURCES IN ENVIRONMENTAL SCIENCES

EnviroLink. <http://www.envirolink.org> • A clearinghouse for information on the environment and a network for nonprofit environmental organizations. The site provides a library of documents, links to government and nonprofit organizations and publications, daily environmental news, and discussion forums. The site is sponsored by Networkforchange.com, an activist organization.

Environmental Protection Agency. <http://www.epa.gov> • Information on the EPA and related organizations. This site provides environmental databases with information on a variety of issues including safe drinking water and hazardous waste. The site also provides links to libraries, environmental publications, and EPA dockets and reports.

National Council for Science and the Environment: National Library for the Environment. <http://www.cnie.org> • Provides the full texts of Congressional Research Service reports on environmental issues, reference resources, state of the environment reports from a variety of sources, and more. The National Council for Science and the Environment (NCSE) was established in 1990 to provide "accurate and complete science-based information on the environment" to environmental policymakers. It is endorsed by a number of universities and environmental and scientific organizations.

The Nature Conservancy. <http://www.tnc.org> • Provides information on the Nature Conservancy's programs and research, with databases in taxonomy, nomenclature, status, distribution, habitat, ecology, and management. The site also links to government conservation efforts, such as the National Biological Information Infrastructure, which provides press releases on endangered species and specialized pages full of facts for researchers. The Nature Conservancy is an international nonprofit conservation group.

World Resources Institute. <http://www.wri.org/facts> • Sponsored by an organization dedicated to improving the environment. The site provides links to information on environmental issues including World Resources publications, statistics, and maps as well as news and educational materials about the global environment. The site covers topics such as biodiversity, climate change, sustainable agriculture, and water resources.

WWW Virtual Library: Environment. <http://earthsystems.org /Environment.shtml> • An encyclopedic set of links on the environment sorted into categories such as atmosphere, biosphere, hydrosphere, and lithosphere. Users can search the site or view a list of all the links. This site is edited and maintained by Earthsystems.org, a nonprofit environmental and educational organization; it is part of the *WWW Virtual Library* <http://www.vlib.org>.

REFERENCE BOOKS IN ENVIRONMENTAL SCIENCES

Beacham's Guide to Environmental Issues and Sources. Ed. Walton Beacham. 5 vols. Washington, D.C.: Beacham, 1993. • A bibliography and guide to various aspects of environmental sciences arranged by subject.

Encyclopedia of Energy, Technology, and the Environment. Ed. Attilio Bisio and Sharon Boots. 4 vols. New York: Wiley, 1995. • Provides lengthy articles on the technologies used to produce energy and the effects of these technologies on the environment. The book includes many tables, graphs, and diagrams; most articles, written by experts in the field, are followed by extensive bibliographies.

Encyclopedia of the Environment. Ed. Ruth A. Eblen and William R. Eblen. Boston: Houghton Mifflin, 1994. • Offers concise articles on environmental problems, the impact of business and social institutions on the natural environment, government involvement, legislation, and other topics.

Environmental Encyclopedia. Ed. T. H. Cooper and M. T. Hepworth. 2nd ed. Detroit: Gale Group, 1998. • Offers concise definitions and discussions of organizations, people, places, economic and political issues, and terminology related to the environment; includes illustrations and tables.

The Environmentalist's Bookshelf: A Guide to the Best Books. By Robert W. Merideth. New York: G. K. Hall, 1993. • A selective, annotated guide to classic and high-quality reading material in environmental studies, including a list of the most influential books on the environment and environmental issues.

HarperCollins Dictionary of Environmental Science. Ed. G. Jones et al. New York: HarperCollins, 1992. • Briefly defines terms related to natural and built environments as well as to the agricultural and economic infrastructures worldwide.

The State of the World: A Worldwatch Institute Report on Progress toward a Sustainable Society. Ed. Lester R. Brown et al. New York: Norton, 1984–. • An annual survey of the global condition of the environment offering an excellent overview of environmental problems and controversies.

The Water Encyclopedia. Ed. Frits Van der Leeden et al. 2nd ed. Chelsea, Mich.: Lewis, 1990. • Offers tables and maps concerning climate, water resources, water use, environmental policy, water law, and other issues as well as a directory of relevant organizations and a list of colleges and universities offering programs in water use and conservation.

World Resources. Washington, D.C.: World Resources Institute, 1986–. • An annual report on global environmental issues including land use, water resources, population, and pollution, with many comparative statistical tables and maps. This work is a joint publication of the World Resources Institute, the United Nations Environment Program (UNEP) and Development Program (UNDP), and the World Bank. The World Resources Institute Web site provides some of the organization's publications online, including statistics and maps, with additional news and educational materials about the global environment <http://www.wri.org/facts>.

Geology

DATABASES AND INDEXES IN GEOLOGY

GeoRef. Alexandria, Va.: American Geological Institute, 1966–. • A comprehensive index of more than 2.3 million bibliographic citations to articles, books, maps, papers, reports, and theses covering the geosciences internationally. This index is maintained and updated monthly by the AGI. The print version of this work is the *Bibliography and Index of Geology.*

WEB RESOURCES IN GEOLOGY

Structural Geology and Metamorphic Petrology on the WWW. <http://craton.geol.brocku.ca/guest/jurgen/struct.htm> • Covers the various subfields of structural geology and petrology and includes information on electronic mailing lists and journals, conferences, job opportunities, databases, and software. The site is maintained by Jurgen Kraus of Brock University, Ontario, Canada.

U.S. Geological Survey <http://www.usgs.gov> • Access to more than 100 years' worth of data collected by the USGS. Resources include numerous databases that offer reports, maps, and surveys of geological places and features. The Geological Survey's publications are also available in any library that is a federal documents repository, and there is an index to its publications, available in print (*Publications of the Geological Survey*) and online <http://usgs -georef.cos.com>.

U.S. Geological Survey: Minerals Yearbook. <http://minerals.usgs .gov/minerals/pubs/myb.html> • Provides information on 90 minerals, including production, foreign trade, outlook, and current research, and reports on the mining industry in each state and in over 175 countries. Maps and statistics are included. The *Minerals Yearbook* is also available in print format, published by the U.S. Government Printing Office.

West's Geology Directory. <http://www.soton.ac.uk/~imw /index.htm> • A large, selective list of links that cover paleontology, stratigraphy, sedimentology, and mineralogy. The site's emphasis is on U.K. geology, but there are links to sites worldwide. It is maintained by Ian West of Southampton University.

WWW Virtual Library: Earth Science. <http://www.vlib.org /EarthScience.html> • A directory of earth science resources online, organized by topic including cartography, environment, forestry, geophysics, geotechnical engineering, and oceanography. The general directory for the *WWW Virtual Library* is <http:// www.vlib.org>.

REFERENCE BOOKS IN GEOLOGY

Cambridge Encyclopedia of Earth Sciences. Ed. David G. Smith. New York: Crown, 1981. • A topically arranged overview of the field, covering topics in lengthy survey chapters; includes an alphabetical index.

Encyclopedia of Earth Sciences Series. Ed. Rhodes W. Fairbridge et al. 20 vols. Boston: Kluwer Academic Publishers, 1966–99. • Offers lengthy, scholarly articles on oceanography, atmospheric sciences and astrogeology, geochemistry, world regional geography, climatology, and structural geology.

Glossary of Geology. Ed. Robert L. Bates and Julia A. Jackson. 4th ed. Washington, D.C.: American Geological Institute, 1997.   • Defines more than 37,000 geological terms and provides bibliographic references for disputed or controversial ones. This work is available in electronic format.

Lexicon of Geologic Names of the United States (including Alaska). 2 vols. Washington, D.C.: Government Printing Office, 1936. With supplements.   • Provides information from records kept since the 1880s by the U.S. Geological Survey, Geological Names Committee. This work identifies the names of geological features by time period and location and provides reviews of the literature referring to the names. Supplements provide information on more recently named features. Most (90 percent) of the names from the print volumes are provided at <http://ngmdb.usgs.gov/Geolex/geolex_home.html>.

Publications of the Geological Survey. Washington, D.C.: Government Printing Office, 1962–.   • Indexes the contents of several U.S. Geological Survey series: bulletins, circulars, open file reports, professional papers, water data reports, and water supply papers. The USGS Web site also offers an index to its publications at <http://usgs-georef.cos.com>.

Mathematics

DATABASES AND INDEXES IN MATHEMATICS

MathSciNet. Providence: American Mathematical Society, 1980–. • An electronic index providing bibliographic citations and descriptive abstracts to articles and books relevant to mathematical research. This index is updated daily. *Mathematical Reviews* and *Current Mathematical Publications*, both publications of the American Mathematical Society, are available in print with coverage beginning in 1940. These works provide detailed abstracts and include quarterly updates of new publications in mathematics and an annual subject index.

WEB RESOURCES IN MATHEMATICS

American Mathematical Society: e-math. <http://e-math.ams
.org> • Encompasses a broad range of information including conferences, journals, and books, with links to math resources on the
Web such as university departments and online publications and
bibliographies.

The Geometry Center. <http://www.geom.umn.edu> • A comprehensive and innovative site offering geometric and visual represen-
tations of mathematical concepts and multimedia research papers
and conference proceedings. This site brings geometry to life. The
Geometry Center, located at the University of Minnesota, is funded
by the National Science Foundation.

MacTutor History of Mathematics Archive. <http://www-history
.mcs.st-and.ac.uk/~history> • Devoted to the history of math,
with biographies of more than 1,100 mathematicians, articles on
the development of mathematical ideas, more than 60 articles on
famous curves that include graphics, and a mathematician of the
day. This site is regularly edited by members of the School of Mathematics and Statistics at the University of St. Andrews in Scotland.

Math Archives: Topics in Mathematics. <http://archives.math
.utk.edu/topics> • A directory of math Web resources covering a
broad range of topics. Users can search by keyword or choose a
topic from the table of contents, which includes algebra, geometry,
calculus, fractals, trigonometry, number theory, and statistics among
its forty topics. Links are marked for level of education: K–6; 7–12;
lower-division college; upper-division college; and graduate and
professional. The site is maintained by the Mathematics Department at the University of Tennessee, Knoxville.

WWW Virtual Library: Mathematics. <http://euclid.math.fsu.edu
/Science/math.html> • A comprehensive listing of Web sites in
mathematics with links to bibliographies, mathematics newsgroups,
electronic journals, and specialized fields. This site is maintained
by the Mathematics Department at Florida State University. It is
part of the *WWW Virtual Library* <http://www.vlib.org>.

LIBRARY RESOURCES IN MATHEMATICS

*Companion Encyclopedia of the History and Philosophy of Mathemati-
cal Sciences.* Ed. Ivor Gratton-Guinness. 2 vols. London: Routledge
Reference, 1994. • Offers lengthy, well-documented articles on

the historical and cultural basis of mathematics and mathematical understanding.

CRC Handbook of Mathematical Sciences. Ed. William H. Beyer. 6th ed. Boca Raton: CRC, 1987.   •   A collection of tables for many areas of the field, designed for those interested in both pure and applied mathematics.

Encyclopedic Dictionary of Mathematics. Ed. Kiyoshi Ito. 2nd ed. 4 vols. Cambridge: MIT Press, 1993.   •   Offers detailed discussions of mathematical concepts, with excellent bibliographies.

International Dictionary of Applied Mathematics. Ed. W. F. Freiberger. Princeton: Van Nostrand, 1960.   •   Though dated for some purposes, a useful source for technical definitions and discussions of applications.

Mathematics Dictionary. By Robert C. James. 5th ed. New York: Van Nostrand Reinhold, 1992.   •   Offers concise definitions and brief explanations of topics in the field.

Tables of Integrals, Series, and Products. By I. S. Gradshteyn and I. M. Ryzhik. 6th ed. Boston: Academic Press, 2000.   •   A collection of tables covering elementary and special mathematical functions and their definite and indefinite integrals; available in electronic format.

Nursing and health sciences

DATABASES AND INDEXES IN NURSING AND HEALTH SCIENCES

The CINAHL Database. Glendale: Cinahl Information Systems, 1982–. • An electronic database of publications related to nursing research and practice. The database provides references to articles, books and book chapters, pamphlets and other documents, as well as standards of professional practice and research. This work provides bibliographic citations, descriptive abstracts, and the full texts of materials; it is updated monthly. The print version, *Cumulative Index to Nursing and Allied Health Literature,* covers 1977 to the present.

PubMed. <http://www.ncbi.nlm.nih.gov/entrez/query.fcgi> • A free Web site hosted by the National Library of Medicine. The site offers access to *MEDLINE,* the most complete index to medical research with over 11 million abstracts of medical publications. (An alternative search engine is provided through Internet Grateful Med at <http://igm.nlm.nih.gov>, which also offers access to other databases, including *AIDSLINE* and *BIOETHICSLINE.*)

WEB RESOURCES IN NURSING AND HEALTH SCIENCES

Centers for Disease Control and Prevention. <http://www.cdc.gov>
• A wealth of current information on disease and public health topics; includes a search engine.

HealthWeb. <http://healthweb.org/index.cfm> • A vast collection of sites selected by librarians at 20 health sciences libraries. The site provides links on specialty areas such as pediatrics, nursing, and sports medicine as well as on topics such as bioethics, rural health, and alternative medicine. *HealthWeb* is a collaborative project of a number of health sciences libraries and is supported by the National Library of Medicine. It is hosted by the University of Illinois, Chicago.

The Merck Manual Home Edition. <http://www.merck.com/pubs /mmanual_home> • Full text of the standard medical handbook, written for the nonspecialist. This work can be searched or viewed by table of contents. The more technical version is also available online at <http://www.merck.com/pubs/mmanual>. *The Merck Manual Home Edition* and *The Merck Manual* are also available in print format.

National Center for Health Statistics. <http://www.cdc.gov /nchs> • A source for public health and vital statistics of all kinds gathered by a unit of the Centers for Disease Control.

Virtual Hospital. <http://www.vh.org> • A digital health sciences library from the University of Iowa intended to provide current and authoritative information for health-care providers and patients. The site offers materials organized by type (from a health professional's perspective) and by problem or symptom (from a patient's perspective).

REFERENCE BOOKS IN NURSING AND HEALTH SCIENCES

Cambridge World History of Human Disease. Ed. Kenneth F. Kiple. Cambridge and New York: Cambridge University Press, 1993. • A scholarly guide to the history of specific diseases across time and in all parts of the world.

Cecil Textbook of Medicine. Ed. Lee Goldman and J. Claude Bennet. 21st ed. Philadelphia: Saunders, 2000. • A general textbook of medicine; available in electronic format.

Conn's Current Therapy 2001. Ed. Robert E. Rackel and Edward T. Bope. Philadelphia: Saunders, 2001. • A guide to current diagnosis and treatment of diseases and injuries.

Gale Encyclopedia of Medicine. Ed. Karen Boyden et al. 5 vols. Detroit: Gale Group, 1999. • Covers basic consumer information on hundreds of medical disorders, tests, and treatments.

Handbook of Clinical Nursing Research. Ed. Ada Sue Hinshaw et al. Newbury Park, Calif.: Sage, 1999. • Provides a comprehensive review and critique of current nursing research.

The Oxford Medical Companion. Ed. John Nicholas Walton et al. Oxford: Oxford University Press, 1994. • An alphabetical set of articles, some brief and others quite long, on the knowledge base and practice of medicine, including medicine and government, medical ethics, and medical law. Some short biographies of important figures in medicine are also included.

Stedman's Medical Dictionary. Ed. Thomas Stedman. 27th ed. Philadelphia: Lippincott Williams and Wilkins, 2000. • Brief definitions of medical terms; available in electronic format.

Physics and astronomy

DATABASES AND INDEXES IN PHYSICS AND ASTRONOMY

CRC Handbook of Chemistry and Physics, Online. Ed. David R. Lide. Boca Raton: CRC, 1999–. • A compilation of formulas, numeric data, tables, lists, and charts of interest to scientists. The electronic database, searchable by keyword and subject, provides the full texts of these materials. The print version of this work, *CRC Handbook of Chemistry and Physics*, provides coverage beginning in 1913; it is updated annually.

INSPEC. London: IEEE, 1969–. • A leading database in the fields of physics, electrical and electronics engineering, computers, and information technology. This work provides bibliographic citations and descriptive abstracts of research literature of the field. The print version is *Physics Abstracts*, with coverage beginning in 1941.

WEB RESOURCES IN PHYSICS AND ASTRONOMY

AstroWeb: Astronomy/Astrophysics on the Internet. <http://www.stsci.edu/astroweb/astronomy.html> • A simply designed but comprehensive collection of resources for astronomers including information on observations, data, publications, people, and research. The site is maintained by the AstroWeb Consortium, a collaborative effort of nine scientists at seven institutions.

PhysicsWeb: Global News and Information. <http://physicsweb.org/TIPTOP> • Selected physics links from around the world of interest to scientists, teachers, and students. The site also includes a database of physics departments, bulletin boards, and notification services. Multimedia features demonstrate how certain physics rules and concepts work. (Most of the site is available free of charge, but users must register to enter some areas.)

NASA. <http://www.nasa.gov> • Provides information gathered by NASA and its affiliates, with daily news stories on current astronomical events, data received from space probes, and the latest information on shuttle launches.

The NASA Astrophysics Data System. <http://adswww.harvard.edu> • Provides a searchable database of descriptive abstracts for astrophysics papers divided into categories such as Astronomy and Astrophysics, Instrumentation, Physics and Geophysics, and Los Alamos Preprint Server. The site, funded by NASA and maintained by Harvard University personnel and professors, also provides access to the full text of articles and translations of abstracts written in different languages.

PubScience. <http://pubsci.osti.gov/index.html> • Indexes articles in over 1,000 journals focused on the physical sciences. Provided by the Department of Energy's Office of Scientific and Technical Information, the site includes over 1.8 million citations to articles related to physics and energy. Contributors to the site include a number of well-known science institutions and publishers.

REFERENCE BOOKS IN PHYSICS AND ASTRONOMY

The Astronomy and Astrophysics Encyclopedia. Ed. Stephen P. Maran. New York: Cambridge University Press, 1999. • A handbook of current information in astronomy and astrophysics.

The Cambridge Encyclopedia of Astronomy. Ed. Simon Mitton. New York: Crown, 1977. • A topical survey of astronomy geared to the interested layperson and arranged by broad topic.

Encyclopedia of Physics. Ed. Rita G. Lerner and George L. Trigg. 2nd ed. New York: Wiley, 1990. • Provides brief discussions of basic concepts in physics.

Information Sources in Physics. Ed. Dennis F. Shaw. 3rd ed. London: Bowker Saur, 1994. • A guide to reference resources in physics, arranged in chapters by subdiscipline. Each chapter is written by an expert. Especially helpful is the chapter explaining the scope of physics literature.

Macmillan Encyclopedia of Physics. Ed. John S. Rigden. 4 vols. New York: Macmillan Library Reference, 1996. • Covers laws, concepts, fundamental theories, and the lives and work of important physicists throughout history.

A Physicist's Desk Reference. Ed. Herbert Lawrence Anderson. 2nd ed. New York: American Institute of Physics, 1995. • A concise source of tables, formulas, and bibliographies in 22 subdisciplines related to physics.

PART IV. DOCUMENTATION STYLES

MLA Style: English and Other Humanities

In academic research papers and in any other writing that borrows information from sources, the borrowed information — quotations, summaries, paraphrases, and any facts or ideas that are not common knowledge — must be clearly documented.

The various academic disciplines use their own editorial styles for citing sources and for listing the works that have been cited. The style described in this section is that of the Modern Language Association (MLA), contained in the *MLA Handbook for Writers of Research Papers*, 5th ed. (New York: MLA, 1999). (Other styles of documentation are described elsewhere in this booklet.)

MLA in-text citations

MLA in-text citations are made with a combination of signal phrases and parenthetical references. A signal phrase indicates that something taken from a source (such as a quotation, summary, or paraphrase) is about to be used; usually the signal phrase includes the author's name. The parenthetical reference includes at least a page number (unless the work has no page numbers or is organized alphabetically).

IN-TEXT CITATION

One driver, Peter Cohen, says that after he was rear-ended, the guilty party emerged from his vehicle still talking on the phone (127).

Directory to MLA in-text citation models

Readers can look up the author's last name in the alphabetized list of works cited, where they will find information about the work's title, publisher, and place and date of publication. When readers decide to consult the source, the page number will take them straight to the passage that has been cited.

Basic rules for print and electronic sources

The MLA system of in-text citations, which depends heavily on authors' names and page numbers, was created in the late 1970s with print sources in mind. Because some of today's electronic sources have unclear authorship and lack page numbers, they present a special challenge. Nevertheless, the basic rules are the same for both print and electronic sources.

The models in this section (items 1–5) show how the MLA system usually works and explain what to do if your source has no author or page numbers.

1. AUTHOR NAMED IN A SIGNAL PHRASE   Ordinarily, introduce the material being cited with a signal phrase that includes the author's name. In addition to preparing readers for the source, the signal phrase allows you to keep the parenthetical citation brief.

> Christine Haughney reports that shortly after
> Japan made it illegal to use a handheld phone
> while driving, "accidents caused by using the
> phones dropped by 75 percent" (A8).

The signal phrase — "Christine Haughney reports that" — names the author; the parenthetical citation gives the page number where the quoted words may be found.

Notice that the period follows the parenthetical citation. When a quotation ends with a question mark or an exclamation point, leave the end punctuation inside the quotation mark and add a period after the parentheses: ". . . ?" (8).

2. AUTHOR NAMED IN PARENTHESES   If the signal phrase does not include the author's name (or if there is no signal phrase), the author's last name must appear in parentheses along with the page number.

> Most states do not keep adequate records on the
> number of times cell phones are a factor in acci-
> dents; as of December 2000, only ten states were
> trying to keep such records (Sundeen 2).

Use no punctuation between the name and the page number.

3. AUTHOR UNKNOWN If the author is unknown, either use
the complete title in a signal phrase or use a short form of
the title in parentheses. Titles of books are underlined (or
italicized); titles of articles are put in quotation marks.

> As of 2001, at least three hundred towns and
> municipalities had considered legislation regulat-
> ing use of cell phones while driving ("Lawmakers"
> 2).

CAUTION: Before assuming that a Web source has no author, do some detective work. Often the author's name is
available but is not easy to find. For example, it may appear
at the end of the source, in tiny print. Or it may appear on
another page of the site, such as the home page.

NOTE: If a source has no author and is sponsored by a corporate entity, such as an organization or a government
agency, name the corporate entity as the author (see item 9
on p. 132).

4. PAGE NUMBER UNKNOWN You may omit the page number if a work lacks page numbers, as is the case with many
Web sources. Although printouts from Web sites usually show
page numbers, different printers may provide different page
breaks; for this reason, MLA recommends treating such
sources as unpaginated.

> The California Highway Patrol opposes restrictions
> on the use of phones while driving, claiming that

```
distracted drivers can already be prosecuted
(Jacobs).
```

When the pages of a Web source are stable (as in pdf files), however, supply a page number in your in-text citation. (For example, the Web source by Sundeen cited in the example on p. 129 has stable pages, so a page number is included in the citation.)

NOTE: If a Web source uses paragraph or section numbers, give the abbreviation "par." or "sec." in the parentheses: (Smith, par. 4).

5. ONE-PAGE SOURCE   If the source is one page long, MLA allows (but does not require) you to omit the page number. Many instructors will want you to supply the page number because without it readers may not know where your citation ends or, worse yet, may not realize that you have provided a citation at all.

NO PAGE NUMBER GIVEN

```
Milo Ippolito reports that the driver who struck
and killed a two-year-old while using her cell
phone got off with a light sentence even though
she left the scene of the accident and failed to
call 911 for help. In this and in similar cases,
traffic offenders distracted by cell phones have
not been sufficiently punished under laws on
reckless driving.
```

PAGE NUMBER GIVEN

```
Milo Ippolito reports that the driver who struck
and killed a two-year-old while using her cell
phone got off with a light sentence even though
she left the scene of the accident and failed to
```

```
call 911 for help (J1). In this and in similar
cases, traffic offenders distracted by cell phones
have not been sufficiently punished under laws on
reckless driving.
```

Variations on the basic rules

This section describes the MLA guidelines for handling a variety of situations not covered by the basic rules just given. Again, these rules on in-text citations are the same for both traditional print sources and electronic sources.

6. TWO OR MORE TITLES BY THE SAME AUTHOR   If your list of works cited includes two or more titles by the same author, mention the title of the work in the signal phrase or include a short version of the title in the parentheses.

```
On December 6, 2000, reporter Jamie Stockwell
wrote that distracted driver Jason Jones had been
charged with "two counts of vehicular manslaughter
[. . .] in the deaths of John and Carole Hall"
("Phone" B1). The next day Stockwell reported the
judge's ruling: Jones "was convicted of negligent
driving and fined $500, the maximum penalty al-
lowed" ("Man" B4).
```

Titles of articles are placed in quotation marks, as in the example just given. Titles of books are underlined or italicized.

In the rare case when both the author's name and a short title must be given in parentheses, separate them with a comma.

```
According to police reports, there were no skid
marks indicating that the distracted driver who
killed John and Carole Hall had even tried to stop
(Stockwell, "Man" B4).
```

7. TWO OR THREE AUTHORS   If your source has two or three authors, name them in the signal phrase, as in the following example, or include their last names in the parenthetical reference: (Redelmeier and Tibshirani 453).

> Redelmeier and Tibshirani found that "the risk of
> a collision when using a cellular telephone was
> four times higher than the risk when a cellular
> telephone was not being used" (453).

When three authors are named in the parentheses, separate the names with commas: (Alton, Davies, and Rice 56).

8. FOUR OR MORE AUTHORS   If your source has four or more authors, you may name all of the authors or you may include only the first author's name followed by "et al." (Latin for "and others"). Make sure that your parenthetical citation matches the way you handle the entry in the list of works cited (see also item 2 on p. 140).

> The study was extended for two years, and only
> after results were reviewed by an independent
> panel did the researchers publish their findings
> (Blaine et al. 35).

9. CORPORATE AUTHOR   When the author is a corporation or an organization, name the corporate author either in the signal phrase or in the parentheses.

> Researchers at the Harvard Center for Risk Analy-
> sis found that the risks of driving while phoning
> were small compared with other driving risks
> (3-4).

In the list of works cited, the Harvard Center for Risk Analysis is treated as the author and alphabetized under *H*.

10. AUTHORS WITH THE SAME LAST NAME If your list of works cited includes works by two or more authors with the same last name, include the first initial of the author in the signal phrase or parentheses. (If the authors share an initial as well as a last name, spell out the first name.)

> Estimates of the number of accidents caused by
> distracted drivers vary because little evidence is
> being collected (D. Smith 7).

11. INDIRECT SOURCE (SOURCE QUOTED IN ANOTHER SOURCE) When a writer's or a speaker's quoted words appear in a source written by someone else, begin the citation with the abbreviation "qtd. in."

> According to Richard Retting, "As the comforts of
> home and the efficiency of the office creep into
> the automobile, it is becoming increasingly at-
> tractive as a work space" (qtd. in Kilgannon A23).

12. ENCYCLOPEDIA OR DICTIONARY Unless an encyclopedia or a dictionary has an author, it will be alphabetized in the list of works cited under the word or entry that you consulted — not under the title of the reference work itself. Either in your text or in your parenthetical reference, mention the word or the entry. No page number is required, since readers can easily look up the word or entry.

> The word <u>crocodile</u> has a surprisingly complex
> etymology ("Crocodile").

13. MULTIVOLUME WORK If your paper cites more than one volume of a multivolume work, indicate in the parentheses the volume you are referring to, followed by a colon and the page number.

> Terman's studies of gifted children reveal a
> pattern of accelerated language acquisition (2:
> 279).

If your paper cites only one volume of a multivolume work, you will include the volume number in the list of works cited and will not need to include it in the parentheses.

14. TWO OR MORE WORKS When you want to document a particular point with more than one source, separate the citations with a semicolon.

```
The dangers of mountain lions to humans have been
well documented (Rychnovsky 40; Seidensticker 114;
Williams 30).
```

Multiple citations can be distracting, however, so you should not overuse the technique. If you want to alert readers to several sources that discuss a particular topic, consider using an information note instead (see p. 162).

15. AN ENTIRE WORK To cite an entire work, use the author's name in a signal phrase or a parenthetical reference. There is of course no need to use a page number.

```
Robinson succinctly describes the status of the
mountain lion controversy in California.
```

16. WORK IN AN ANTHOLOGY Put the name of the author of the work (not the editor of the anthology) in the signal phrase or the parentheses.

```
In Susan Glaspell's "A Jury of Her Peers," Mrs.
Hale describes both a style of quilting and a
murder weapon when she utters the last words of
the story: "We call it--knot it, Mr. Henderson"
(302).
```

In the list of works cited, the work is alphabetized under Glaspell, not under the name of the editor of the anthology.

```
Glaspell, Susan. "A Jury of Her Peers." Literature
     and Its Writers: An Introduction to Fiction,
```

<u>Poetry, and Drama</u>. Ed. Ann Charters and
Samuel Charters. 2nd ed. Boston: Bedford,
2001. 286-302.

Literary works and sacred texts

Literary works and sacred texts are usually available in a variety of editions. Your list of works cited will specify which edition you are using, and your in-text citation will usually consist of a page number from the edition you consulted (see item 17).

However, MLA suggests that when possible you should give enough information — such as book parts, play divisions, or line numbers — so that readers can locate the cited passage in any edition of the work (see items 18–20).

17. LITERARY WORKS WITHOUT PARTS OR LINE NUMBERS Many literary works, such as most short stories and many novels and plays, do not have parts or line numbers that you can refer to. In such cases, simply cite the page number.

At the end of Kate Chopin's "The Story of an
Hour," Mrs. Mallard drops dead upon learning that
her husband is alive. In the final irony of the
story, doctors report that she has died of a "joy
that kills" (25).

18. VERSE PLAYS AND POEMS For verse plays, MLA recommends omitting page numbers in the parenthetical citation. Instead, include act, scene, and line numbers that can be located in any edition of the work. Use arabic numerals, and separate the numbers with periods.

In his famous advice to players, Shakespeare's
Hamlet defines the purpose of theater, "whose end,
both at the first and now, was and is, to hold, as
'twere, the mirror up to nature" (3.2.21-23).

For a poem, cite the part (if there are a number of parts) and the line numbers, separated by a period.

```
When Homer's Odysseus comes to the hall of Circe,
he finds his men "mild / in her soft spell, fed on
her drug of evil" (10.209-11).
```

For poems that are not divided into parts, use line numbers. For a first reference, use the word "lines": (lines 5-8). Thereafter use just the numbers: (12-13).

19. NOVELS WITH NUMBERED DIVISIONS   When a novel has numbered divisions, put the page number first, followed by a semicolon, and then indicate the book, part, or chapter in which the passage may be found. Use abbreviations such as "bk." and "ch."

```
One of Kingsolver's narrators, teenager Rachel,
pushes her vocabulary beyond its limits. For
example, Rachel complains that being forced to
live in the Congo with her missionary family is "a
sheer tapestry of justice" because her chances of
finding a boyfriend are "dull and void" (117; bk.
2, ch. 10).
```

20. SACRED TEXTS   When citing a sacred text such as the Bible or the Koran, name the edition you are using in your works cited entry (see p. 144). In your parenthetical citation, give the chapter and verse (or their equivalent), separated by periods. Common abbreviations for chapters of the Bible are acceptable.

```
Consider the words of Solomon: "If your enemies
are hungry, give them food to eat. If they are
thirsty, give them water to drink" (Holy Bible,
Prov. 25.21).
```

MLA list of works cited

An alphabetized list of works cited, which appears at the end of your research paper, gives publication information for each of the sources you have cited in the paper. (For a sample list of works cited, see p. 174.)

NOTE: Unless your instructor asks for them, omit sources not actually cited in the paper, even if you read them.

General guidelines for listing authors

Alphabetize entries in the list of works cited by authors' last names (if a work has no author, alphabetize it by its title). The author's name is important because citations in the text of the paper refer to it and readers will be looking for it at the beginning of an entry in the alphabetized list.

NAME CITED IN TEXT

According to Matt Sundeen, . . .

BEGINNING OF WORKS CITED ENTRY

Sundeen, Matt.

The following examples show how to begin an entry for a work with (1) a single author, (2) multiple authors, (3) a corporate author, (4) an unknown author, and (5) multiple works by the same author. What comes after this first element of your citation will depend on the kind of source you are citing. (See items 6–56.)

NOTE: For a book, an entry in the works cited list will sometimes begin with an editor (see item 7).

Directory to MLA works cited entries

1. SINGLE AUTHOR   For a work with one author, begin the entry with the author's last name, followed by a comma; then give the author's first name, followed by a period.

```
Tannen, Deborah.
```

2. MULTIPLE AUTHORS   For works with two or three authors, name the authors in the order in which they are listed in the source. Reverse the name of only the first author.

```
Walker, Janice R., and Todd Taylor.

Wilmut, Ian, Keith Campbell, and Colin Tudge.
```

For a work with four or more authors, either name all of the authors or name the first author, followed by "et al." (Latin for "and others").

```
Sloan, Frank A., Emily M. Stout, Kathryn Whetten-
    Goldstein, and Lan Liang.

Sloan, Frank A., et al.
```

3. CORPORATE AUTHOR   When the author of a print document or Web site is a corporation, a government agency, or some other organization, begin your entry with the name of the group.

```
Bank of Boston.

United States. Bureau of the Census.

American Automobile Association.
```

NOTE: Make sure that your in-text citation also treats the organization as the author (see item 9 on p. 132).

4. UNKNOWN AUTHOR   When the author of a work is unknown, begin with the work's title. Titles of articles and other short works are put in quotation marks. Titles of books and Web sites are underlined (or italicized). (For titles of works within Web sites, see items 28 and 29.)

ARTICLE

"Cell Phone Use Increases Risk of Accidents, but
Users Willing to Take the Risk."

BOOK

Atlas of the World.

WEB SITE

Caracol: The Official Website of the Caracol
Archaeological Project.

Before concluding that the author of a work such as a Web
source is unknown, check carefully (see the caution on p.
129). Also remember that an organization may be the author (see item 3).

5. TWO OR MORE WORKS BY THE SAME AUTHOR If your list
of works cited includes two or more works by the same author, use the author's name only for the first entry. For other
entries use three hyphens followed by a period. The three
hyphens must stand for exactly the same name or names as
in the first entry. List the titles in alphabetical order.

Atwood, Margaret. Alias Grace: A Novel. New York:
Doubleday, 1996.

---. The Robber Bride. New York: Doubleday, 1993.

Books

Items 6–19 apply to print books. For online books, see item
29.

6. BASIC FORMAT FOR A BOOK For most books, arrange the
information into three units, each followed by a period and
one space: (1) the author's name; (2) the title and subtitle,

underlined (or italicized); and (3) the place of publication, the publisher, and the date.

```
Tan, Amy. The Bonesetter's Daughter. New York:
     Putnam, 2001.
```

Take the information about the book from its title page and copyright page. You may use a short form of the publisher's name as long as it is easily identifiable; omit terms such as *Press, Inc.*, and *Co.* except when naming university presses (Harvard UP, for example). If the copyright page lists more than one date, use the most recent one.

7. EDITORS   An entry for an editor is similar to that for an author except that the name is followed by a comma and the abbreviation "ed." for "editor" (or "eds." for "editors").

```
Powell, Kevin, ed. Step into a World: A Global
     Anthology of the New Black Literature. New
     York: Wiley, 2000.
```

8. AUTHOR WITH AN EDITOR   Begin with the author and title, followed by the name of the editor. In this case the abbreviation "Ed." means "Edited by," so it is the same for one or multiple editors.

```
Plath, Sylvia. The Unabridged Journals of Sylvia
     Plath. Ed. Karen V. Kukil. New York: Anchor-
     Doubleday, 2000.
```

9. AUTHOR WITH A TRANSLATOR   Begin with the name of the author. After the title, write "Trans." (for "Translated by") and the name of the translator.

```
Allende, Isabel. Daughter of Fortune. Trans.
     Margaret Sayers Peden. New York: Harper,
     2000.
```

10. EDITION OTHER THAN THE FIRST If you are citing an edition other than the first, include the number of the edition after the title: 2nd ed., 3rd ed., and so on.

Boyce, David George. The Irish Question and
British Politics, 1868-1996. 2nd ed. New
York: St. Martin's, 1996.

11. MULTIVOLUME WORK Include the total number of volumes before the city and publisher, using the abbreviation "vols."

Conway, Jill Ker, ed. Written by Herself. 2 vols.
New York: Random, 1996.

If your paper cites only one of the volumes, give the volume number before the city and publisher and give the total number of volumes after the date.

Conway, Jill Ker, ed. Written by Herself. Vol. 2.
New York: Random, 1996. 2 vols.

12. ENCYCLOPEDIA OR DICTIONARY ENTRY When an encyclopedia or a dictionary is well known, simply list the author of the entry, the title of the entry, the title of the reference work, the edition number (if any), and the date of the edition.

Posner, Rebecca. "Romance Languages." The New
Encyclopaedia Britannica: Macropaedia. 15th
ed. 1987.

"Sonata." The American Heritage Dictionary of the
English Language. 4th ed. 2000.

Volume and page numbers are not necessary because the entries in the source are arranged alphabetically and therefore are easy to locate.

If a reference work is not well known, provide full publication information as well.

13. SACRED TEXT   Give the title of the edition of the sacred text (taken from the title page), underlined; the editor's name (if any); and publication information.

```
Holy Bible: New Living Translation. Wheaton:
     Tyndale, 1996.
```

14. WORK IN AN ANTHOLOGY   Begin with the name of the author of the selection, not with the name of the editor of the anthology. Then give the title of the selection, the title of the anthology, the name of the editor, publication information, and the pages on which the selection appears.

```
Odell, Noell. "Mallory and Irvine's Attempt."
     Points Unknown: A Century of Great Explora-
     tion. Ed. David Roberts. New York: Norton,
     2000. 161-72.
```

If an anthology gives the original publication information for a selection and if your instructor prefers that you use it, cite that information first. Follow with "Rpt. in" (for "Reprinted in") and the title of the anthology, along with the other information about the anthology as in the model just given.

```
Alvarez, Julia. "Picky Eater." Something to
     Declare. Chapel Hill: Algonquin, 1998. 75-86.
     Rpt. in The Norton Book of American Autobiog-
     raphy. Ed. Jay Parini. New York: Norton,
     1999. 619-26.
```

15. FOREWORD, INTRODUCTION, PREFACE, OR AFTER-WORD   Begin with the author of the foreword or other book part, followed by the name of that part. Then give the title of the book; the author of the book, preceded by the word "By"; and the editor of the book (if any). After the publication information, give the page numbers for the part of the book being cited.

Pipher, Mary. Foreword. Can't Buy My Love:
How Advertising Changes the Way We Think
and Feel. By Jean Kilbourne. New York:
Touchstone-Simon, 1999. 11-13.

If the book part being cited has a title, include it immediately after the author's name.

Ozick, Cynthia. "Portrait of the Essay as a Warm
Body." Introduction. The Best American Essays
1998. Ed. Ozick. Boston: Houghton, 1998. xv-
xxi.

16. BOOK WITH A TITLE WITHIN ITS TITLE If the book contains a title normally underlined (or italicized), neither underline (nor italicize) the internal title nor place it in quotation marks.

Vanderham, Paul. James Joyce and Censorship: The
Trials of Ulysses. New York: New York UP,
1997.

If the title within is normally enclosed within quotation marks, retain the quotation marks and underline (or italicize) the entire title.

Faulkner, Dewey R., ed. Twentieth Century Interpretations of "The Pardoner's Tale."
Englewood Cliffs: Prentice, 1973.

17. BOOK IN A SERIES Before the publication information, cite the series name as it appears on the title page, followed by the series number, if any.

```
Malena, Anne. The Dynamics of Identity in
     Francophone Caribbean Narrative. Francophone
     Cultures and Lits. Ser. 24. New York: Lang,
     1998.
```

18. REPUBLISHED BOOK   After the title of the book, cite the original publication date, followed by the current publication information. If the republished book contains new material, such as an introduction or afterword, include information about the new material after the original date.

```
Dietz, Lew, and Kosti Ruohomaa. Night Train at
     Wiscasset Station. 1977. Foreword Andrew Wyeth.
     Camden: Down East, 1998.
```

19. PUBLISHER'S IMPRINT   If a book was published by an imprint (a division) of a publishing company, link the name of the imprint and the name of the publisher with a hyphen, putting the imprint first.

```
Truan, Barry. Acoustic Communication. Westport:
     Ablex-Greenwood, 2000.
```

Articles in periodicals

This section shows how to prepare works cited entries for articles in magazines, scholarly journals, and newspapers. In addition to consulting the models in this section, you will at times need to turn to other models as well:

- More than one author: see item 2
- Corporate author: see item 3
- Unknown author: see item 4
- Online article: see item 32
- Article from a subscription service: see item 31

NOTE: For articles appearing on consecutive pages, provide the range of pages (see items 21 and 22). When an article does not appear on consecutive pages, give the number of the first page followed by a plus sign: 32+.

20. ARTICLE IN A MAGAZINE List, in order, separated by periods, the author's name; the title of the article, in quotation marks; and the title of the magazine, underlined (or italicized). Then give the date and the page numbers, separated by a colon. If the magazine is issued monthly, give just the month and year. Abbreviate the names of the months except May, June, and July.

Kaplan, Robert D. "History Moving North." Atlantic
    Monthly Feb. 1997: 21+.

If the magazine is issued weekly, give the exact date.

Lord, Lewis. "There's Something about Mary Todd."
    U.S. News and World Report 19 Feb. 2001: 53.

21. ARTICLE IN A JOURNAL PAGINATED BY VOLUME Many scholarly journals continue page numbers throughout the year instead of beginning each issue with page 1; at the end of the year, the issues are collected in a volume. To find an article, readers need only the volume number, the year, and the page numbers.

Ryan, Katy. "Revolutionary Suicide in Toni Morrison's
    Fiction." African American Review 34 (2000): 389-
    412.

22. ARTICLE IN A JOURNAL PAGINATED BY ISSUE If each issue of the journal begins with page 1, you need to indicate the number of the issue. Simply place a period after the volume number and follow it with the issue number.

Wood, Michael. "Broken Dates: Fiction and the
    Century." Kenyon Review 22.3 (2000): 50-64.

23. ARTICLE IN A DAILY NEWSPAPER   Begin with the name of the author, if there is one, followed by the title of the article. Next give the name of the newspaper, the date, and the page number (including the section letter). Use a plus sign (+) after the page number if the article does not appear on consecutive pages.

```
Murphy, Sean P. "Decisions on Status of Tribes Draw
     Fire." Boston Globe 27 Mar. 2001: A2.
```

If the section is marked with a number rather than a letter, handle the entry as follows:

```
Wilford, John Noble. "In a Golden Age of Discovery,
     Faraway Worlds Beckon." New York Times 9 Feb.
     1997, late ed., sec. 1: 1+.
```

When an edition of the newspaper is specified on the masthead, name the edition after the date and before the page reference (eastern ed., late ed., natl. ed., and so on), as in the example just given.

24. EDITORIAL IN A NEWSPAPER   Cite an editorial as you would an unsigned article, adding the word "Editorial" after the title.

```
"All Wet." Editorial. Boston Globe 12 Feb. 2001: 14.
```

25. LETTER TO THE EDITOR   Cite the writer's name, followed by the word "Letter" and the publication information for the newspaper or magazine in which the letter appears.

```
Shrewsbury, Toni. Letter. Atlanta Journal-
     Constitution 17 Feb. 2001: A13.
```

26. BOOK OR FILM REVIEW   Cite first the reviewer's name and the title of the review, if any, followed by the words "Rev. of" and the title and author or director of the work reviewed.

Add the publication information for the publication in which the review appears.

Gleick, Elizabeth. "The Burdens of Genius." Rev. of
    The Last Samurai, by Helen DeWitt. Time 4 Dec.
    2000: 171.

Denby, David. "On the Battlefield." Rev. of The
    Hurricane, dir. Norman Jewison. New Yorker 10
    Jan. 2000: 90-92.

Electronic sources

MLA's current guidelines for documenting electronic sources can be found in the *MLA Handbook for Writers of Research Papers* (5th ed., 1999). For more help with citing electronic sources in MLA style, see the list of frequently asked questions in the section "MLA Style" on MLA's Web site, <http://www.mla.org>.

NOTE: When a Web address in a works cited entry must be divided at the end of a line, MLA recommends that you break it after a slash. Do not insert a hyphen.

27. AN ENTIRE WEB SITE   Begin with the name of the author or corporate author (if known) and the title of the site, underlined (or italicized). Then give the names of any editors, the date of publication or last update, the name of any sponsoring organization, the date of access, and the URL in angle brackets. Provide as much of this information as is available.

WITH AUTHOR

Peterson, Susan Lynn. The Life of Martin Luther.
    1999. 9 Mar. 2001 <http://pweb.netcom.com/
    ~supeters/luther.htm>.

WITH CORPORATE (GROUP) AUTHOR

United States. Environmental Protection Agency.
     <u>Values and Functions of Wetlands</u>. 25 May
     1999. 24 Mar. 2001 <http://www.epa.gov-owow/
     wetlands/facts/fact2.html>.

AUTHOR UNKNOWN

<u>Margaret Sanger Papers Project</u>. 18 Oct. 2000.
     History Dept., New York U. 3 Apr. 2001
     <http://www.nyu.edu/projects/sanger/>.

WITH EDITOR

<u>Exploring Ancient World Cultures</u>. Ed. Anthony F.
     Beavers. 1997. U of Evansville. 12 Mar. 2001
     <http://eawc.evansville.edu/index.htm>.

NOTE: If the site has no title, substitute a description, such as "Home page," for the title. Do not underline the words or put them in quotation marks.

Block, Marylaine. Home page. 5 Mar. 2001. 12 Apr.
     2001 <http://www.marylaine.com>.

28. SHORT WORK FROM A WEB SITE   "Short" works are those that appear in quotation marks in MLA style: articles, poems, and other documents that are not book length. For a short work from a Web site, include as many of the following elements as apply and as are available:

- Author's name
- Title of the short work, in quotation marks
- Title of the site, underlined (or italicized)
- Date of publication or last update
- Sponsor of the site (if not named as the author)

- Date you accessed the source
- The URL in angle brackets

Usually at least some of these elements will not apply or will be unavailable. For example, in the following model, no date of publication was available. (The date given is the date on which the researcher accessed the source.)

WITH AUTHOR

Shiva, Vandana. "Bioethics: A Third World Issue."
     NativeWeb. 24 Feb. 2001 <http://
     www.nativeweb.org/pages/legal/shiva.html>.

AUTHOR UNKNOWN

"Media Giants." The Merchants of Cool. 2001. PBS
     Online. 7 Mar. 2001 <http://www.pbs.org/wgbh/
     pages/frontline/shows/cool/giants>.

If your source appears within a scholarly Web site, see also item 30.

29. ONLINE BOOK   When a book or a book-length work such as a play or a long poem is posted on the Web as its own site, give as much publication information as is available, followed by your date of access and the URL. (See also the models for print books: items 5–19.)

Rawlins, Gregory J. E. Moths to the Flame. Cambridge:
     MIT P, 1996. 3 Apr. 2001 <http://
     mitpress.mit.edu/e-books/Moths/contents.html>.

If the book-length work appears within a scholarly Web site, see item 30.

30. WORK WITHIN A SCHOLARLY PROJECT   For a work within a Web-based scholarly project, you may need to include more information than is necessary for an ordinary Web site or document (see items 28–29). For example, the project may contain information about the authors, translators, and editors (along with dates, if available) for both the source you are citing and for the entire scholarly project.

SHORT WORK WITHIN A SCHOLARLY PROJECT

Swift, Jonathan. "A Modest Proposal." 1729.
Eighteenth-Century Studies. Ed. Geoffrey
Sauer. The English Server. U of Washington. 7
Mar. 2001 <http://eserver.org/18th/
swiftmodest.txt>.

BOOK WITHIN A SCHOLARLY PROJECT

Jacobs, Harriet Ann. Incidents in the Life of a
Slave Girl. Boston, 1861. Documenting the
American South: The Southern Experience in
Nineteenth-Century America. Ed. Ji-Hae Yoon
and Natalia Smith. 1998. Academic Affairs
Lib., U of North Carolina, Chapel Hill. 14
Mar. 2001 <http://docsouth.unc.edu/jacobs/
jacobs.html>.

31. WORK FROM A SUBSCRIPTION SERVICE Libraries pay for access to databases through subscription services such as *Lexis-Nexis* and *ProQuest Direct.* When you retrieve a work from a subscription service, give as much of the following information as is available:

- Publication information for the source (see items 20–26)
- The name of the database, underlined (or italicized)
- The name of the service, neither underlined nor in quotation marks

- The name of the library where you retrieved the article
- The date on which you retrieved the article

Here is a model for an article retrieved through *Expanded Academic ASAP.* The source being cited is a scholarly article paginated by issue (see also item 22).

Fitzgerald, Jill. "How Will Bilingual/ESL Programs in
    Literacy Change in the Next Millennium?" Reading
    Research Quarterly 35.4 (2000). Expanded Academic
    ASAP. InfoTrac. Salem State Coll. Lib., Salem,
    MA. 16 Feb. 2001.

If you know the URL of the subscription service, add it at the end of the entry.

NOTE: When you access a work through a personal subscription service such as *America Online,* give the information about the source, followed by the name of the service, the date of access, and the keyword used to retrieve the source.

Conniff, Richard. "The House That John Built."
    Smithsonian Feb. 2001. America Online. 11 Mar.
    2001. Keyword: Smithsonian Magazine.

32. ARTICLE IN AN ONLINE PERIODICAL When citing online articles, follow the guidelines for printed articles (see items 20–26), giving whatever information is available in the online source. End the citation with your date of access and the URL.

NOTE: In some online articles, paragraphs are numbered. For such articles, include the total number of paragraphs in your citation, as in the next example.

FROM AN ONLINE SCHOLARLY JOURNAL

Belau, Linda. "Trauma and the Material Signifier."
    Postmodern Culture 11.2 (2001): 37 pars. 30

> Mar. 2001 <http://jefferson.village.virginia
> .edu/pmc/current.issue/11.2belau.html>.

FROM AN ONLINE MAGAZINE

Morgan, Fiona. "Banning the Bullies." <u>Salon.com</u> 15
> Mar. 2001. 2 Apr. 2001 <http://www.salon.com/
> news/feature/2001/03/15/bullying/index.html>.

FROM AN ONLINE NEWSPAPER

Barabak, Mark Z. "Californians Endorse New Power
> Plants, Environmental Rules." <u>Los Angeles
> Times</u> 17 Feb. 2001. 18 Feb. 2001 <http://
> www.latimes.com/news/timespoll/state/
> lat_poll0010217.htm>.

33. CD-ROM Treat a CD-ROM as you would any other
source, but name the medium before the publication information.

"Pimpernel." <u>The American Heritage Dictionary of the
> English Language</u>. 4th ed. CD-ROM. Boston:
> Houghton, 2000.

Wattenberg, Ruth. "Helping Students in the Middle."
> <u>American Educator</u> 19.4 (1996): 2-18. <u>ERIC</u>. CD-
> ROM. SilverPlatter. Sept. 1996.

34. E-MAIL To cite an e-mail, begin with the writer's name
and the subject line. Then write "E-mail to" followed by the
name of the recipient. End with the date of the message.

O'Donnell, Patricia. "Re: Interview questions." E-
> mail to the author. 15 Mar. 2001.

35. ONLINE POSTING   For an online posting, begin with the author's name, followed by the title or subject line (in quotation marks), the words "Online posting," the date of posting, the list or group name, the date of access, and the URL.

Keirn, Kellie. "Evaluation Criteria." Online posting.

6 Feb. 2001. Speakeasy Café. 7 Feb. 2001 <http://

morrison.wsu.edu/ExchangeDetail.asp?i+274925>.

36. REAL-TIME COMMUNICATION   To cite a real-time communication, include the writer's name (if relevant), a description and date of the event, the title of the forum, the date of access, and the URL.

Carbone, Nick. Planning for the future. 1 Mar. 2001.

TechRhet's Thursday night MOO. 1 Mar. 2001

<telnet://connections.moo.mud.org:3333>.

Multimedia sources

Multimedia sources include visuals (such as works of art), audio works (such as sound recordings), audiovisuals (such as films), and live events (such as the performance of a play).

When citing online multimedia sources, consult the appropriate model in this section and give whatever information is available for the online source; then end the citation with your date of access and the URL. (See item 37 for an example.)

37. WORK OF ART   Cite the artist's name, followed by the title of the artwork, usually underlined, and the institution and city in which the artwork can be found. If you want to indicate the work's date, include it after the title. For a work of art you viewed online, end your citation with your date of access and the URL.

Constable, John. <u>Dedham Vale</u>. Victoria and Albert

Museum, London.

```
van Gogh, Vincent. Starry Night. June 1889. Museum of
     Mod. Art, New York. 27 Feb. 2001 <http://
     www.moma.org/docs/collection/paintsculpt/
     c58.htm>.
```

38. CARTOON   Begin with the cartoonist's name, the title of the cartoon (if it has one) in quotation marks, the word "Cartoon," and the publication information for the publication in which the cartoon appears.

```
Rall, Ted. "Search and Destroy." Cartoon. Village
     Voice 23 Jan. 2001: 6.
```

39. ADVERTISEMENT   Name the product or company being advertised, followed by the word "Advertisement." Give publication information for the source in which the advertisement appears.

```
Truth by Calvin Klein. Advertisement. Vogue Dec. 2000:
     95-98.
```

40. MAP OR CHART   Cite a map or chart as you would a book or a short work within a longer work. Add the word "Map" or "Chart" following the title.

```
New Jersey. Map. Chicago: Rand, 2000.

Joseph, Lori, and Bob Laird. "Driving While Phoning Is
     Dangerous." Chart. USA Today 16 Feb. 2001: 1A.
```

41. MUSICAL COMPOSITION   Cite the composer's name, followed by the title of the work. Underline the title of an opera, a ballet, or a composition identified by name, but do not underline or use quotation marks around a composition identified by number or form.

```
Ellington, Duke. Conga Brava.

Haydn, Franz Joseph. Symphony no. 88 in G.
```

42. SOUND RECORDING   Begin with the name of the person you want to emphasize: the composer, conductor, or performer. For a long work, give the title, underlined (or italicized), followed by names of pertinent artists (such as performers, readers, or musicians) and the orchestra and conductor (if relevant). End with the manufacturer and the date.

Bizet, Georges. <u>Carmen</u>. Perf. Jennifer Laramore,
    Thomas Moser, Angela Gheorghiu, and Samuel Ramey.
    Bavarian State Orch. and Chorus. Cond. Giuseppe
    Sinopoli. Warner, 1996.

For a song, put the title in quotation marks. If you include the name of the album, underline it.

Chapman, Tracy. "Paper and Ink." <u>Telling Stories</u>.
    Elektra, 2000.

43. FILM OR VIDEO   Begin with the title, underlined (or italicized). For a film, cite the director and the lead actors or narrator ("Perf." or "Narr."), followed by the name of the distributor and the year of the film's release. For a videotape or DVD, add "Videocassette" or "DVD" before the name of the distributor.

<u>Chocolat</u>. Dir. Lasse Hallström. Perf. Juliette
    Binoche, Judi Dench, Alfred Molina, Lena Olin,
    and Johnny Depp. Miramax, 2001.

<u>High Fidelity</u>. Dir. Stephen Frears. Perf. John
    Cusack, Iben Hjejle, Jack Black, and Todd Louiso.
    2000. Videocassette. Walt Disney Video, 2001.

44. RADIO OR TELEVISION PROGRAM   Begin with the title of the radio segment or television episode (if there is one) in quotation marks, followed by the title of the program, underlined (or italicized). Next give relevant information about the program's writer ("By"), director ("Dir."), performers ("Perf."), or host ("Host"). Then name the network, the local station (if any), and the date the program was broadcast.

"American Limbo." <u>This American Life</u>. Host Ira Glass.
    Public Radio Intl. WBEZ, Chicago. 9 Feb. 2001.

If there is a series title, include it after the title of the program, neither underlined nor in quotation marks.

<u>Mysteries of the Pyramids</u>. On the Inside. Discovery
    Channel. 7 Feb. 2001.

45. RADIO OR TELEVISION INTERVIEW Begin with the name of the person who was interviewed, followed by the word "Interview." End with the information about the program as in item 44.

McGovern, George. Interview. <u>Charlie Rose</u>. PBS. WNET,
    New York. 1 Feb. 2001.

46. LIVE PERFORMANCE OF A PLAY Begin with the title of the play, followed by the author ("By"). Then include information about the performance: the director ("Dir."), major actors ("Perf."), the theater company, the theater and its location, and the date of the performance.

<u>Mother Courage</u>. By Bertolt Brecht. Dir. János Szász.
    Perf. Karen McDonald, Mirjana Jokovic, Jonathon
    Roberts, Tim Kang, and Amos Lichtman. Amer.
    Repertory Theatre, Cambridge. 18 Mar. 2001.

47. LECTURE OR PUBLIC ADDRESS Cite the speaker's name, followed by the title of the lecture (if any), the organization sponsoring the lecture, the location, and the date.

Cohran, Kelan. "Slavery and Astronomy." Adler
    Planetarium, Chicago. 21 Feb. 2001.

48. PERSONAL INTERVIEW   To cite an interview that you conducted, begin with the name of the person interviewed. Then write "Personal interview," followed by the date of the interview.

```
Shaikh, Michael. Personal interview. 22 Mar. 2001.
```

Other sources

This section includes a variety of traditional print sources not covered elsewhere. For sources obtained on the Web, consult the appropriate model in this section and give whatever information is available for the online source; then end the citation with the date on which you accessed the source and the URL. (See item 49 for an example.)

49. GOVERNMENT PUBLICATION   Treat the government agency as the author, giving the name of the government followed by the name of the agency.

```
United States. Natl. Council on Disability. Promises
    to Keep: A Decade of Federal Enforcement of the
    Americans with Disabilities Act. Washington: GPO,
    2000.
```

For government documents published online, give as much publication information as is available and end your citation with the date of access and the URL.

```
United States. Dept. of Transportation. Natl. Highway
    Traffic Safety Administration. An Investigation
    of the Safety Implications of Wireless Communica-
    tions in Vehicles. Nov. 1999. 20 May 2001
    <http://www.nhtsa.dot.gov/people/injury/research/
    wireless>.
```

50. LEGAL SOURCE   For most legal documents, cite the name of the document (without underlining or quotation marks), the article and section numbers, and the year if relevant.

```
US Const. Art. 4, sec. 2.
```

For an act, include its Public Law number ("Pub. L."), the date it was enacted, and its Statutes at Large number ("Stat.").

```
Electronic Freedom of Information Act Amendments of
     1996. Pub. L. 104-418. 2 Oct. 1996. Stat. 3048.
```

51. PAMPHLET   Cite a pamphlet as you would a book.

```
Commonwealth of Massachusetts. Dept. of Jury
     Commissioner. A Few Facts about Jury Duty.
     Boston: Commonwealth of Massachusetts, 1997.
```

52. DISSERTATION   Begin with the author's name, followed by the dissertation title in quotation marks, the abbreviation "Diss.," the name of the institution, and the year the dissertation was accepted.

```
Vallecillo, Maria Fernando. "At the Edge of the Abyss:
     The Concentration Camp Experience in the Novels
     of Jorge Semprún." Diss. U of North Carolina,
     2001.
```

For dissertations that have been published in book form, underline the title. After the title and before the book's publication information, add the abbreviation "Diss.," the name of the institution, and the year the dissertation was accepted.

```
Damberg, Cheryl L. Healthcare Reform: Distributional
     Consequences of an Employer Mandate for Workers
     in Small Firms. Diss. Rand Graduate School, 1995.
     Santa Monica: Rand, 1996.
```

53. ABSTRACT OF A DISSERTATION   Cite an abstract as you would an unpublished dissertation. After the dissertation date, give the abbreviation "*DA*" or "*DAI*" (for *Dissertation*

Abstracts or *Dissertation Abstracts International*), followed by the volume number, the date of publication, and the page number.

Goldman, Dara. "Lost and Found: Insularity and the
    Construction of Subjectivity in Hispanic Carib-
    bean Literature." Diss. Emory U, 2000. DAI 61
    (2000): 1431A.

54. PUBLISHED PROCEEDINGS OF A CONFERENCE   Cite published conference proceedings as you would a book, adding information about the conference after the title.

Kartiganer, Donald M., and Ann J. Abadie. Faulkner at
    100: Retrospect and Prospect. Proc. of Faulkner
    and Yoknapatawpha Conf., 27 July-1 Aug. 1997, U
    of Mississippi. Jackson: UP of Mississippi, 2000.

55. PUBLISHED INTERVIEW   Name the person interviewed, followed by the title of the interview (if there is one). If the interview does not have a title, include the word "Interview" followed by a period after the interviewee's name. Give publication information for the work in which the interview was published.

Renoir, Jean. "Renoir at Home: Interview with Jean
    Renoir." Film Quarterly 50.1 (1996): 2-8.

If the name of the interviewer is relevant, include it after the name of the interviewee, as in the following example.

Prince. Interview with Bilge Ebiri. Yahoo! Internet
    Life 7.6 (2001): 82-85.

56. PERSONAL LETTER   To cite a letter that you have received, begin with the writer's name and add the phrase "Letter to the author," followed by the date.

Coggins, Christopher. Letter to the author. 6 May, 2001.

MLA information notes (optional)

Researchers who use the MLA system of parenthetical documentation (see pp. 126–36) may also use information notes for one of two purposes:

1. to provide additional material that might interrupt the flow of the paper yet is important enough to include
2. to refer readers to any sources not discussed in the paper

Information notes may be either footnotes or endnotes. Footnotes appear at the foot of the page; endnotes appear on a separate page at the end of the paper, just before the list of works cited. For either style, the notes are numbered consecutively throughout the paper. The text of the paper contains a raised arabic numeral that corresponds to the number of the note.

TEXT

Local governments are more likely than state governments to pass legislation against using a cell phone while driving.[1]

NOTE

[1] For a discussion of local laws banning cell phone use, see Sundeen 8.

MLA manuscript format

In most English and humanities classes, you will be asked to use MLA (Modern Language Association) guidelines for formatting a paper and preparing a list of the works you have cited. The following guidelines are consistent with advice given in the *MLA Handbook for Writers of Research Papers*,

5th ed. (New York: MLA, 1999). For a sample MLA paper, see pages 167–75.

Formatting the paper

The following MLA recommendations have been endorsed by most English instructors.

MATERIALS   Use good-quality 8½" × 11" white paper. Secure the pages with a paper clip. Unless your instructor suggests otherwise, do not staple the pages together or use any sort of binder.

TITLE AND IDENTIFICATION   MLA does not require a title page. On the first page of your paper, place your name, your instructor's name, the course title, and the date on separate lines against the left margin. Then center your title. (See p. 167 for a sample first page.)

If your instructor requires a title page, ask for guidelines on formatting it. A format similar to the one on page 227 will most likely be acceptable.

PAGINATION   Put the page number preceded by your last name in the upper right corner of each page, one-half inch below the top edge. Use arabic numerals (1, 2, 3, and so on).

MARGINS, LINE SPACING, AND PARAGRAPH INDENTS Leave margins of one inch on all sides of the page. Do not justify (align) the right margin.

Double-space throughout the paper. Do not add extra line spaces above or below the title of the paper or between paragraphs.

Indent the first line of each paragraph one-half inch (or five spaces) from the left margin.

LONG QUOTATIONS   When a quotation is longer than four typed lines of prose or three lines of verse, set it off from the text by indenting the entire quotation a full inch (or ten spaces) from the left margin. Double-space the indented quotation, and don't add extra space above or below it.

Quotation marks are not needed when a quotation has been set off from the text by indenting. See page 169 for an example.

WEB ADDRESSES   When a Web address mentioned in the text of your paper must be divided at the end of a line, do not insert a hyphen (a hyphen could appear to be part of the address). For MLA rules on dividing Web addresses in your list of works cited, see page 165.

HEADINGS   MLA neither encourages nor discourages the use of headings and currently provides no guidelines for their use. If you would like to insert headings in a long essay or research paper, check first with your instructor. Although headings are not used as frequently in English and the humanities as in other disciplines, the trend seems to be changing.

VISUALS   MLA classifies visuals as tables and figures (figures include graphs, charts, maps, photographs, and drawings). Label each table with an arabic numeral (Table 1, Table 2, and so on) and provide a clear caption that identifies the subject. The label and caption should appear on separate lines above the table, flush left. Below the table, give its source in a note like this one:

```
Source: John M. Violanti, "Cellular Phones and
Fatal Traffic Collisions," Accident Analysis and
Prevention 30 (1998): 521.
```

For each figure, place a label and a caption below the figure, flush left. They need not appear on separate lines. The word "Figure" may be abbreviated to "Fig." Include source information following the caption.

Visuals should be placed in the text, as close as possible to the sentences that relate to them unless your instructor prefers them in an appendix. See page 169 for an example of a visual in the text of a paper.

Preparing the list of works cited

Begin the list of works cited on a new page at the end of the paper. Center the title Works Cited about one inch from the top of the page. Double-space throughout. See pages 174–75 for a sample list of works cited.

ALPHABETIZING THE LIST Alphabetize the list by the last names of the authors (or editors); if a work has no author or editor, alphabetize by the first word of the title other than *A, An,* or *The.*

If your list includes two or more works by the same author, use the author's name only for the first entry. For subsequent entries use three hyphens followed by a period. List the titles in alphabetical order. See also page 141.

INDENTING Do not indent the first line of each works cited entry, but indent any additional lines one-half inch (or five spaces). This technique highlights the names of the authors, making it easy for readers to scan the alphabetized list.

WEB ADDRESSES Do not insert a hyphen when dividing a Web address at the end of a line. Break the line after a slash. Also insert angle brackets around the URL.

If your word processing program automatically turns Web addresses into hot links (by underlining them and highlighting them in color), turn off this feature. For advice on how to do this, visit the MLA Web site at <http://www.mla.org> and consult the list of frequently asked questions.

Sample research paper: MLA style

On the following pages is a research paper on the topic of cell phones and driving, written by Angela Daly, a student in a composition class. Daly's paper is documented with the MLA style of in-text citations and a list of works cited.

Angela Daly
Professor Chavez
English 101
14 March 2001

A Call to Action:

Regulate Use of Cell Phones on the Road

When a cell phone goes off in a classroom or at a concert, we are irritated, but at least our lives are not endangered. When we are on the road, however, irresponsible cell phone users are more than irritating: They are putting our lives at risk. Many of us have witnessed drivers so distracted by dialing and chatting that they resemble drunk drivers, weaving between lanes, for example, or nearly running down pedestrians in crosswalks. A number of bills to regulate use of cell phones on the road have been introduced in state legislatures, and the time has come to push for their passage. Regulation is needed because drivers using phones are seriously impaired and because laws on negligent and reckless driving are not sufficient to punish offenders.

No one can deny that cell phones have caused traffic deaths and injuries. Cell phones were implicated in three fatal accidents in November 1999 alone. Early in November, two-year-old Morgan Pena was killed by a driver distracted by his cell phone. Morgan's mother, Patti Pena, reports that the driver "ran a stop sign at 45 mph, broadsided my vehicle and killed Morgan as she sat in her car seat." A week later, corrections officer Shannon Smith, who was guarding

prisoners by the side of the road, was killed by a
woman distracted by a phone call (Besthoff). On
Thanksgiving weekend that same month, John and Carole
Hall were killed when a Naval Academy midshipman
crashed into their parked car. The driver said in
court that when he looked up from the cell phone he
was dialing, he was three feet from the car and had no
time to stop (Stockwell B8).

Expert testimony, public opinion, and even
cartoons suggest that driving while phoning is dangerous. Frances Bents, an expert on the relation between
cell phones and accidents, estimates that between 450
and 1,000 crashes a year have some connection to cell
phone use (Layton C9). In a survey published by
Farmers Insurance Group, 87% of those polled said that
cell phones affect a driver's ability, and 40% reported having close calls with drivers distracted by
phones. Many cartoons have depicted the very real
dangers of driving while distracted (see Fig. 1 for an
example).

Scientific research confirms the dangers of using
phones while on the road. In 1997 an important study
appeared in the New England Journal of Medicine. The
authors, Donald Redelmeier and Robert Tibshirani,
studied 699 volunteers who made their cell phone bills
available in order to confirm the times when they had
placed calls. The participants agreed to report any
nonfatal collision in which they were involved. By
comparing the time of a collision with the phone
records, the researchers assessed the dangers of
driving while phoning. Here are their results:

Fig. 1 Chan Lowe, cartoon, Washington Post 22 July
2000: A21.

> We found that using a cellular telephone
> was associated with a risk of having a
> motor vehicle collision that was about four
> times as high as that among the same driv-
> ers when they were not using their cellular
> telephones. This relative risk is similar
> to the hazard associated with driving with
> a blood alcohol level at the legal limit.
> (456)

In reports by news media, the latter claim was
exaggerated ("similar to" is not "equal to"), but the

comparison with drunk driving is startling nonethe-
less.

A 1998 study focused on Oklahoma, one of the few
states to keep records on fatal accidents involving
cell phones. Using police records, John M. Violanti of
the Rochester Institute of Technology investigated the
relation between traffic fatalities in Oklahoma and
the use or presence of a cell phone. He found a
ninefold increase in the risk of fatality if a phone
was being used and a doubled risk simply when a phone
was present in a vehicle (522-23). The latter statis-
tic is interesting, for it suggests that those who
carry phones in their cars may tend to be more negligent (or prone to distractions of all kinds) than
those who do not.

Some groups have argued that state traffic laws
make legislation regulating cell phone use unnecessary. Sadly, this is not true. Laws on traffic safety
vary from state to state, and drivers distracted by
cell phones can get off with light punishment even
when they cause fatal accidents. For example, although
the midshipman mentioned earlier was charged with
vehicular manslaughter for the deaths of John and
Carole Hall, the judge was unable to issue a verdict
of guilty. Under Maryland law, he could only find the
defendant guilty of negligent driving and impose a
$500 fine (Layton C1). Such a light sentence is not
unusual. The driver who killed Morgan Lee Pena in
Pennsylvania received two tickets and a $50 fine--and
retained his driving privileges (Pena). In Georgia, a
young woman distracted by her phone ran down and

killed a two-year-old; her sentence was ninety days in
boot camp and five hundred hours of community service
(Ippolito J1). The families of the victims are under-
standably distressed by laws that lead to such light
sentences.

When certain kinds of driver behavior are shown
to be especially dangerous, we wisely draft special
laws making them illegal and imposing specific punishments. Running red lights, failing to stop for a
school bus, and drunk driving are obvious examples;
phoning in a moving vehicle should be no exception.
Unlike more general laws covering negligent driving,
specific laws leave little ambiguity for law officers
and for judges and juries imposing punishments. Such
laws have another important benefit: They leave no
ambiguity for drivers. Currently, drivers can tease
themselves into thinking they are using their car
phones responsibly because the definition of "negligent driving" is vague.

As of December 2000, twenty countries were
restricting use of cell phones in moving vehicles
(Sundeen 8). In the United States, it is highly
unlikely that legislation could be passed on the
national level, since traffic safety is considered a
state and local issue. To date, only a few counties
and towns have passed traffic laws restricting cell
phone use. For example, in Suffolk County, New York,
it is illegal for drivers to use a handheld phone for
anything but an emergency call while on the road
(Haughney A8). The first town to restrict use of
handheld phones was Brooklyn, Ohio (Layton C9).

Brooklyn, the first community in the country to pass a seat belt law, has once again shown its concern for traffic safety.

Laws passed by counties and towns have had some effect, but it makes more sense to legislate at the state level. Local laws are not likely to have the impact of state laws, and keeping track of a wide variety of local ordinances is confusing for drivers. Even a spokesperson for Verizon Wireless has said that statewide bans are preferable to a "crazy patchwork quilt of ordinances" (qtd. in Haughney A8). Unfortunately, although a number of bills have been introduced in state legislatures, as of early 2001 no state law seriously restricting use of the phones has passed--largely because of effective lobbying from the wireless industry.

Despite the claims of some lobbyists, tough laws regulating phone use can make our roads safer. In Japan, for example, accidents linked to cell phones fell by 75% just a month after the country prohibited using a handheld phone while driving (Haughney A8). Research suggests and common sense tells us that it is not possible to drive an automobile at high speeds, dial numbers, and carry on conversations without significant risks. When such behavior is regulated, obviously our roads will be safer.

Because of mounting public awareness of the dangers of drivers distracted by phones, state legislators must begin to take the problem seriously. "It's definitely an issue that is gaining steam around the

country," says Matt Sundeen of the National Conference
of State Legislatures (qtd. in Layton C9). Lon Anderson of the American Automobile Association agrees:
"There is momentum building," he says, to pass laws
(qtd. in Layton C9). The time has come for states to
adopt legislation restricting the use of cell phones
in moving vehicles.

Works Cited

Besthoff, Len. "Cell Phone Use Increases Risk of
     Accidents, but Users Willing to Take the Risk."
     <u>WRAL Online</u>. 11 Nov. 1999. 12 Jan. 2001 <http://
     www.wral-tv.com/news/wral/1999/
     1110-talking-driving>.

Farmers Insurance Group. "New Survey Shows
     Drivers Have Had 'Close Calls' with Cell Phone
     Users." 8 May 2000. 12 Jan. 2001 <http://
     www.farmersinsurance.com/news_cellphones.html>.

Haughney, Christine. "Taking Phones Out of Drivers'
     Hands." <u>Washington Post</u> 5 Nov. 2000: A8.

Ippolito, Milo. "Driver's Sentence Not Justice, Mom
     Says." <u>Atlanta Journal-Constitution</u> 25 Sept.
     1999: J1.

Layton, Lyndsey. "Legislators Aiming to Disconnect
     Motorists." <u>Washington Post</u> 10 Dec. 2000: C1+.

Lowe, Chan. Cartoon. <u>Washington Post</u> 22 July 2000:
     A21.

Pena, Patricia N. "Patti Pena's Letter to Car Talk."
     <u>Cars.com</u>. Car Talk. 10 Jan. 2001 <http://
     cartalk.cars.com/About/Morgan-Pena/
     letter.html>.

Redelmeier, Donald A., and Robert J. Tibshirani.
     "Association between Cellular-Telephone Calls and
     Motor Vehicle Collisions." <u>New England Journal of
     Medicine</u> 336 (1997): 453-58.

Stockwell, Jamie. "Phone Use Faulted in Collision."
    Washington Post 6 Dec. 2000: B1+.

Sundeen, Matt. "Cell Phones and Highway Safety: 2000
    State Legislative Update." Dec. 2000. Natl. Conf.
    of State Legislatures. 27 Feb. 2001 <http://
    ncsl.org/programs/esnr/cellphone.pdf>.

Violanti, John M. "Cellular Phones and Fatal Traffic
    Collisions." Accident Analysis and Prevention 30
    (1998): 519-24.

APA Style: The Social Sciences

In most social science classes, you will be asked to use the APA (American Psychological Association) system for documenting sources, which is set forth in the *Publication Manual of the American Psychological Association,* 5th ed. (Washington: APA, 2001). APA recommends in-text citations that refer readers to a list of references.

An in-text citation names the author of the source (often in a signal phrase), gives the date of publication, and at times includes a page number in parentheses. At the end of the paper, a list of references provides publication information about the source; the list is alphabetized by authors' last names (or by titles for works without authors). There is a direct link between the in-text citation and the alphabetical listing. In the following example, that link is underlined.

IN-TEXT CITATION

Rumbaugh (1995) reported that "Kanzi's comprehension of over 600 novel sentences of request was very comparable to Alia's; both complied with requests without assistance on approximately 70% of the sentences" (p. 722).

ENTRY IN THE LIST OF REFERENCES

Rumbaugh, D. (1995). Primate language and cognition: Common ground. *Social Research, 62,* 711-730.

NOTE: Indent the entry in your list of references as shown here unless your instructor suggests otherwise (see pp. 196–98).

Directory to APA in-text citations

APA in-text citations

The APA's in-text citations provide at least the author's last name and the date of publication. For direct quotations and some paraphrases, a page number is given as well.

NOTE: In the models that follow, notice that APA style requires the use of the past tense or the present perfect tense in signal phrases introducing material that has been cited: *Smith reported, Smith has argued.*

1. BASIC FORMAT FOR A QUOTATION   Ordinarily, introduce the quotation with a signal phrase that includes the author's last name followed by the date of publication in parentheses. Put the page number (preceded by "p.") in parentheses at the end of the quotation.

```
Hart (1996) wrote that some primatologists "won-
dered if apes had learned Language, with a capital
L" (p. 109).
```

If the signal phrase does not name the author, place the author's name, the date, and the page number in parentheses at the end of the quotation. Use commas between items in the parentheses: (Hart, 1996, p. 109).

2. BASIC FORMAT FOR A SUMMARY OR A PARAPHRASE   For a summary or a paraphrase, include the author's last name and the date either in a signal phrase or in parentheses at the end. A page number is not required for a summary or a paraphrase, but include one if it would help readers find the passage in a long work.

According to Hart (1996), researchers took Terrace's conclusions seriously, and funding for language experiments soon declined (p. 110).

Researchers took Terrace's conclusions seriously, and funding for language experiments soon declined (Hart, 1996, p. 110).

3. A WORK WITH TWO AUTHORS   Name both authors in the signal phrase or parentheses each time you cite the work. In the parentheses, use "&" between the authors' names; in the signal phrase, use "and."

Greenfield and Savage-Rumbaugh (1990) have acknowledged that Kanzi's linguistic development was slower than that of a human child (p. 567).

Kanzi's linguistic development was slower than that of a human child (Greenfield & Savage-Rumbaugh, 1990, p. 567).

4. A WORK WITH THREE TO FIVE AUTHORS   Identify all authors in the signal phrase or parentheses the first time you cite the source.

> The chimpanzee Nim was raised by researchers who
> trained him in American Sign Language by molding
> and guiding his hands (Terrace, Petitto, Sanders,
> & Bever, 1979, p. 891).

In subsequent citations, use the first author's name followed by "et al." in either the signal phrase or the parentheses.

> Nim was able to string together as many as 16
> signs, but their order appeared quite random
> (Terrace et al., 1979, p. 895).

5. A WORK WITH SIX OR MORE AUTHORS Use only the first author's name followed by "et al." in the signal phrase or parentheses.

> The ape language experiments are shedding light on
> the language development of very young children
> and children with linguistic handicaps (Savage-
> Rumbaugh et al., 1993).

6. UNKNOWN AUTHOR If the author is unknown, mention the work's title in the signal phrase or give the first word or two of the title in the parenthetical citation. Titles of articles and chapters are put in quotation marks; titles of books and reports are italicized.

> Chimpanzees living in separate areas of Africa
> differ in a range of behaviors: in their methods
> of cracking nuts or gathering ants, for example,
> or in their grooming rituals. An international
> team of researchers has concluded that many of the
> differing behaviors are cultural, not just re-
> sponses to varying environmental factors
> ("Chimps," 1999).

NOTE: In the rare case when "Anonymous" is specified as the author, treat it as if it were a real name: (Anonymous, 2001). In the list of references, also use the name Anonymous as author.

7. ORGANIZATION AS AUTHOR   If the author is a government agency or other corporate organization, give the full name of the organization in the signal phrase or in the parenthetical citation the first time you cite the source.

> According to the Language Research Center (2000), linguistic research with apes has led to new methods of treating humans with learning disabilities such as autism and dyslexia.

If the organization has a familiar abbreviation, you may include it in brackets the first time you cite the source and use the abbreviation alone in later citations.

> **FIRST CITATION**   (National Institute of Mental Health [NIMH], 2001)
>
> **LATER CITATIONS**   (NIMH, 2001)

8. TWO OR MORE WORKS IN THE SAME PARENTHESES   When your parenthetical citation names two or more works, put them in the same order that they appear in the reference list, separated by semicolons.

> Researchers argued that the apes in the early language experiments were merely responding to cues (Sebeok & Umiker-Sebeok, 1979; Terrace, 1979).

9. AUTHORS WITH THE SAME LAST NAME   To avoid confusion, use initials with the last names if your bibliography lists two or more authors with the same last name.

> Research by E. Smith (1989) revealed that . . .

10. PERSONAL COMMUNICATION Interviews, memos, letters, e-mail, and similar unpublished person-to-person communications should be cited by initials, last name, and precise date.

> One of Patterson's former aides, who worked for
> seven months with the gorilla Michael, is con-
> vinced that he was capable of joking and lying in
> sign language (E. Robbins, personal communication,
> January 4, 2000).

It is not necessary to include personal communications in the bibliographic references at the end of your paper.

11. AN ELECTRONIC DOCUMENT When possible, cite an electronic document as you would any other document (using the author-date style).

> R. Fouts and D. Fouts (1999) have explained one
> benefit of ape language research: It has shown us
> how to teach children with linguistic disabili-
> ties.

Electronic sources may lack authors' names or dates. In addition, they may lack page numbers (required in some citations). Here are APA's guidelines for handling sources without authors' names, dates, or page numbers.

Unknown author

If no author is named, mention the title of the document in a signal phrase or give the first word or two of the title in parentheses (see also item 6). (If an organization serves as the author, see item 7.)

> According to the BBC article "Chimps Are Cultured
> Creatures" (1999), chimpanzees at sites in West
> Africa, Tanzania, and Uganda exhibit culture-

```
specific patterns of behavior when grooming one
another.
```

Unknown date

When the date is unknown, APA recommends using the abbreviation "n.d." (for "no date").

```
Attempts to return sign-language-using apes to the
wild have had mixed results (Smith, n.d.).
```

No page numbers

APA ordinarily requires page numbers for direct quotations, and it recommends them for summaries or paraphrases from long sources. When an electronic source lacks stable numbered pages, your citation should include — if possible — information that will help readers locate the particular passage being cited.

When an electronic document has numbered paragraphs, use the paragraph number preceded by the symbol ¶ or by the abbreviation "para.": (Hall, 2001, ¶ 5) *or* (Hall, 2001, para. 5). If neither a page nor a paragraph number is given and the document contains headings, cite the appropriate heading and indicate which paragraph under that heading you are referring to:

```
According to Kirby (1999), some critics have
accused activists in the Great Ape Project of
"exaggerating the supposed similarities of the
apes [to humans] to stop their use in experiments"
(Shared Path section, para. 6).
```

NOTE: Some electronic sources post articles in files using portable document format (pdf). When such a file contains page numbers, give the page number in the parenthetical citation.

Williams, Brakke, and Savage-Rumbaugh (1997)
reported that three chimpanzees who were exposed
to language after they were two years old could
learn symbols but could not understand speech,
even after years of hearing it (p. 302).

APA list of references

In APA style, the alphabetical list of works cited is titled "References." Following are models illustrating the form APA recommends for entries in the list of references. Observe all details: capitalization, punctuation, use of italics, and so on. For advice on preparing the reference list, see pages 196–98. For a sample reference list, see pages 207–8.

General guidelines for listing authors

Alphabetize entries in the list of references by authors' last names; if a work has no author, alphabetize it by its title. The first element of each entry is important because citations in the text of the paper refer to it and readers will be looking for it in the alphabetized list. The date of publication always appears immediately after the first element of the citation.

NAME AND DATE CITED IN TEXT

Duncan (2001) has reported that . . .

BEGINNING OF ENTRY IN THE LIST OF REFERENCES

Duncan, B. (2001).

Items 1–4 show how to begin an entry for a work with a single author, multiple authors, an organization as author, and an unknown author. Items 5 and 6 show how to begin an entry when your list includes two or more works by the

Directory to APA references (bibliographic entries)

Directory to APA references (continued)

---

same author or two or more works by the same author in the same year. What comes after the first element of your citation will depend on the kind of source you are citing (see items 7–30).

1. SINGLE AUTHOR Begin the entry with the author's last name, followed by a comma and the author's initial(s). Then give the date in parentheses.

```
Conran, G. (2001).
```

2. MULTIPLE AUTHORS List up to six authors by last names followed by initials. Use an ampersand (&) between the names of two authors or, if there are more than two authors, before the name of the last author.

```
Walker, J. R., & Taylor, T. (1998).
```

```
Sloan, F. A., Stout, E. M., Whetten-Goldstein, K., &
     Liang, (2000).
```

If there are more than six authors, list the first six and "et al." (meaning "and others") to indicate that there are others.

3. ORGANIZATION AS AUTHOR When the author is an organization, begin with the name of the organization.

```
American Psychiatric Association. (2000).
```

NOTE: If the organization is also the publisher, see item 28.

4. UNKNOWN AUTHOR   Begin the entry with the work's title. Titles of books are italicized. Titles of articles are neither italicized nor put in quotation marks. (For rules on capitalization of titles, see pp. 197–98.)

> *Oxford essential world atlas.* (1996).
>
> EMFs on the brain. (1995, January 21).

5. TWO OR MORE WORKS BY THE SAME AUTHOR   Use the author's name for all entries. List the entries by date, the earliest first.

Schlechty, P. C. (1997).

Schlechty, P. C. (2001).

6. TWO OR MORE WORKS BY THE SAME AUTHOR IN THE SAME YEAR   List the works alphabetically by title. In the parentheses, following the year, add lowercase letters beginning with "a," "b," and so on. Use these same designations when giving the date in the in-text citation.

> Kennedy, C. H. (2000a).
>
> Kennedy, C. H. (2000b).

Articles in periodicals

This section shows how to prepare an entry for an article in a periodical such as a scholarly journal, a magazine, or a newspaper. In addition to consulting the models in this section, you may need to refer to items 1–6 (general guidelines for listing authors).

NOTE: For articles on consecutive pages, provide the range of pages. When an article does not appear on consecutive pages, give all page numbers (see item 10 for an example).

7. ARTICLE IN A JOURNAL PAGINATED BY VOLUME   Many professional journals continue page numbers throughout the year instead of beginning each issue with page 1; at the end of the year, the issues are collected in a volume. After the italicized title of the journal, give the volume number (also italicized), followed by the page numbers.

Morawski, J. (2000). Social psychology a century ago.
    American Psychologist, 55, 427-431.

8. ARTICLE IN A JOURNAL PAGINATED BY ISSUE   When each issue of a journal begins with page 1, include the issue number in parentheses after the volume number. Italicize the volume number but not the issue number.

Scruton, R. (1996). The eclipse of listening. *The New*
    Criterion, 15(3), 5-13.

9. ARTICLE IN A MAGAZINE   In addition to the year of publication, list the month and, for weekly magazines, the day. If there is a volume number, include it following the title (italicized).

Raloff, J. (2001, May 12). Lead therapy won't help
    most kids. *Science News,* 159, 292.

10. ARTICLE IN A NEWSPAPER   Begin with the name of the author, if there is one, followed by the year, month, and day of publication. (For an article with an unknown author, see also item 4.) Page numbers are introduced with "p." (or "pp." for multiple pages).

Haney, D. Q. (1998, February 20). Finding eats at
    mystery of appetite. *The Oregonian,* pp. A1, A17.

11. LETTER TO THE EDITOR   Letters to the editor appear in scholarly journals, in magazines, and in newspapers. Follow the appropriate model and insert the words "Letter to the editor" in brackets before the name of the periodical.

```
Carter, R. (2000). New York, New York [Letter to the
    editor]. Scientific American, 238(1), 8.
```

12. REVIEW Reviews of books and other media appear in a variety of periodicals. Follow the appropriate model for the periodical. For a book, give the title of the review (if there is one), followed by the words "Review of the book" and the title of the book in brackets.

```
Gleick, E. (2000, December 14). The burdens of genius
    [Review of the book The Last Samurai]. Time, 156,
    171.
```

For a film review, write "Review of the motion picture," and for a TV review, write "Review of the television program." Treat other media in a similar way.

Books

In addition to consulting the items in this section, you may need to turn to other models. See items 1–6 for general guidelines on listing authors.

13. BASIC FORMAT FOR A BOOK Begin with the author's name followed by the date and the book's title. End with the place of publication and the name of the publisher.

```
Bernstein, N. (2001). The lost children of Wilder: The
    epic struggle to change foster care. New York:
    Pantheon.
```

14. EDITORS For a book with an editor but no author, begin with the name of the editor (or editors) followed by the abbreviation "Ed." (or "Eds." for more than one editor) in parentheses.

Duncan, G. J., & Brooks-Gunn, J. (Eds.). (1997).
Consequences of growing up poor. New York:
Russell Sage Foundation.

For a book with an author and an editor, begin with the author's name. Give the editor's name in parentheses after the title of the book, followed by the abbreviation "Ed." (or "Eds.").

Plath, Sylvia. (2000). *The unabridged journals* (K. V.
Kukil, Ed.). New York: Anchor.

15. TRANSLATION   After the title, name the translator, followed by the abbreviation "Trans.," in parentheses. Add the original date of the work's publication in parentheses at the end of the entry.

Singer, I. B. (1998). *Shadows on the Hudson* (J.
Sherman, Trans.). New York: Farrar, Straus and
Giroux. (Original work published 1957)

16. EDITION OTHER THAN THE FIRST   Include the number of the edition in parentheses after the title.

Helfer, M. E., Keme, R. S., & Drugman, R. D. (1997).
The battered child (5th ed.). Chicago: University
of Chicago Press.

17. ARTICLE OR CHAPTER IN AN EDITED BOOK   Begin with the author, the year of publication, and the title of the article or chapter. Then write "In" and give the editor's name, followed by "Ed." in parentheses; the title of the book; and the page numbers of the article or chapter in parentheses. End with the book's publication information.

Luban, D. (2000). The ethics of wrongful obedience. In
D. L. Rhode (Ed.), *Ethics in practice: Lawyers'*

> *roles, responsibilities, and regulation* (pp. 94-
> 120). New York: Oxford University Press.

18. MULTIVOLUME WORK   Give the number of volumes after the title.

Wiener, P. (Ed.). (1973). *Dictionary of the history of
ideas* (Vols. 1-4). New York: Scribner's.

Electronic sources

The following guidelines for electronic sources are based on
the fifth edition of the *Publication Manual of the American
Psychological Association* (2001). Any updates will be posted
on the APA Web site, <http://www.apastyle.org>.

19. ARTICLE FROM AN ONLINE PERIODICAL   When citing
online articles, follow the guidelines for printed articles (see
items 7–12), giving whatever information is available in the
online source. If the article also appears in a printed journal, a URL is not required; instead, include "Electronic version" in brackets after the title of the article.

Williams, S. L., Brakke, K. E., & Savage-Rumbaugh, E.
S. (1977). Comprehension skills of language-
competent and nonlanguage-competent apes [Elec-
tronic version]. *Language and Communication,
17*(4), 301-317.

If there is no print version, include the date you accessed
the source and the article's URL.

Ashe, D. D., & McCutcheon, L. E. (2001, May 4).
Shyness, loneliness, and attitude toward celebrities. *Current Research in Social Psychology,
6*(9). Retrieved July 3, 2001, from http://
www.uiowa.edu/~grpproc/crisp/crisp.6.9.htm

NOTE: When you have retrieved an article from a newspaper's searchable Web site, give the URL for the site, not for the exact source.

Cary, B. (2001, June 18). Mentors of the mind. *Los
    Angeles Times.* Retrieved July 5, 2001, from
    http://www.latimes.com

20. ARTICLE FROM A DATABASE Libraries pay for access to electronic databases such as *PsycInfo* and *JSTOR,* which are not otherwise available to the public. To cite an article from an electronic database, include the publication information from the source (see items 7–12). End the citation with your date of access, the name of the database, and the document number (if applicable).

Holliday, R. E., & Hayes, B. K. (2001, January).
    Dissociating automatic and intentional processes
    in children's eyewitness memory. *Journal of
    Experimental Child Psychology, 75*(1), 1-5.
    Retrieved February 21, 2001, from Expanded
    Academic ASAP database (A59317972).

21. NONPERIODICAL WEB DOCUMENT To cite a nonperiodical Web document, such as a report, list as many of the following elements as are available.

Author's name

Date of publication (if there is no date, use "n.d.")

Title of document (in italics)

Date you accessed the source

A URL that will take readers directly to the source

In the first model, the source has both an author and a date; in the second, the source lacks a date. If a source has no author, begin with the title.

Cain, A., & Burris, M. (1999, April). *Investigation of the use of mobile phones while driving.* Retrieved January 15, 2000, from http://www.cutr.eng.usf.edu/its/mobile_phone_text.htm

Archer, Z. (n.d.). *Exploring nonverbal communication.* Retrieved July 18, 2001, from http://zzyx.ucsc.edu/~archer

NOTE: If you retrieved the source from a university program's Web site, name the program in your retrieval statement.

Cosmides, L., & Tooby, J. (1997). *Evolutionary psychology: A primer.* Retrieved July 5, 2001, from the University of California, Santa Barbara, Center for Evolutionary Psychology Web site: http://www.psych.ucsb.edu/research/cep/primer.html

22. CHAPTER OR SECTION IN A WEB DOCUMENT Begin with the author, the year of publication, and the title of the chapter or section. Then write "In" and give the title of the document, followed by any identifying information in parentheses. End with your date of access and the URL for the chapter or section.

Heuer, R. J., Jr. (1999). Keeping an open mind. In *Psychology of intelligence analysis* (chap. 6). Retrieved July 7, 2001, from http://www.cia.gov/csi/books/19104/art9.html

23. E-MAIL E-mail messages are personal communications and are not included in the list of references.

24. ONLINE POSTING If an online posting cannot be retrieved (because the newsgroup or forum does not maintain archives), cite it as a personal communication in the text of your paper and do not include it in the list of references. If the posting can be retrieved from an archive, treat it as follows, giving as much information as is available.

Eaton, S. (2001, June 12). Online transactions [Msg
      2]. Message posted to news://
      sci.psychology.psychotherapy.moderated

25. COMPUTER PROGRAM Add the words "Computer software" in brackets after the title of the program.

Kaufmann, W. J., III, & Comins, N. F. (1998). Discov-
      ering the universe (Version 4.1) [Computer
      software]. New York: Freeman.

Other sources

26. DISSERTATION ABSTRACT

Hu, X. (1996). Consumption and social inequality in
      urban Guangdong, China (Doctoral dissertation,
      University of Hawaii, 1996). *Dissertation
      Abstracts International, 57,* 3280A.

27. GOVERNMENT DOCUMENT

U.S. Census Bureau. (2000). *Statistical abstract of
      the United States.* Washington, DC: U.S. Govern-
      ment Printing Office.

28. REPORT FROM A PRIVATE ORGANIZATION If the publisher is the author, give the word "Author" as the publisher. If the report has an author, begin with the author's name, and name the publisher at the end.

American Psychiatric Association. (2000). *Practice
      guidelines for the treatment of patients with
      eating disorders* (2nd ed.). Washington, DC:
      Author.

29. CONFERENCE PROCEEDINGS

Schnase, J. L., & Cunnius, E. L. (Eds.). (1995).
*Proceedings of CSCL '95: The First International
Conference on Computer Support for Collaborative
Learning.* Mahwah, NJ: Erlbaum.

30. MOTION PICTURE To cite a motion picture in any format (film, video, or DVD), list the director and the producer (if available) and the year of the picture's release. Give the title, followed by "Motion picture" in brackets, the country where it was made, and the name of the studio. If the motion picture is difficult to find, include instead the name and address of its distributor.

Soderbergh, S. (Director). (2000). *Traffic* [Motion
picture]. United States: Gramercy Pictures.

Donohew, P. (Producer/Director). (1999). *Seven
sisters: A Kentucky portrait* [Motion picture].
(Available from Sour Mash Films, 55 Cumberland
Street, San Francisco, CA 94110)

APA manuscript format

The American Psychological Association makes a number of recommendations for formatting a paper and preparing a list of references. The following guidelines are consistent with advice given in the *Publication Manual of the American Psychological Association,* 5th ed. (Washington: APA, 2001).

Formatting the paper

APA guidelines for formatting a paper are endorsed by many instructors in the social sciences.

MATERIALS AND TYPEFACE   Use good-quality 8½" × 11" white paper. Avoid a typeface that is unusual or hard to read.

TITLE PAGE   The APA manual does not provide guidelines for preparing the title page of a college paper, but most instructors will want you to include one. See page 199 for an example.

PAGE NUMBERS AND RUNNING HEAD   In the upper right-hand corner of each page, type a short version of your title, followed by five spaces and the page number. Number all pages, including the title page.

MARGINS, LINE SPACING, AND PARAGRAPH INDENTS   Use margins of one inch on all sides of the page. Do not justify (align) the right margin.

Double-space throughout the paper, and indent the first line of each paragraph one-half inch (or five spaces).

LONG QUOTATIONS   When a quotation is longer than forty words, set it off from the text by indenting it one-half inch (or five spaces) from the left margin. Double-space the quotation. Quotation marks are not needed when a quotation has been set off from the text. See page 204 for an example.

ABSTRACT   If your instructor requires one, include an abstract immediately after the title page. Center the word Abstract one inch from the top of the page; double-space the abstract as you do the body of your paper.

An abstract is a 75-to-100-word paragraph that provides readers with a quick overview of your essay. It should express your main idea and your key points; it might also briefly suggest any implications or applications of the research you discuss in the paper.

HEADINGS Although headings are not always necessary, their use is encouraged in the social sciences. For most undergraduate papers, one or two levels of headings will usually be sufficient.

In APA style, major headings are centered and second-level headings are placed flush left and italicized. Capitalize the first word of the heading, along with all important words. Do not capitalize minor words — articles, short prepositions, and coordinating conjunctions — unless they are the first word.

VISUALS The APA classifies visuals as tables and figures (figures include graphs, charts, drawings, and photographs). Keep visuals as simple as possible. Label each table with an arabic numeral (Table 1, Table 2, and so on) and provide a clear title that identifies the subject. The label and title should appear on separate lines above the table, flush left. Below the table, give its source in a note like this one:

Note. From "Innovation Roles: From Souls of Fire to Devil's Advocates," by Marcy Meyer, 2000, *The Journal of Business Communication, 37,* p. 338.

For each figure, place a label and a caption below the figure, flush left. They need not appear on separate lines.

In the text of your paper, discuss the most significant features of each visual. Place the visual as close as possible to the sentences that relate to them unless your instructor prefers them in an appendix.

Preparing the list of references

Begin your list of references on a new page at the end of the paper. Center the title "References" about one inch from the top of the page. Double-space throughout. For a sample reference list, see pages 207–8.

INDENTING ENTRIES APA recommends using hanging indents, which highlight the authors' names and thus make it easy for readers to scan through the alphabetized list of references. To create a hanging indent, type the first line of an entry flush left and indent any additional lines one-half inch (or five spaces), as shown here.

Stoessinger, J. G. (1998). *Why nations go to war* (7th
     ed.). New York: St. Martin's Press.

Some instructors may prefer a paragraph-style indent, as in the following example.

     Stoessinger, J. G. (1998). *Why nations go to war*
(7th ed.). New York: St. Martin's Press.

ALPHABETIZING THE LIST Alphabetize the reference list by the last names of the authors (or editors); when a work has no author or editor, alphabetize by the first word of the title other than *A, An,* or *The.*

If your list includes two or more works by the same author, arrange the entries by date, the earliest first. If your list includes two or more works by the same author in the same year, arrange them alphabetically by title. Add the lowercase letters "a," "b," and so on within the parentheses immediately following the year: (2001a, July 7).

AUTHORS' NAMES Invert all authors' names and use initials instead of first names. With two or more authors, use an ampersand (&) between the names. Separate the names with commas. Include names for the first six authors; if there are additional authors, end the list with "et al." (Latin for "and others") to indicate that there are others (see also p. 185).

TITLES OF BOOKS AND ARTICLES Italicize the titles and subtitles of books; capitalize only the first word of the title and subtitle (and all proper nouns). Capitalize names of periodicals as you would capitalize them normally.

ABBREVIATIONS FOR PAGE NUMBERS Abbreviations for "page" and "pages" ("p." and "pp.") are used before page numbers of newspaper articles and articles in edited books (see pp. 186–87 and 189) but not before page numbers of articles appearing in magazines and scholarly journals (see pp. 187–88).

NOTE: The sample reference page (see p. 207) shows how to type your list of references.

BREAKING A URL When a URL must be divided, break it after a slash or before a period. Do not insert a hypen.

For information about the exact format of each entry in your list, consult the models on pages 185–94.

Sample research paper: APA style

On the following pages is a research paper written by Karen Shaw, a student in a psychology class. Shaw's assignment was to write a "review of the literature" paper documented with APA-style citations and references.

In preparing her final manuscript, Shaw followed the APA guidelines. She did not include an abstract because her instructor did not require one.

Apes and Language:
A Review of the Literature

Karen Shaw

Psychology 110, Section 2
Professor Verdi
March 2, 2001

Apes and Language:

A Review of the Literature

Over the past thirty years, researchers have demonstrated that the great apes (chimpanzees, gorillas, and orangutans) resemble humans in language abilities more than had been thought possible. Just how far that resemblance extends, however, has been a matter of some controversy. Researchers agree that the apes have acquired fairly large vocabularies in American Sign Language and in artificial languages, but they have drawn quite different conclusions in addressing the following questions:

1. How spontaneously have apes used language?
2. How creatively have apes used language?
3. Can apes create sentences?
4. What are the implications of the ape language studies?

This review of the literature on apes and language focuses on these four questions.

How Spontaneously

Have Apes Used Language?

In an influential article, Terrace, Petitto, Sanders, and Bever (1979) argued that the apes in the language experiments were not using language spontaneously but were merely imitating their trainers, responding to conscious or unconscious cues. Terrace and his colleagues at Columbia University had trained a chimpanzee, Nim, in American Sign Language, so their skepticism about the apes' abilities received much attention. In fact, funding for ape language research was sharply reduced following publication of their 1979 article "Can an Ape Create a Sentence?"

In retrospect, the conclusions of Terrace et al. seem to have been premature. Although some early ape language studies had not been rigorously controlled to eliminate cuing, even as early as the 1970s R. A. Gardner and B. T. Gardner were conducting double-blind experiments that prevented any possibility of cuing (Fouts, 1997, p. 99). Since 1979, researchers have diligently guarded against cuing.

Perhaps the best evidence that apes are not merely responding to cues is that they have signed to one another spontaneously, without trainers present. Like many of the apes studied, gorillas Koko and Michael have been observed signing to one another (Patterson & Linden, 1981). At Central Washington University the baby chimpanzee Loulis, placed in the care of the signing chimpanzee Washoe, mastered nearly fifty signs in American Sign Language without help from humans. "Interestingly," wrote researcher Fouts (1997), "Loulis did *not* pick up any of the seven signs that we [humans] used around him. He learned only from Washoe and [another chimp] Ally" (p. 244).

The extent to which chimpanzees spontaneously use language may depend on their training. Terrace trained Nim using the behaviorist technique of operant condi-tioning, so it is not surprising that many of Nim's signs were cued. Many other researchers have used a conversational approach that parallels the process by which human children acquire language. In an experimental study, O'Sullivan and Yeager (1989) contrasted the two techniques, using Terrace's Nim as their subject. They found that Nim's use of language was significantly more spontaneous under conversational conditions.

How Creatively
Have Apes Used Language?

There is considerable evidence that apes have invented creative names. One of the earliest and most controversial examples involved the Gardners' chimpanzee Washoe. Washoe, who knew signs for "water" and "bird," once signed "water bird" when in the presence of a swan. Terrace et al. (1979) suggested that there was "no basis for concluding that Washoe was characterizing the swan as a 'bird that inhabits water.'" Washoe may simply have been "identifying correctly a body of water and a bird, in that order" (p. 895).

Other examples are not so easily explained away. The bonobo Kanzi has requested particular films by combining symbols on a computer in a creative way. For instance, to ask for *Quest for Fire*, a film about early primates discovering fire, Kanzi began to use symbols for "campfire" and "TV" (Eckholm, 1985). The gorilla Koko, who learned American Sign Language, has a long list of creative names to her credit: "elephant baby" to describe a Pinocchio doll, "finger bracelet" to describe a ring, "bottle match" to describe a cigarette lighter, and so on (Patterson & Linden, 1981, p. 146). If Terrace's analysis of the "water bird" example is applied to the examples just men-

tioned, it does not hold. Surely Koko did not first
see an elephant and then a baby before signing "elephant baby"--or a bottle and a match before signing
"bottle match."

Can Apes Create Sentences?

The early ape language studies offered little
proof that apes could combine symbols into grammati-
cally ordered sentences. Apes strung together various
signs, but the sequences were often random and repeti-
tious. Nim's series of sixteen signs is a case in
point: "give orange me give eat orange me eat orange
give me eat orange give me you" (Terrace et al., 1979,
p. 895).

More recent studies with bonobos at the Language
Research Center in Atlanta have broken new ground.
Kanzi, a bonobo trained by Savage-Rumbaugh, seems to
understand simple grammatical rules about word order.
For instance, Kanzi learned that in two-word utter-
ances action precedes object, an ordering also used by
human children at the two-word stage. In a major
article reporting on their research, Greenfield and
Savage-Rumbaugh (1990) wrote that Kanzi rarely "re-
peated himself or formed combinations that were
semantically unrelated" (p. 556).

More important, Kanzi began on his own to create
certain patterns that may not exist in English but can
be found among deaf children and in other human
languages. For example, Kanzi used his own rules when
combining action symbols. Symbols that involved an
invitation to play, such as "chase," would appear

first; symbols that indicated what was to be done during play ("hide") would appear second. Kanzi also created his own rules when combining gestures and symbols. He would use the symbol first and then gesture, a practice often followed by young deaf children (Greenfield & Savage-Rumbaugh, 1990, p. 560).

In a later study, Kanzi's abilities to understand spoken language were shown to be similar to those of a 2-1/2-year-old human, Alia. Rumbaugh (1995) reported that "Kanzi's comprehension of over 600 novel sentences of request was very comparable to Alia's; both complied with the requests without assistance on approximately 70% of the sentences" (p. 722). A recent monograph provided examples of the kinds of sentences both Kanzi and Alia were able to understand:

> For example, the word *ball* occurred in 76 different sentences, including such different requests as "Put the leaves in your ball," "Show me the ball that's on TV," "Vacuum your ball," and "Go do ball slapping with Liz." Overall, 144 different content words, many of which were presented in ways that required syntactic parsing for a proper response (such as "Knife your ball" vs. "Put the knife in the hat"), were utilized in the study. (Savage-Rumbaugh et al., 2000, p. 101-102).

The researchers concluded that neither Kanzi nor Alia could have demonstrated understanding of such requests without comprehending syntactical relationships among the words in a sentence.

What Are the Implications of the
Ape Language Studies?

Kanzi's linguistic abilities are so impressive that they may help us understand how humans came to acquire language. Pointing out that 99% of our genetic material is held in common with the chimpanzees, Greenfield and Savage-Rumbaugh (1990) have suggested that something of the "evolutionary root of human language" can be found in the "linguistic abilities of the great apes" (p. 540). Noting that apes' brains are similar to those of our human ancestors, Leakey and Lewin (1992) argued that in ape brains "the cognitive foundations on which human language could be built are already present" (p. 244).

The suggestion that there is a continuity in the linguistic abilities of apes and humans has created much controversy. Linguist Noam Chomsky has strongly asserted that language is a unique human characteristic (Booth, 1990). Terrace has continued to be skeptical of the claims made for the apes, as have Petitto and Bever, coauthors of the 1979 article that caused such skepticism earlier (Gibbons, 1991).

Recently, neurobiologists have made discoveries that may cause even the skeptics to take notice. Ongoing studies at the Yerkes Primate Research Center have revealed remarkable similarities in the brains of chimpanzees and humans. Through brain scans of live chimpanzees, researchers have found that, as with humans, "the language-controlling PT [*planum temporale*] is larger on the left side of the chimps'

Apes and Language 8

brain than on the right. But it is not lateralized in monkeys, which are less closely related to humans than apes are" (Begley, 1998, p. 57).

Although the ape language studies continue to generate controversy, researchers have shown over the past thirty years that the gap between the linguistic abilities of apes and humans is far less dramatic than was once believed.

References

Begley, S. (1998, January 19). Aping language. *Newsweek, 131,* 56-58.

Booth, W. (1990, October 29). Monkeying with language: Is chimp using words or merely aping handlers? *The Washington Post,* p. A3.

Eckholm, E. (1985, June 25). Kanzi the chimp: A life in science. *The New York Times,* pp. C1, C3.

Fouts, R. (1997). *Next of kin: What chimpanzees taught me about who we are.* New York: William Morrow.

Gibbons, A. (1991). Déjà vu all over again: Chimp-language wars. *Science, 251,* 1561-1562.

Greenfield, P. M., & Savage-Rumbaugh, E. S. (1990). Grammatical combination in *Pan paniscus:* Processes of learning and invention in the evolution and development of language. In S. T. Parker & K. R. Gibson (Eds.), *"Language" and intelligence in monkeys and apes: Comparative developmental perspectives* (pp. 540-578). Cambridge: Cambridge University Press.

Leakey, R., & Lewin, R. (1992). *Origins reconsidered: In search of what makes us human.* New York: Doubleday.

O'Sullivan, C., & Yeager, C. P. (1989). Communicative context and linguistic competence: The effect of social setting on a chimpanzee's conversational skill. In R. A. Gardner, B. T. Gardner, & T. E. Van Cantfort (Eds.). *Teaching sign language to chimpanzees* (pp. 269-279). Albany: SUNY Press.

Patterson, F., & Linden, E. (1981). The education of
    Koko. New York: Holt, Rinehart & Winston.

Rumbaugh, D. (1995). Primate language and cognition:
    Common ground. Social Research, 62, 711-730.

Savage-Rumbaugh, E. S., Murphy, J. S., Sevcik, R. A.,
    Brakke, K. E., Williams, S. L., Rumbaugh, D. M.,
    et al. (2000). Language comprehension in ape and
    child: Monograph. Atlanta, GA: The Language
    Research Center. Retrieved January 6, 2000, from
    the Language Research Center Web site: http://
    www.gsu.edu/~www1rc/monograph.html

Terrace, H. S., Petitto, L. A., Sanders, R. J., &
    Bever, T. G. (1979). Can an ape create a
    sentence? Science, 206, 891-902.

Chicago Style: History

Most assignments in history and other humanities classes are based to some extent on reading. At times you will be asked to respond to one or two readings, such as essays or historical documents. At other times you may be asked to write a research paper that draws on a wide variety of sources.

Most history instructors and some humanities instructors require you to document sources with footnotes or endnotes based on *The Chicago Manual of Style,* 14th ed. (Chicago: U of Chicago P, 1993). When you write a paper using sources, you face three main challenges in addition to documenting your sources: (1) supporting a thesis, (2) citing your sources and avoiding plagiarism, and (3) integrating quotations and other source material.

Chicago documentation style (footnotes or endnotes)

Professors in history and some humanities courses often require footnotes or endnotes based on *The Chicago Manual of Style.* When you use *Chicago*-style notes, you will usually be asked to include a bibliography at the end of your paper (see p. 231).

TEXT

A Union soldier, Jacob Thomas, claimed to have seen Forrest order the killing, but when asked to describe the six-foot-two general, he called him "a little bit of a man."[12]

FOOTNOTE OR ENDNOTE

> 12. Brian Steel Wills, A Battle from the
> Start: The Life of Nathan Bedford Forrest (New
> York: HarperCollins, 1992), 187.

BIBLIOGRAPHY ENTRY

> Wills, Brian Steel. A Battle from the Start: The
> Life of Nathan Bedford Forrest. New York:
> HarperCollins, 1992.

First and subsequent references to a source

The first time you cite a source, the note should include publishing information for that work as well as the page number on which the passage being cited may be found.

> 1. Peter Burchard, One Gallant Rush: Robert
> Gould Shaw and His Brave Black Regiment (New York:
> St. Martin's Press, 1965), 85.

For subsequent references to a source you have already cited, give only the author's last name, followed by a comma and the page or pages cited.

> 4. Burchard, 31.

If you cite more than one work by the same author, include a short form of the title in subsequent citations. A short form of the title of a book is underlined or italicized; a short form of the title of an article is put in quotation marks.

> 8. Burchard, One Gallant Rush, 31.

> 10. Burchard, "Civil War," 10.

NOTE: *Chicago* style no longer requires the use of "ibid." to refer to the work cited in the previous note. The Latin abbreviations "op. cit." and "loc. cit." are also no longer used.

Chicago-style bibliography

A bibliography, which appears at the end of your paper, lists every work you have cited in your notes; in addition, it may include works that you consulted but did not cite. For advice on constructing the list, see page 225. A sample bibliography appears on page 231.

Model notes and bibliography entries

The following models are consistent with guidelines set forth in *The Chicago Manual of Style,* 14th ed. For each type of source, a model note appears first, followed by a model bibliography entry. The model note shows the format you should use when citing a source for the first time. For subsequent citations of a source, use shortened notes (as just described).

Books

1. BASIC FORMAT FOR A BOOK

    1. William H. Rehnquist, The Supreme Court: A History (New York: Knopf, 2001), 204.

Rehnquist, William H. The Supreme Court: A History. New York: Knopf, 2001.

2. TWO OR THREE AUTHORS

    2. Lesley Adkins and Roy Adkins, The Keys of Egypt: The Obsession to Decipher Egyptian Hieroglyphs (New York: HarperCollins, 2000), 117-23.

Adkins, Lesley, and Roy Adkins. The Keys of Egypt: The Obsession to Decipher Egyptian Hieroglyphs. New York: HarperCollins, 2000.

Directory to Chicago-style notes and bibliography entries

3. FOUR OR MORE AUTHORS

3. Joan N. Burstyn et al., Preventing Violence in Schools: A Challenge to American Democracy (Mahwah, N.J.: Lawrence Erlbaum, 2001), 22.

Burstyn, Joan N., et al. Preventing Violence in Schools: A Challenge to American Democracy. Mahwah, N.J.: Lawrence Erlbaum, 2001.

4. UNKNOWN AUTHOR

4. The Men's League Handbook on Women's Suffrage (London, 1912), 23.

The Men's League Handbook on Women's Suffrage. London, 1912.

5. AUTHOR'S NAME IN TITLE

5. Long Walk to Freedom: The Autobiography of Nelson Mandela (Boston: Little, Brown, 1995), 435.

Mandela, Nelson. Long Walk to Freedom: The Autobiography of Nelson Mandela. Boston: Little, Brown, 1995.

6. EDITED WORK WITHOUT AN AUTHOR

6. Jon Meacham, ed., <u>Voices in Our Blood: America's Best on the Civil Rights Movement</u> (New York: Random House, 2001), 312.

Meacham, Jon, ed. <u>Voices in Our Blood: America's Best on the Civil Rights Movement</u>. New York: Random House, 2001.

7. EDITED WORK WITH AN AUTHOR

7. Ted Poston, <u>A First Draft of History</u>, ed. Kathleen A. Hauke (Athens: University of Georgia Press, 2000), 46.

Poston, Ted. <u>A First Draft of History</u>. Edited by Kathleen A. Hauke. Athens: University of Georgia Press, 2000.

8. TRANSLATED WORK

8. Sergei Nikolaevich Bulgakov, <u>Philosophy of Economy: The World as Household</u>, trans. Catherine Evtuhov (New Haven: Yale University Press, 2000), 167.

Bulgakov, Sergei Nikolaevich. <u>Philosophy of Economy: The World as Household</u>. Translated by Catherine Evtuhov. New Haven: Yale University Press, 2000.

9. EDITION OTHER THAN THE FIRST

9. Andrew F. Rolle, <u>California: A History</u>, 5th ed. (Wheeling, Ill.: Harlan Davidson, 1998), 243-46.

Rolle, Andrew F. <u>California: A History</u>. 5th ed. Wheeling, Ill.: Harlan Davidson, 1998.

10. UNTITLED VOLUME IN A MULTIVOLUME WORK

10. New Cambridge Modern History (Cambridge: Cambridge University Press, 1957), 1:52-53.

New Cambridge Modern History. Vol. 1. Cambridge: Cambridge University Press, 1957.

11. TITLED VOLUME IN A MULTIVOLUME WORK

11. Horst Boog et al., The Attack on the Soviet Union, vol. 4 of Germany and the Second World War (Cambridge: Oxford University Press, 1998), 70-72.

Boog, Horst, et al. The Attack on the Soviet Union. Vol. 4 of Germany and the Second World War. Cambridge: Oxford University Press, 1998.

12. WORK IN AN ANTHOLOGY

12. Zora Neale Hurston, "From Dust Tracks on a Road," in The Norton Book of American Autobiography, ed. Jay Parini (New York: Norton, 1999), 336.

Hurston, Zora Neale. "From Dust Tracks on a Road." In The Norton Book of American Autobiography, edited by Jay Parini, 333-43. New York: Norton, 1999.

13. LETTER IN A PUBLISHED COLLECTION

13. Bartolomeo Vanzetti to Dante Sacco, 21 August 1927, Letters of the Century: America, 1900-1999, ed. Lisa Grunwald and Stephen J. Adler (New York: Dial, 1999), 180-81.

Vanzetti, Bartolomeo. Letter to Dante Sacco, 21 August 1927. In Letters of the Century: America, 1900-1999, edited by Lisa Grunwald and Stephen J. Adler, 180-81. New York: Dial, 1999.

14. WORK IN A SERIES

14. R. Keith Schoppa, <u>The Columbia Guide to Modern Chinese History</u>, Columbia Guides to Asian History (New York: Columbia University Press, 2000), 256-58.

Schoppa, R. Keith. <u>The Columbia Guide to Modern Chinese History</u>. Columbia Guides to Asian History. New York: Columbia University Press, 2000.

15. ENCYCLOPEDIA OR DICTIONARY ENTRY

15. <u>Encyclopaedia Britannica</u>, 15th ed., s.v. "Monroe Doctrine."

NOTE: The abbreviation "s.v." is for the Latin *sub verbo* ("under the word").

Encyclopedias and dictionaries are usually not included in the bibliography.

16. BIBLICAL REFERENCE

16. Matt. 20.4-9 Revised Standard Version.

The Bible is usually not included in the bibliography.

Articles in periodicals

For articles in periodicals, a footnote or endnote should cite an exact page number. In the bibliography entry, include the page range for the entire article.

NOTE: If you accessed an article through an online database such as *Lexis-Nexis*, see also item 26.

17. ARTICLE IN A JOURNAL PAGINATED BY VOLUME

17. Virginia Guedea, "The Process of Mexican Independence," <u>American Historical Review</u> 105 (2000): 120.

Guedea, Virginia. "The Process of Mexican Independence." <u>American Historical Review</u> 105 (2000):
116-31.

18. ARTICLE IN A JOURNAL PAGINATED BY ISSUE

18. Jonathon Zimmerman, "Ethnicity and the
History Wars in the 1920s," <u>Journal of American
History</u> 87, no. 1 (2000): 101.

Zimmerman, Jonathon. "Ethnicity and the History Wars
in the 1920s." <u>Journal of American History</u> 87,
no. 1 (2000): 92-111.

19. ARTICLE IN A MAGAZINE

19. Joy Williams, "One Acre," <u>Harper's</u>, February
2001, 62.

Williams, Joy. "One Acre." <u>Harper's</u>, February 2001,
59-65.

20. ARTICLE IN A NEWSPAPER

20. Dan Barry, "A Mill Closes, and a Hamlet Fades
to Black," <u>New York Times</u>, 16 February 2001, sec. A.

Barry, Dan. "A Mill Closes, and a Hamlet Fades to
Black." <u>New York Times</u>, 16 February 2001, sec. A.

21. UNSIGNED ARTICLE

21. "Radiation in Russia," <u>U.S. News and World
Report</u>, 9 August 1993, 41.

"Radiation in Russia." <u>U.S. News and World Report</u>, 9
August 1993, 40-42.

22. BOOK REVIEW

    22. Nancy Gabin, review of <u>The Other Feminists:</u> <u>Activists in the Liberal Establishment</u>, by Susan M. Hartman, <u>Journal of Women's History</u> 12 (2000): 230.

Gabin, Nancy. Review of <u>The Other Feminists: Activists</u>
    <u>in the Liberal Establishment</u>, by Susan M.
    Hartman. <u>Journal of Women's History</u> 12 (2000):
    227-34.

Electronic sources

Although *The Chicago Manual of Style* does not include guidelines for documenting online sources, the University of Chicago Press recommends following the system developed by Andrew Harnack and Eugene Kleppinger in *Online! A Reference Guide to Using Internet Sources* (Boston: Bedford/St. Martin's, 2000). The examples of online sources given in this section are based on Harnack and Kleppinger's guidelines.

23. AN ENTIRE WEB SITE Begin with the name of the author or corporate author (if known) and the title of the site (underlined). Then give the date of publication, the site's URL (in angle brackets), and the date of access (in parentheses).

    23. Kevin Rayburn, <u>The 1920s</u>, 9 April 2000, <http://www.louisville.edu/~kprayb01/1920s.html>(6 March 2001).

Rayburn, Kevin. <u>The 1920s</u>. 9 April 2000. <http://
    www.louisville.edu/~kprayb01/1920s.html> (6 March
    2001).

24. SHORT DOCUMENT FROM A WEB SITE "Short" works are those that appear in quotation marks in *Chicago* style: articles and other documents that are not book length. (For online books, see item 25.)

When citing a short work, include as many of the following elements as apply and as are available: author's name, title of the short work (in quotation marks), title of the site (underlined), date of publication, the URL (in angle brackets), date of access (in parentheses), and page number (if available). Many Web documents are not marked with page numbers; when possible, give the text division instead. In the following example, "Origins and Inspiration" is a heading breaking up the text of the article being cited.

WITH AUTHOR

>   24. Sheila Connor, "Historical Background,"
> <u>Garden and Forest</u>, Library of Congress, 23 Decem-
> ber 1999, <http://lcweb.loc.gov/preserv/prd/
> gardfor/historygf.html> (20 January 2001), Origins
> and Inspiration.

> Connor, Sheila. "Historical Background." <u>Garden
>   and Forest</u>. Library of Congress. 23 December
>   1999. <http://lcweb.loc.gov/preserv/prd/
>   gardfor/historygf.html> (20 January 2001).

AUTHOR UNKNOWN

>   24. "Media Giants," <u>The Merchants of Cool</u>,
> <u>PBS Online</u>, 2001, <http://www.pbs.org/wgbh/pages/
> frontline/shows/cool/giants> (7 March 2001).

> "Media Giants." <u>The Merchants of Cool</u>. <u>PBS
>   Online</u>. 2001. <http://www.pbs.org/wgbh/
>   pages/frontline/shows/cool/giants> (7 March
>   2001).

25. ONLINE BOOK When a book or a book-length work is posted on the Web, give as much publication information as is available, followed by the URL (in angle brackets), your date of access (in parentheses), and page numbers.

25. Booker T. Washington, "Up from Slavery," in The Autobiographical Writings, vol. 1 of The Booker T. Washington Papers, 2000, <http://stills.nap.edu/btw/ Vol.1/html/264.html> (16 Feb. 2001), 213.

Washington, Booker T. "Up from Slavery." In The Autobiographical Writings. Vol. 1 of The Booker T. Washington Papers, 2000, 211-388. <http:// stills.nap.edu/btw/Vol.1/html/264.html> (16 Feb. 2001).

26. DOCUMENT FROM A DATABASE When you retrieve a document from an online database, give as much of the following information as is available: publication information for the source, the name of the database (underlined), the name of the service, and the access date (in parentheses).

26. Anna Clark, "The New Poor Law and the Bread-winner Wage: Contrasting Assumptions," Journal of Social History 34, no. 2 (2000): 261. Expanded Academic ASAP, InfoTrac (20 March 2001).

Clark, Anna. "The New Poor Law and the Breadwinner Wage: Contrasting Assumptions." Journal of Social History 34, no. 2 (2000): 261. Expanded Academic ASAP, InfoTrac (20 March 2001).

27. E-MAIL MESSAGE To cite an e-mail message, include the writer's name, the subject line (in quotation marks), date sent, and the type of e-mail (personal e-mail or distribution list). End with the date you read it (in parentheses).

27. Kathleen Veslany, "Public Policy Initiative," 25 January 2001, personal e-mail (25 January 2001).

Veslany, Kathleen. "Public Policy Initiative." 25
    January 2001. Personal e-mail (25 January 2001).

28. ONLINE POSTING To cite a posting to a Web forum, an online mailing list, or a newsgroup, include the name of the author, the title or subject of the posting (in quotation marks), the date of the posting, the URL (in angle brackets), and the date of access (in parentheses).

28. Nancy Stegall, "Web Publishing and Censorship," 2 February 1997, <acw-1@ttacs6.ttu.edu> (18
March 1997).

Stegall, Nancy. "Web Publishing and Censorship." 2
    February 1997. <acw-1@ttacs6.ttu.edu> (18 March
    1997).

29. REAL-TIME COMMUNICATION Cite the name of the speaker or the site; the title, date, and description of the event; the URL (in angle brackets); and the date of access (in parentheses).

29. Diversity University MOO, 16 March 2001,
group discussion, <http://moo.du.org> (16 March 2001).

Diversity University MOO. 16 March 2001. Group discus-
    sion. <http://moo.du.org> (16 March 2001).

Other sources

30. GOVERNMENT DOCUMENT

30. U.S. Department of State, Foreign Relations
of the United States: Diplomatic Papers, 1943 (Washington, D.C.: GPO, 1965), 562.

U.S. Department of State. Foreign Relations of the
    United States: Diplomatic Papers, 1943. Washing-
    ton, D.C.: GPO, 1965.

31. UNPUBLISHED DISSERTATION

31. Stephanie Lynn Budin, "The Origins of Aphrodite (Greece)" (Ph.D. diss., University of Pennsylvania, 2000), 301-2.

Budin, Stephanie Lynn. "The Origins of Aphrodite (Greece)." Ph.D. diss., University of Pennsylvania, 2000.

32. PERSONAL COMMUNICATION

32. Sara Lehman, letter to author, 13 August 2000.

Personal communications are not included in the bibliography.

33. INTERVIEW

33. Ron Haviv, interview by Charlie Rose, The Charlie Rose Show, Public Broadcasting System, 12 February 2001.

Haviv, Ron. Interview by Charlie Rose. The Charlie Rose Show. Public Broadcasting System, 12 February 2001.

34. FILM OR VIDEOTAPE

34. North by Northwest, prod. and dir. Alfred Hitchcock, 2 hr. 17 min., MGM/UA, 1959, videocassette.

North by Northwest. Produced and directed by Alfred Hitchcock. 2 hr. 17 min. MGM/UA, 1959. Videocassette.

35. SOUND RECORDING

35. Gustav Holst, The Planets, Royal Philharmonic, André Previn, Telarc compact disc 80133.

Holst, Gustav. The Planets. Royal Philharmonic. André
    Previn. Telarc compact disc 80133.

36. SOURCE QUOTED IN ANOTHER SOURCE

    36. George Harmon Knoles, The Jazz Age Revisited:
British Criticism of American Civilization during the
1920s (Stanford: Stanford University Press, 1955), 31,
quoted in C. Vann Woodward, The Old World's New World
(Oxford: Oxford University Press, 1991), 46.

Knoles, George Harmon. The Jazz Age Revisited: British
    Criticism of American Civilization during the
    1920s, 31. Stanford: Stanford University Press,
    1955. Quoted in C. Vann Woodward, The Old World's
    New World (Oxford: Oxford University Press,
    1991), 46.

Chicago-style manuscript format

The following guidelines for formatting a *Chicago*-style paper and preparing its endnotes and bibliography are based
on *The Chicago Manual of Style*, 14th ed. For a sample *Chicago*-style paper, see pages 227–31.

Formatting the paper

Chicago manuscript guidelines are fairly generic, since they
were not created with a specific type of writing in mind.

   TITLE PAGE   On the title page, include the full title of
your paper and your name. Your instructor will usually want
you to include the course title, the instructor's name, and
the date as well. Do not type a number on the title page but
count it in the manuscript numbering; that is, the first page
of the text will usually be numbered 2. See page 227 for a
sample title page.

PAGINATION   Using arabic numerals, number all pages except the title page in the upper right corner. Depending on your instructor's preference, you may also use a short title or your last name before the page numbers to help identify pages in case they come loose from your manuscript.

MARGINS AND LINE SPACING   Leave margins of at least one inch at the top, bottom, and sides of the page. Double-space the entire manuscript, including long quotations that have been set off from the text.

LONG QUOTATIONS   When a quotation is fairly long, set it off from the text by indenting. Indent the full quotation one-half inch (five spaces) from the left margin. Quotation marks are not needed when a quotation has been set off from the text.

VISUALS   *The Chicago Manual* classifies visuals as tables and illustrations (illustrations, or figures, include drawings, photographs, maps, and charts). Keep visuals as simple as possible. Label each table with an arabic numeral (Table 1, Table 2, and so on) and provide a clear title that identifies the subject. The label and title should appear on separate lines above the table, flush left. Below the table, give its source in a note like this one:

```
Source: Edna Bonacich and Richard P. Appelbaum,
Behind the Label (Berkeley: University of  Cali-
fornia Press, 2000), 145.
```

For each figure, place a label and a caption below the figure, flush left. The label and caption need not appear on separate lines. The word "Figure" may be abbreviated to "Fig."

In the text of your paper, discuss the most significant features of each visual. Place visuals as close as possible to the sentences that relate to them unless your instructor prefers them in an appendix.

Preparing the endnotes

Begin the endnotes on a new page at the end of the paper. Center the title Notes about one inch from the top of the page, and number the pages consecutively with the rest of the manuscript. See page 230 for an example.

INDENTING AND NUMBERING Indent the first line of each entry one-half inch (or five spaces) from the left margin; do not indent additional lines in an entry. Begin the note with the arabic numeral that corresponds to the number in the text. Put a period after the number.

LINE SPACING Double-space throughout. Do not add extra lines of space between entries.

Preparing the bibliography

Typically, the notes in *Chicago*-style papers are followed by a bibliography, an alphabetically arranged list of all the works cited or consulted (see p. 231 for an example). Center the title "Bibliography" about one inch from the top of the page. Number bibliography pages consecutively with the rest of the paper.

ALPHABETIZING THE LIST Alphabetize the bibliography by the last names of the authors (or editors); when a work has no author or editor, alphabetize by the first word of the title other than *A, An,* or *The.*

If your list includes two or more works by the same author, use three hyphens instead of the author's name in all entries after the first. You may arrange the entries alphabetically by title or chronologically; be consistent throughout the bibliography.

INDENTING AND LINE SPACING Begin each entry at the left margin, and indent any additional lines one-half inch (or five spaces). Double-space throughout; do not add extra lines of space between entries.

Sample pages from a research paper: *Chicago*-style

Following are sample pages from a research paper by Ned Bishop, a student in a history class. Bishop was asked to document his paper using *Chicago*-style endnotes and a bibliography. In preparing his manuscript, Bishop also followed *Chicago* guidelines.

SAMPLE *CHICAGO* TITLE PAGE

The Massacre at Fort Pillow:
Holding Nathan Bedford Forrest Accountable

Ned Bishop

History 214
Professor Citro
22 March 2001

SAMPLE CHICAGO PAGE

Although Northern newspapers of the time no doubt exaggerated some of the Confederate atrocities at Fort Pillow, most modern sources agree that a massacre of Union troops took place there on 12 April 1864. It seems clear that Union soldiers, particularly black soldiers, were killed after they had stopped fighting or had surrendered or were being held prisoner. Less clear is the role played by Major General Nathan Bedford Forrest in leading his troops. Although we will never know whether Forrest directly ordered the massacre, evidence suggests that he was responsible for it.

What happened at Fort Pillow?

Fort Pillow, Tennessee, which sat on a bluff overlooking the Mississippi River, had been held by the Union for two years. It was garrisoned by 580 men, 292 of them from the Sixth United States Colored Heavy and Light Cavalry, 285 from the white Thirteenth Tennessee Cavalry. Nathan Bedford Forrest's troops numbered about 1,500 men.[1]

The Confederates attacked Fort Pillow on 12 April 1864 and had virtually surrounded the fort by the time Forrest arrived on the battlefield. At 3:30 P.M., Forrest displayed a flag of truce and sent in a demand for unconditional surrender of the sort he had used before: "The conduct of the officers and men garrisoning Fort Pillow has been such as to entitle them to being treated as prisoners of war. . . . Should my

SAMPLE CHICAGO PAGE

demand be refused, I cannot be responsible for the fate of your command."[2] Union Major William Bradford, who had replaced Major Booth, killed earlier by sharpshooters, asked for an hour to consult. Forrest, worried that vessels in the river were bringing in more troops, shortened the time to twenty minutes. Bradford refused to surrender, and Forrest quickly ordered the attack.

The Confederates charged across the short distance between their lines and the fort, helping one another scale the parapet, from which they fired into the fort. Victory came quickly, with the Union forces running toward the river or surrendering. Shelby Foote describes the scene like this:

> Some kept going, right into the river, where a number drowned and the swimmers became targets for marksmen on the bluff. Others, dropping their guns in terror, ran back toward the Confederates with their hands up, and of these some were spared as prisoners, while others were shot down in the act of surrender.[3]

The complete text of the paper appears at <www.bedfordstmartins.com/hacker/resdoc>.

SAMPLE *CHICAGO* ENDNOTES

Bishop 8

Notes

1. John Cimprich and Robert C. Mainfort Jr., "Fort Pillow Revisited: New Evidence about an Old Controversy," Civil War History 28 (1982): 293-94.

2. Quoted in Brian Steel Wills, A Battle from the Start: The Life of Nathan Bedford Forrest (New York: HarperCollins, 1992), 182.

3. Shelby Foote, The Civil War, a Narrative: Red River to Appomattox (New York: Vintage, 1986), 110.

4. Nathan Bedford Forrest, "Report of Maj. Gen. Nathan B. Forrest, C. S. Army, Commanding Cavalry, of the Capture of Fort Pillow," Shotgun's Home of the American Civil War, 7 January 1997, <http://www.civilwarhome.com/forrest.htm> (23 April 1999).

5. Jack Hurst, Nathan Bedford Forrest: A Biography (New York: Knopf, 1993), 174.

6. Foote, 111.

7. Cimprich and Mainfort, 305.

8. Cimprich and Mainfort, 299.

9. Foote, 110.

10. Wills, 187.

11. Albert Castel, "The Fort Pillow Massacre: A Fresh Examination of the Evidence," Civil War History 4 (1958): 44-45.

12. Cimprich and Mainfort, 300.

13. Hurst, 177.

14. Hurst, 177.

SAMPLE *CHICAGO* BIBLIOGRAPHY

Bibliography

Castel, Albert. "The Fort Pillow Massacre: A Fresh
    Examination of the Evidence." Civil War History 4
    (1958): 37-50.

Cimprich, John, and Robert C. Mainfort Jr. "Fort
    Pillow Revisited: New Evidence about an Old
    Controversy." Civil War History 28 (1982): 293-
    306.

Cornish, Dudley Taylor. The Sable Arm: Black Troops in
    the Union Army, 1861-1865. Lawrence, Kans.:
    University Press of Kansas, 1987.

Foote, Shelby. The Civil War, a Narrative: Red River
    to Appomattox. New York: Vintage, 1986.

Forrest, Nathan Bedford. "Report of Maj. Gen. Nathan
    B. Forrest, C. S. Army, Commanding Cavalry, of
    the Capture of Fort Pillow." Shotgun's Home of
    the American Civil War. 7 January 1997. <http://
    www.civilwarhome.com/forrest.htm> (23 April
    1999).

Hurst, Jack. Nathan Bedford Forrest: A Biography. New
    York: Knopf, 1993.

McPherson, James M. Battle Cry of Freedom: The Civil
    War Era. New York: Oxford University Press, 1988.

Wills, Brian Steel. A Battle from the Start: The Life
    of Nathan Bedford Forrest. New York: Harper-
    Collins, 1992.

CBE Style: Biology and Other Sciences

CBE number system

Though scientific publications document sources in similar ways, the details of presenting source information vary from journal to journal. Often publications provide prospective authors with style sheets that outline formats for presenting sources. Before submitting an article to a scientific publication, you should request its style sheet. If one is not available, examine a copy of the publication to see how sources are listed. When writing for a science course, check with your instructor about which format to use.

Biologists, zoologists, earth scientists, geneticists, and other scientists may use an author-date system of documentation (one type of author-date system is shown in the APA documentation section of this booklet). Or they may use a number system in which each source is given a number in the text. Following the text, full publication information for each numbered source is provided in a list of references. Entries in this list are given in the order in which they are mentioned in the paper.

One type of number system is outlined in *Scientific Style and Format*, published by the Council of Biology Editors (6th ed., 1994).

In the paper, the source is referenced by a superscript number:

IN-TEXT CITATION

Scientists are beginning to question the validity of linking genes to a number of human traits and disorders[1].

At the end of the paper, on a page titled "References" or "Cited References," the source is fully identified according to CBE style.

ENTRY IN THE REFERENCE LIST

```
1 Horgan J. Eugenics revisited. Sci Am 1993;
  268:122-31.
```

The number format for citing sources is less cumbersome and distracting than the author-date method, especially when you need to refer to many works one after another in the text of your paper. However, it is much less informative for the reader. If the author or publication date of a particular work is important to your discussion, you must add this information to the sentence.

```
Smith[11], studying three species of tree frogs in
South Carolina, was the first to observe. . . .
```

```
This species was not listed in early floras of New
York; however, in 1985 it was reported in a bo-
tanical survey of Chenango County[13].
```

As in the author-date format, if you need to refer to specific portions of a source, make this clear in the citation. Some writers also include the page number for a direct quotation.

```
My data thus differ markedly from Markam's study
on the same species in New York[5](Figs 2,7).
```

```
"Tailbeating" behavior, as defined by Cheevers and
Briggs[3](p 25) is. . . .
```

CBE reference list

BASIC FORMAT Center the title "References" (or "Cited References") and then list the works you have cited in the paper; do not include other works you may have read. Double-space throughout.

ORGANIZATION OF THE LIST   Number the entries in the order in which they appear in the text. If your paper contains tables or figures, you may cite them along with your text references in one numeric sequence. Or you may cite the tables and figures in a separate list, using a second numeric sequence.

AUTHORS' NAMES   Invert all authors' names. Use initials for first and middle names, with no periods after the initials and no space between them. Do not use a comma between the last name and the initials. Use all authors' names; do not use "et al."

TITLES OF BOOKS AND ARTICLES   Capitalize only the first word in the title of a book or article (along with all proper nouns). Do not underline or italicize the titles of books; do not place titles of articles in quotation marks.

TITLES OF JOURNALS   Abbreviate titles of journals that consist of more than one word. Capitalize all the words or abbreviated words in the title (for example, Science, Sci Am, J Clin Psychopharmacol). Do not underline or italicize the title.

PAGE RANGES   Abbreviate page ranges for articles in journals or periodicals and for chapters in edited volumes (for example, 51–3, 129–34). When an article appears on discontinuous pages, list all pages or page ranges (for example, 145–9, 162–74). Give the total number of pages for a book or an unpublished dissertation, followed by the abbreviation "p" (for example, 365 p).

Books

1. BASIC FORMAT FOR A BOOK   After the author(s) and title, give the place of publication, the name of the publisher, and the date of publication. End with the number of pages in the book.

Directory to CBE reference list

```
1 Melchias, G. Biodiversity and conservation. Enfield
   (NH): Science; 2001. 250 p.
```

2. TWO OR MORE AUTHORS   List the authors in the order in which they appear on the title page.

```
2 Ennos R, Sheffield E. Plant life. Boston: Blackwell
   Sci; 2000. 217.
```

3. EDITION OTHER THAN THE FIRST   Include the number of the edition after the title.

```
3 Tate RL. Soil microbiology. 2nd ed. New York: J
   Wiley; 2000. 536 p.
```

4. ARTICLE OR CHAPTER IN AN EDITED VOLUME   Begin with the name of the author and the title of the article or chapter. Then write "In:" and name the editor or editors, followed by a comma and the word "editor" or "editors." Place the title of the volume and publication information next. End with the page numbers on which the article or chapter appears.

```
4 Underwood AJ, Chapman MG. Intertidal ecosystems. In:
   Levin SA, editor. Encyclopedia of biodiversity.
   5 volumes. San Diego: Academic Pr; 2000. Vol 3:
   485-99.
```

Articles

5. ARTICLE IN A MAGAZINE   Provide the year, month, and day (for weekly publications), followed by the page numbers of the article.

```
5 Cerio G. Artificial sight. Discover 2001 Aug:50-55.
```

6. ARTICLE IN A JOURNAL PAGINATED BY VOLUME   After the author(s) and the title of the article, give the journal title, the year, the volume number, and the page numbers on which the article appears.

6 Gulbins E, Lang F. Pathogens, host-cell invasion and disease. Am Sci 2001;89:406-13.

7. ARTICLE IN A JOURNAL PAGINATED BY ISSUE If each issue of the journal begins with page 1, indicate the number of the issue in parentheses after the volume number.

7 Chang C. Sunscreen for birds. Audubon 2001;103 (4):18-20.

8. ARTICLE IN A NEWSPAPER After the name of the newspaper and the date of publication, give the section letter (or number), the page number, and the column number. If the newspaper does not have section designations, use a colon between the date and the page number.

8 O'Neil J. A closer look at medical marijuana. New York Times 2001 Jul 17;Sect D:6(col 4).

9. ARTICLE WITH MULTIPLE AUTHORS

9 Vogler DW, Kalisz S. Sex among the flowers: the distribution of plant mating systems. Evolution 2001 Jan;55[(1)]:202-4.

10. ARTICLE WITH A CORPORATE OR ANONYMOUS AUTHOR When a work has a corporate author, begin with the authoring organization, followed by the article title, journal title, year, month, volume number, issue number in parentheses, and page span.

10 National Vaccine Advisory Committee. Strategies to sustain success in childhood immunizations. Jnl Am Med Assoc 2001 Jul;282(4):363-70.

If the work's author is anonymous, begin the entry with the word "Anonymous" in brackets.

```
10 [Anonymous]. A survivor's story. Esquire
   2001;135(1):106-8.
```

Electronic sources

The sixth edition of *Scientific Style and Format*, published in 1994, does not provide extensive guidelines for citing electronic sources. However, the CBE, which plans to publish a seventh edition in 2003, recommends the guidelines recently created by the National Library of Medicine. This document, titled the *National Library of Medicine Recommended Formats for Bibliographic Citation Supplement: Internet Formats*, was published in July 2001 and is available at http://www.nlm.nih.gov/pubs/formats/internet.pdf. The guidelines included here are based on the NLM document.

11. HOME PAGE OF A WEB SITE Begin with the author, whether an individual or an organization, and the author's affiliation. Include the title of the home page, followed by the word [Internet] or the more specific phrase [homepage on the Internet]. Provide the place of publication, the publisher, and date of publication or copyright. If the name of the publishing organization appears earlier in the citation, the name may be abbreviated here as publisher (for example, the University of Arizona can appear later in the citation as "The Univ"). Include in brackets the date the page was revised or updated; provide in separate brackets the date you accessed the site: [rev May 2001; cited 27 Sep 2001]. Use the phrase "Available from:" followed by the URL. Note that only URLs that end in a slash are followed by a period.

```
11 Amer Soc of Gene Therapy [homepage on the
   Internet]. Milwaukee: The Soc; c2000-2001
   [cited 2001 Sep 18]. Available from: http://
   www.asgt.org/.
```

12. SHORT WORK FROM A WEB SITE   Begin this citation as you would a home page from a Web site, but following the author and affiliation, include the title of the short work or document followed by the bracketed word [Internet] or a more descriptive phrase such as [brochure on the Internet], [report on the Internet], or [bibliography on the Internet]. Continue the citation as you would for a home page. If you are citing a specific portion of a work and it has a distinct title or number, provide that information following your citation date (for example, "Chapter 1, environmental impact," or "Transmission of foot-and-mouth disease"). Indicate a page number, if available, or an estimate of the number of pages, screens, or lines: [about 5 p.], [about 2 screens], or [about 26 lines]. As in other electronic citations, use the phrase "Available from:" followed by the URL.

```
12 Univ of Wisconsin, Inst for Molecular Virology.
   Rhinoviruses [report on the Internet]. Madison
   (WI): The Univ; c1994-98 [rev 2000 Nov 14;
   cited 2001 Sep 20]. Icosahedral capsid [about
   3 screens]. Available from: http://
   www.bocklabs.wisc.edu/rhinovirusascii.html
```

13. ONLINE BOOK   To site an online book, referred to by the CBE as a monograph, follow the instructions for a home page, but include the description [monograph on the Internet] following the title.

```
13 Wilson DE, Reeder DM, editors. Mammal species of
   the world [monograph on the Internet]. Wash-
   ington: Smithsonian Inst Pr, c1993 [cited
   2001 Sep 18]. [about 200 screens]. Available
   from: http://www.nmnh.si.edu/cgi-bin/wdb/msw/.
```

NOTE: If you are referring to a specific chapter or section within an online book, begin the citation with the author and the title of that specific work. Follow with the word "In:"

and the author, editor, and title of the entire book, as shown
in the following example.

```
13 Liphardt J. The path to a Ph.D. In: Olson S,
   editor. Beyond bio 101: the transformation of
   undergraduate biology education [monograph on
   the Internet]. Chevy Chase (MD): Howard Hughes
   Med Inst; c2001 [cited 2001 Sep 18]. [about 2
   screens]. Available from: http://www.hhmi.org/
   beyondbio101/phdpath.htm
```

14. WORK FROM A SUBSCRIPTION SERVICE To cite the full
text of an article or other document from a subscription database (such as InfoTrac or the databases published by
EBSCO), begin with the author and affiliation, followed by
the title of the work and the original source of the work. For
an article, include the name of the journal, date, volume,
and pagination; for text from a book, include the place of
publication, publisher, and date of publication. Write "In:"
followed by information about the database. Include, if available, the database author and affiliation, the title of the database (such as Health Source: Consumer Ed), followed by
the bracketed term [Internet] or the more descriptive phrase
[database on the Internet]. Provide the place of publication,
the publisher of the database, and date of publication or
copyright of the database. Include the date the page was
updated, followed by the date you accessed the site. Include
in brackets the number of pages, if available, or an estimate
of the number of bytes, pages, screens, or lines: [about 5 p.],
[about 2 screens], [about 26 lines]. As in other electronic
citations, include the URL and availability statement. If the
database provides further locating information, such as an
accession number, include that information last (Available
from: http://www.bio.com; Accession No.: FN191001444).

14 Sinha G. A gene that heals. Popular Sci 2001
   Sep;259(3):41. In: Health Source: Consumer Ed
   [database on the Internet]. Ipswich (MA): EBSCO;
   c1984-[cited 2001 Sep 20]. [about 25 lines].
   Available from: http://ehostweb17.epnet.com/ehost.
   asp?key=204.179.122.140_8000_1570184348&site=
   ehost&return=n&custid=noble&profile=web; Accession
   No.: 4928058.

15. ARTICLE IN AN ONLINE PERIODICAL   Begin with the name
of the author and the author's affiliation followed by the title
of the article. If the article is identified as an editorial, letter,
news, or abstract, you may indicate that in brackets (The
cost of the harvest [editorial]). Next include the name of the
journal, followed by [Internet] or the more descriptive phrase
[serial on the Internet]. Follow this with special information
about the edition (such as "Internet ed."), and the date of
publication. If no publication date is given, use the copyright date preceded by a "c" with no space between (c2001).
Next include in brackets the date the piece was updated or
revised and the date you accessed it. Then provide the volume number, issue number, and page numbers with no space
between. If there are no page numbers, estimate the length,
whether in bytes, pages, screens, or lines, and include in
brackets: [about 27 p.]. Follow this information with "Available From:" and the URL.

15 Dove AW. Putting cell polarity on the map. Jnl of
   Cell Biol Online [serial on the Internet]. 2001 Aug
   6 [cited 2001 Sep 18];154(3):478. Available from:
   http://www.jcb.org/cgi/content/full/154/3/478

16. E-MAIL   Begin with the author of the message and the
author's affiliation. Next include in brackets the title, which
is the subject line of the message, followed by the bracketed

term [Internet] or the more descriptive phrase [electronic mail on the Internet]. Provide the recipient's name, preceded by the phrase "Message to:" and followed by the date and time the message was sent. Include in brackets the date you accessed the e-mail. Finally, indicate the total length of the message in screens, paragraphs, or lines: [about 3 screens].

16 McNeil T. AIDS research [electronic mail on the
    Internet]. Message to: Melanie Sherwin. 2001 Mar 2,
    10:50 am [cited 2001 Sep 24]. [about 2 screens].

17. ONLINE POSTING   Begin with the author initiating the mail message to the discussion list (a category that includes the LISTSERV, newsgroup, forum, or bulletin board), the author's affiliation, and the title of the message found in the subject line. Next use the word "In:" followed by the name of the host system. Include in brackets the word [Internet] or the more descriptive phrase [discussion list on the Internet], followed in separate brackets by the city where the discussion list is issued and the individual or organization that hosts the discussion list. Provide the date and time the message was posted, followed in brackets by the date you accessed it. Finally, indicate the total length of the message in bytes, screens, paragraphs, or lines and end with the phrase "Available from:" followed by the e-mail address by which the list can be accessed.

17 Jovelin F. Genomic sequencing. In: BIOSCI: Elec
    Newsgroup Network for Biol [discussion list on the
    Internet]. [London: Med Research Council]; 2001 Jul
    20, 1:37 pm [cited 2001 Sep 20]. [about 4 lines].
    Available from: http://www.bio.net/hypermail/
    autoseq/autoseq.200107/0024.html

Other sources (print and electronic)

The advice in this section refers to the print versions of the following sources, but in each case an example is also given for an electronic version.

18. GOVERNMENT REPORT   Begin with the name of the performing organization (such as the Nat Inst of Health), the country of origin in parentheses, and the abbreviation of the performing organization in brackets. Next include the title of the report, a description of the report, place of publication, publisher, year and month of publication, and total number of pages or volumes. After the phrase "Available from:" provide the name, city, and state of the organization that makes the report available, along with any other relevant identifying information such as a product number.

```
18 Dept of Health and Human Services (US) [DHHS].
   Diabetes: a serious public health problem, 2001.
   Public health report. Atlanta (GA): Centers for
   Disease Control and Prevention [CDC]; 2001 Apr. 4
   p. Available from: CDC, Atlanta, GA 30341-3717;
   PB99-4994.

18 Dept of Health and Human Services (US) [DHHS].
   Diabetes: a serious public health problem, 2001
   [report on the Internet]. Atlanta (GA): Centers for
   Disease Control and Prevention [CDC]; 2001 Apr
   [cited 2001 Sep 27]. [about 4 screens]. Available
   from: http://www.cdc.gov/diabetes/pubs/glance.htm;
   PB99-4994.
```

19. REPORT FROM A PRIVATE ORGANIZATION   Begin with the name of the sponsoring organization and the abbreviation of the sponsoring organization in brackets. Next include the title of the report, a description of the report, place of publi-

cation, publisher, year and month of publication, product
number (if any), and total number of pages.

19 Assoc of Chemical Biochemists [ACB]. The association of clinical biochemists annual report and
   accounts, 2001. Annual report. London: ACB; 2001
   Jan. 30 p.

19 Assoc of Chemical Biochemists [ACB]. The association of clinical biochemists annual report and
   accounts, 2001 [report on the Internet]. London:
   ACB; 2001 Jan. [about 30 screens]. Available from:
   http://www.acb.org.uk/news/annreps.htm

20. UNPUBLISHED DISSERTATION OR THESIS   After the author and title of the work, indicate the type of work in brackets. List the city and state of the institution granting the
degree, followed by the name of the institution, the date of
the degree, and the number of pages.

20 Warner DA. Phenotypes and survival of hatchling
   lizards [thesis]. Blacksburg (VA): Virginia Polytechnic Inst and State Univ; 2001 Jan 16. 125 p.

20 Warner DA. Phenotypes and survival of hatchling
   lizards [thesis on the Internet]. Blacksburg (VA):
   Virginia Polytechnic Inst and State Univ; 2001 Jan
   16 [cited 2001 Sep 27]. [125 p.]. Available from:
   http://scholar.lib.vt.edu/theses/available/etd
   -01232001-123230/.

21. CONFERENCE PUBLICATION   Begin with the author and
title of the publication. Provide the name of the conference if
it is not included in the title of the publication. Give the
dates and location of the conference, followed by publication
information and the total number of pages.

21 Ortiz-Lopez A, Rebeiz C, Ort D, Whitmarsh J. The green seed problem in canola. American Soc of Plant Physiologists [ASPP]: Plant Biology 2000 Conference; 2000 Jul 15-19; San Diego (CA): ASPP; 2001, 21 p.

21 Ortiz-Lopez A, Rebeiz C, Ort D, Whitmarsh J. The green seed problem in canola [conference paper on the Internet]. American Soc of Plant Physiologists [ASPP]: Plant Biology 2000 Conference. San Diego (CA): ASPP; 2000 Jul 15-19 [cited 2001 Sep 27]. [21 p.]. Available from: http://www.rycomusa.com/aspp2000/public/M15/1057.html

22. MAP When citing a map, the name of the area represented takes the place of the author's name. Include the title of the map and, in brackets, the type of map. Provide the place of publication, publisher, date of publication, and a brief physical description of the map: if it is a sheet map, include the number of sheets; if it is a map in an atlas, include the page span. Indicate whether the map is in color and provide its scale, if available.

22 Northeastern United States. West Nile virus: wild bird cases [demographic map]. Washington: US Dept of the Interior; 2001 Jun 1. 1 sheet, color.

22 Northeastern United States. West Nile virus: wild bird cases [demographic map on the Internet]. Washington: US Dept of the Interior; 2001 Jun 1 [cited 2001 Sep 27]. [1 screen] color. Available from: http://nationalatlas.gov/virusprint.html

23. AUDIO AND VIDEO RECORDING Begin with the title of the work, followed by a description in brackets. Next include the author, editor, and producer. Provide the place of publication in brackets, followed by the publisher and date of publication. Give a brief physical description of the work. End the citation with "Available from:" followed by the name, city, and state of the organization that makes the work available.

```
23 NOVA: Cancer warrior [videocassette]. Quade D,
     editor. WGBH Boston, producer. [Boston]: WGBH Ed
     Foundation; 2001 Feb 27. 1 videocassette: 60 min,
     sound, color. Available from: WGBH Boston Video,
     Boston, MA; NOVA #2805.

23 NOVA: Cancer warrior [video on the Internet]. Quade
     D, editor. WGBH Boston, producer. [Boston]: WGBH Ed
     Foundation; 2001 Feb 27 [cited 2001 Sep 27]. [60
     min], sound, color. Available from: wysiwyg://183/
     http://www.pbs.org/wgbh/nova/cancer/program.html;
     NOVA #2805.
```

CBE manuscript format

Although the style manual of the Council of Biology Editors does not include manuscript guidelines for student papers, most instructors will want you to format your manuscript in ways consistent with common scientific practice. The following guidelines for student writers have been adapted from CBE advice directed to professional authors. When in doubt, check with your instructor. For sample pages of a college biology paper, see pages 249–53.

MATERIALS Use good-quality $8^1/_2$" × 11" white paper. Secure the pages with a paper clip.

TITLE Begin a college paper with an unnumbered title page. Center all information on the page: the title of your paper, your name, the name of the course, and the date. See page 249 for an example.

PAGINATION Although the title page is unnumbered, treat the first page of the paper as page 2. Type the number in the top right corner of the page. Many instructors will want you to use an abbreviated form of the title of your paper before the page number.

MARGINS, SPACING, AND INDENTATION Leave margins of at least one inch on all sides of the page, and double-space throughout the paper. Indent the first line of each paragraph one-half inch (or five spaces). When a quotation is set off from the text, indent it one-half inch (or five spaces) from the left margin.

ABSTRACT Many science instructors require an abstract, a single paragraph that summarizes your paper. If your paper reports on research you conducted, use the abstract to describe research methods, findings, and conclusions. Do not include bibliographic references in the abstract.

HEADINGS CBE encourages the use of headings to help readers follow the organization of a paper. Common headings for papers reporting research are "Introduction," "Methods" (or "Methods and Materials"), "Results," and "Discussion." If you use both headings and subheadings for a long paper, make sure to distinguish clearly between them with your choice of typography.

VISUALS A visual should be placed as close as possible to the text that discusses it. In general, try to place visuals at the top of a page.

APPENDIXES Appendixes may be used for relevant information that is too long to include in the body of the paper. Label each appendix and give it a title (for example, "Appendix 1: Methodologies Used by Previous Researchers").

ACKNOWLEDGMENTS An acknowledgments section is common in scientific writing because research is often conducted with help from others. For example, you might give credit to colleagues who reviewed your work, to organizations that funded your work, and to writers who allowed you to cite their unpublished work.

LIST OF REFERENCES For advice on constructing a CBE reference list, see pages 233–46.

Sample pages: CBE style

The following sample pages are based on guidelines set forth in the CBE style manual, *Scientific Style and Format*, 6th edition, and on the guidelines for citing electronic sources provided in the *National Library of Medicine Recommended Formats for Bibliographic Citation Supplement: Internet Formats* (July 2001).

SAMPLE CBE TITLE PAGE

Hypothermia, the Diving Reflex,
and Survival

Briana Martin

Biology 281
Professor McMillan
April 17, 200-

SAMPLE CBE PAGES

Hypothermia and Diving Reflex 2

ABSTRACT

This paper reviews the contributions of hypothermia and the mammalian diving reflex (MDR) to human survival of cold-water immersion incidents. It also examines the relationship between the victim's age and MDR and considers the protective role played by hypothermia. Hypothermia is the result of a reduced metabolic rate and lowered oxygen consumption by body tissues. Although hypothermia may produce fatal cardiac arrhythmias such as ventricular fibrillation, it is also associated with bradycardia and peripheral vasoconstriction, both of which enhance oxygen supply to the heart and brain. The MDR also causes bradycardia and reduced peripheral blood flow as well as laryngospasm, which protects victims against rapid inhalation of water. Studies of drowning and near drowning of children and adults suggest that victim survival depends on the presence of both hypothermia and the MDR, as neither alone can provide adequate cerebral protection during long periods of hypoxia. Future research is suggested to improve patient care.

INTRODUCTION

Drowning and near-drowning incidents are leading causes of mortality and morbidity in both children[1] and adults[2]. Over the past 30 years, there has been considerable interest in cold-water immersion incidents, particularly the reasons why some victims survive under seemingly fatal conditions. Research suggests that both hypothermia and a "mammalian diving

Hypothermia and Diving Reflex 3

reflex" (MDR) may account for survival in many near-drowning episodes[3]. However, the extent to which these two processes interact is not fully understood. There is further controversy regarding the effect of the victim's age on the physiological responses to cold-water immersion. In this paper, I provide an overview of recent research on the protective value of hypo-thermia and the MDR in cold-water immersions. I also examine hypotheses concerning the effects of age on these processes and conclude with suggestions about future lines of research that may lead to improved patient care.

Hypoxia during drowning and near-drowning incidents

The major physiological problem facing drowning victims is hypoxia, or lack of adequate oxygen perfu-sion to body cells[4]. Hypoxia results in damage to many organs, including the heart, lungs, kidneys, liver, and intestines[5]. Generally, the length of time the body has been deprived of oxygen is closely related to patient prognosis. Only 6-7 minutes of hypoxia may cause unconsciousness; if hypoxia lasts longer than 5 minutes at relatively warm temperatures, the result may be death or irreversible brain damage[6]. However, some victims of cold-water immersion have survived after periods of oxygen deprivation lasting up to two hours.[7] . . .

[*The student goes on to highlight the major controversies and to add interpretation and analysis.*]

Hypothermia and Diving Reflex 4

CONCLUSIONS

Recent research on cold-water immersion incidents has provided a more complete understanding of the physiological processes occurring during drowning and near-drowning accidents. Current findings suggest that the cooperative effect of the MDR and hypothermia plays a critical role in patient survival during a cold-water immersion incident. However, the relationship between the two processes is still unclear. Because it is impossible to provide an exact reproduction of a particular drowning incident within the laboratory, research is hampered by the lack of complete details. Consequently, it is difficult to draw comparisons among published case studies.

More complete and accurate documentation of cold-water immersion incidents--including time of submersion, time of recovery, and a profile of the victim including age, sex, and physical condition--will facilitate easier comparison of individual situations and lead to a more complete knowledge of the processes affecting long-term survival rates for drowning victims. Once we have a clearer understanding of the relationship between hypothermia and the MDR--and of the effect of other factors--physicians and rescue personnel can take steps to improve patient care at the scene and in the hospital.

ACKNOWLEDGMENTS

I would like to thank V. McMillan and D. Huerta for their support, suggestions, and patience through-

Hypothermia and Diving Reflex 5

out the research and writing of this paper. I am also grateful to my classmates in COMP 281 for their thoughtful comments during writing workshops. Finally, I thank Colgate's reference librarians for their tireless efforts to secure the sources I needed for this paper.

SAMPLE CBE LIST OF REFERENCES

CITED REFERENCES

1   Kallas HJ, O'Rourke PP. Drowning and immersion injuries in children. Curr Opin Pediatr [serial on the Internet]. 2000 Sep [cited 2001 Sep 27]; 5:295-302. Available from: http://www.cop.org/drn/text

2   Keatinge WR. Accidental immersion hypothermia and drowning. Practitioner 2000;219:183-7.

3   Gooden BA. Why some people do not drown--hypothermia versus the diving response. Med J [serial on the Internet]. 2001 Aug [cited 2001 Sep 4]; 157:629-32. Available from: http://www.medjourn.org/hypth/text001

4   Gooden BA. Drowning and the diving reflex in man. Med J [serial on the Internet]. 2000 Jul [cited 2001 Sep 7]; 2:583-7. Available from: http://www.medjourn.org/drn/text024

5   Biggart MJ, Bohn DJ. Effect of hypothermia and cardiac arrest on outcome of near-drowning accidents in children. J Pediatr 2000;117:179-83. In: Health Source: Consumer Ed [database on the Internet]. Ipswich (MA): EBSCO; c1984- [cited 2001 Sep 20]. [about 5 screens]. Available from: http://ehostweb17.epnet.com/ehost.asp?key-0043964; Accession No.: 4396401.

6   Bierens JJ, van der Velde EA. Submersion in the Netherlands: prognostic indicators and the results of resuscitation. Ann Emerg Med 2001;19(12):1390-5.

7   Ramey CA, Ramey DN, Hayward JS. Dive response of children in relation to cold-water near drowning. J Appl Physiol 2001;62(2):665-8.

List of Style Manuals

Research and Documentation, 3rd edition, describes four commonly used systems of documentation: MLA, used in English and the humanities (see p. 126); APA, used in psychology and the social sciences (see p. 176); *Chicago*, used primarily in history (see p. 209); and CBE, used in the sciences (see p. 232). Following is a list of style manuals used in a variety of disciplines.

BIOLOGY (SEE P. 232)

Council of Biology Editors. *Scientific Style and Format: The CBE Manual for Authors, Editors, and Publishers.* 6th ed. New York: Cambridge UP, 1994.

CHEMISTRY

Dodd, Janet S., ed. *The ACS Style Guide: A Manual for Authors and Editors.* 2nd ed. Washington: Amer. Chemical Soc., 1997.

ENGINEERING

Institute of Electrical and Electronics Engineers. *IEEE Standards Style Manual.* 7th ed. New York: IEEE, 2000.

ENGLISH AND THE HUMANITIES (SEE P. 126)

Gibaldi, Joseph. *MLA Handbook for Writers of Research Papers.* 5th ed. New York: MLA, 1999.

GEOLOGY

Bates, Robert L., Rex Buchanan, and Marla Adkins-Heljeson, eds. *Geowriting: A Guide to Writing, Editing, and Printing in Earth Science.* 5th ed. Alexandria: Amer. Geological Inst., 1995.

GOVERNMENT DOCUMENTS

Garner, Diane L. *The Complete Guide to Citing Government Information Resources: A Manual for Writers and Librarians.* Rev. ed. Bethesda: Congressional Information Service, 1993.

United States Government Printing Office. *Style Manual.* Washington: GPO, 2000.

HISTORY (SEE P. 209)

The Chicago Manual of Style. 14th ed. Chicago: U of Chicago P, 1993.

JOURNALISM

Goldstein, Norm, ed. *Associated Press Stylebook and Briefing on Media Law.* 35th ed. New York: Associated Press, 2000.

LAW

Harvard Law Review et al. *The Bluebook: A Uniform System of Citation.* 17th ed. Cambridge: Harvard Law Rev. Assn., 2000.

LINGUISTICS

Linguistic Society of America. "LSA Style Sheet." Published annually in the December issue of the *LSA Bulletin.*

MATHEMATICS

American Mathematical Society. *The AMS Author Handbook: General Instructions for Preparing Manuscripts.* Rev. ed. Providence: AMS, 1996.

MEDICINE

Iverson, Cheryl, et al. *American Medical Association Manual of Style: A Guide for Authors and Editors.* 9th ed. Baltimore: Williams, 1998.

MUSIC

Holoman, D. Kern, ed. *Writing about Music: A Style Sheet from the Editors of* 19th-Century Music. Berkeley: U of California P, 1988.

PHYSICS

American Institute of Physics. *Style Manual: Instructions to Authors and Volume Editors for the Preparation of AIP Book Manuscripts.* 5th ed. New York: AIP, 1995.

POLITICAL SCIENCE

American Political Science Association. *Style Manual for Political Science.* Rev. ed. Washington: APSA, 1993.

PSYCHOLOGY AND OTHER SOCIAL SCIENCES (SEE P. 176)

American Psychological Association. *Publication Manual of the American Psychological Association.* 5th ed. Washington: APA, 2001.

SCIENCE AND TECHNICAL WRITING

American National Standard for the Preparation of Scientific Papers for Written or Oral Presentation. New York: Amer. Natl. Standards Inst., 1979.

Rubens, Philip, ed. *Science and Technical Writing: A Manual of Style.* 2nd ed. New York: Routledge, 2001.

SOCIAL WORK

National Association of Social Workers. *Writing for NASW Press: Information for Authors.* Rev. ed. Washington: Natl. Assn. of Social Workers Press, 1995.

PART V. GLOSSARY OF LIBRARY AND WEB TERMS

abstract A summary of an article. An abstract often appears at the beginning of a scholarly or technical article. Databases and indexes often contain abstracts that can help you decide whether an article is relevant for your purposes. Examples include *Chemical Abstracts* and *Psychological Abstracts.*

annotated bibliography A list of sources giving information about each and adding a short description of the item. In some bibliographies the annotation merely describes the content and scope of the item listed; in others the annotation also evaluates its quality.

anthology A collection of writings compiled into a book.

asynchronous communication Communication in which sending, reading, and responding to messages is not simultaneous. E-mail is a form of asynchronous communication; chat is synchronous.

attachment A file sent along with an e-mail message. If the attached file is encoded, transmitted, and decoded properly, the receiver of the e-mail can open the file in its original format. Attachments are sometimes unusable because of differences in hardware or software configurations between a sender and a receiver. They are also used as a means of transmitting computer viruses; network administrators typically advise users to open attachments only if they know the sender and expect an attachment and if the message to which it is attached seems legitimate.

bibliography (1) A list of sources, usually appearing at the end of a research paper, an article, a book, or a chapter in a book that documents evidence used in the work and points out sources that might be useful for further research. Each entry provides enough information about each source so that a reader can track it down. (2) A list of recommended readings on a given topic, usually sorted into subcategories.

bookmark (1) A function in a Web browser that allows users to mark frequently visited Web sites for easy accessibility. When a site is bookmarked, the site's URL is added to a list that the user can return to later. (2) A tag used in a Web page that links directly to a part of the Web page.

Boolean operators The words *and, or,* and *not* used in databases or search engines to relate the contents of two or more sets of data in different ways. When sets are combined with *and,* the resulting set contains only those items that are found in all the sets. When *or* is used, the resulting set includes all items from all sets. *Not* is used to exclude items in one set from the combination of sets.

call number The letter and number combination that indicates where a book is kept on a library's shelves. Call numbers are assigned using a system that locates books on the same subject next to each other for easy browsing. Most academic libraries use the Library of Congress (LC) system; public libraries typically use the Dewey decimal system.

catalog A database containing information about the materials owned by a library and their location. Most catalogs are now computerized, though a library may have all or part of its catalog on cards. Catalogs can usually be searched by author, title, subject heading, or keyword and provide a basic description of the item (book, journal title, video, or other) and a call number.

chat A type of synchronous communication across the Internet in which people communicate with others in real time by typing messages that are posted for all members of the chat to see.

citation A reference to a book, article, Web page, or other source that provides enough information to allow a reader to retrieve the source. Citations in a paper must be given in a standard format (such as MLA, APA, *Chicago*, CBE, or another citation and documentation style).

citation trail   A process used by researchers to track down additional sources on a topic. The tracing of citations to reference works is sometimes referred to as following the path of a "citation trail" or "citation network."

cite   (1) As a verb, to provide a reference to a source. (2) As a noun, a shortened form of *citation.* (**Note:** This term is frequently misused when referring to Web *sites.*)

controlled vocabulary   Descriptive words added to the items in a database that make it easier for researchers to find works on a particular topic. When compilers of a database decide on which words to use in these descriptions (called *descriptors* or *subject headings*), they control the vocabulary users of the database will use. Researchers will retrieve more items searching with controlled vocabulary than they will using synonyms. *See also* **descriptors** and **subject heading**.

corporate author   An organization, an agency, an institution, or a corporation identified as an author of a work. Corporate authors are listed as authors in a citation.

database   A collection of data organized for retrieval. In libraries, databases usually contain references to sources retrievable by a variety of means. Databases may contain bibliographic citations, descriptive abstracts, full-text documents, or a combination.

descriptors   Terms assigned by indexers of a database to describe the subject content of a document. For example, the *PsycLit* database uses *academic achievement* as a descriptor to help researchers locate texts on the subject of scholastic achievement or grade-point average. Descriptors are chosen so that all of the work on that topic can be found with a single word or phrase, even though there may be many different ways of expressing the same idea.

discipline An academic field of study such as history, psychology, or biology. Often books and articles published by members of a discipline intended for other scholars are called *the literature of the discipline* — referring not to literary expression but to research publications in the field.

discussion list An e-mail-based asynchronous conversation among members of a group with a shared interest. E-mail messages are posted to all members of a group using software protocols such as Listserv or Majordomo. Participants have the opportunity to hold a wide-ranging discussion on a common topic with hundreds of others. *See also* **asynchronous communication**.

domain The portion of a URL that indicates the type of Internet server for a Web site or the country where it is located. Common domains are *.edu* (higher education), *.gov* (U.S. federal government), and *.com* (commercial). Recently created domains include *.name* and *.info.* Country domains are two-letter abbreviations such as *.uk* for United Kingdom and *.fr* for France.

fair use A limited set of exemptions to copyright law. Copyright law protects authors and other owners of intellectual property so their expression of ideas cannot be copied by others without payment. Some exemptions to these protections are allowed under the law for limited reproduction of texts for educational purposes.

field A particular area, as in a record in a database, in which the same type of information is regularly recorded. A field in an article database may contain the titles of articles, for example, while another field may contain the names of journals the articles are in. Some search engines allow a user to limit a search to one or more specific fields.

FirstSearch A subscription service that provides access to a number of databases through a common interface. Many academic libraries subscribe to the service, though each chooses which databases it will allow users to search. Access is usually provided through the library's Web page.

full texts Complete documents from databases and Web sites. (**Note:** Illustrations or diagrams may be omitted from a full-text document.) Some databases run searches through full-text documents; others search only the citation or abstract. In some cases researchers can set their own preferences.

hits The list of results called up by a search of a database or the Internet. (**Note:** *Hits* also refers to the number of times a Web site has been visited. Webmasters track hits as a measure of the popularity of a site.)

holdings The exact items a library owns. The term is most typically used to refer to the specific issues of a magazine or journal in a library. This information is often listed in a library's catalog as a *holdings statement.*

index (1) In a book, the alphabetical listing of topics and the pages on which information on them can be found. The index is located at the back of the book. (2) A publication that lists articles or other publications by topic. (3) An alphabetical listing of elements that can be found in a database.

intellectual property The expression of ideas defined by federal and international law as property. Though ideas themselves cannot be owned, the manner in which a particular author, film director, or other creator expresses ideas belongs to him or her and is protected by copyright law from unauthorized reproduction. Materials in the public domain are freely available. Those that are not in the public domain have stringent restrictions (called *fair use*) on how much of a work and under what circumstances copies can be made without payment to the owner. *See also* **fair use** and **public domain**.

IP address A unique numeric identification for every network or computer connected to the Internet. Each IP address consists of four sets of numbers separated by dots. IP addresses for servers hosting Web sites are paired with an alpha-numeric address that users can type into a browser to retrieve the sites.

IP recognition The method by which a subscription service (such as a database) recognizes its subscribers (such as a college library or an individual licensed and authorized to use the database). Many subscription databases, such as *FirstSearch*, identify legitimate users by matching their IP address to a list of subscribing institutions. To access services using IP recognition, users generally must be connected to the Internet through the subscribing institution.

ISP (Internet service provider) A company or organization that provides a connection to the Internet for a group of subscribers. Universities provide Internet services for their communities; AOL and Earthlink are examples of commercial ISPs.

journal A publication containing articles that is issued at regular intervals. Journals are usually written for more specialized or scholarly audiences than magazines.

keyword A word used to search a library database or the Internet. Keyword searches locate results by matching the search word to an item in the database or at the Internet site. For example, a search term using the keyword *third world* will find items with that exact term but may not include related items that use the term *developing countries*. Keyword searches often search very broadly through many database fields. However, researchers who perform a keyword search using terms that are different from those used in the database will not retrieve all of the information in the database related to their topic. *See also* **controlled vocabulary**.

library catalog. *See* **catalog**.

licensed database. *See* **subscription database**.

LISTSERV. *See* **discussion list**.

literature review A descriptive survey of research on a particular topic. Often articles include a literature review section to place their research in the context of other work in the field and to call readers' attention to related work. *See also* **review article**.

magazine　A publication containing articles that is issued at regular intervals. Magazines are generally written for general and popular audiences, are sold on newsstands or by subscription, and earn a part of their revenue through advertising.

meta-search engine　A search engine that sends a request for information to several search engines and compiles the results.

microforms　Formats that reduce texts and reproduce them on plastic film that can be read on a special machine. Microfilm puts pages of text on a continuous strip of film; microfiche puts the pages on flat sheets of film.

MOO (multi-user domain, object-oriented)　A synchronous communication program that allows participants to interact while moving around a virtual space and manipulating virtual objects. MOOs are typically used for educational conferencing and are an extension of MUD systems.

MUD (multi-user dimension)　A synchronous communication program that creates a virtual place where people can take on fictitious identities and communicate with others, usually in a game atmosphere — the basis of MOOs.

newsgroup　An online forum that allows the public to post and read messages on a particular topic.

online catalog. *See* **catalog**.

OPAC (online public access catalog). *See* **catalog**.

peer review　A process during which a group of experts examine a document before it is published to determine whether it is worthy of publication. A peer review process — usually arranged so that the reviewers don't know who the author is — helps provide quality filters for journals and other publications. *See also* **refereed publication.**

periodical　A regularly published magazine, journal, newspaper, or newsletter.

periodical index An index to articles in magazines, journals, newspapers, and newsletters. Many periodical indexes are available as electronic databases, though many electronic versions are limited to articles published in the last ten or twenty years. Print indexes often include all years of a periodical's publication.

plagiarism The unattributed use of a source of information that is not considered common knowledge. Three acts are considered plagiarism: (1) failing to cite quotations and borrowed ideas, (2) failing to enclose borrowed language in quotation marks, and (3) failing to put summaries and paraphrases in your own words.

plug-in A small program that can be downloaded to give a browser additional capabilities, such as the ability to play audio files or display special graphics formats.

primary source An original source, such as a speech, diary, novel, legislative bill, laboratory study, field research report, or eyewitness account. While not necessarily more reliable than a secondary source, a primary source has the advantage of being closely related to the information it conveys and as such is often considered essential for research, particularly in history.

professional journal A journal addressed to a particular professional audience such as doctors, lawyers, teachers, engineers, or accountants.

public domain The status of works that are freely available and not governed by copyright restrictions. Most government documents are in the public domain, as are works for which copyright has expired. Many classic works of literature and primary sources available in full text on the Internet are in the public domain and thus can be copied without restriction. However, many (if not most) of the texts and other works in print and on the Internet are protected by copyright law; users must request permission of the copyright holder to reproduce such works. *See also* **fair use** and **intellectual property**.

record   Each item included in a database. Records contain the information about the books, articles, or other sources that users can search for in a database.

refereed publication   A publication for which every submission is screened through a peer review process. Refereed publications are considered authoritative because disinterested experts have reviewed the material in advance of publication to determine its quality.

reference (1) A source used in research and referred to by a researcher. (2) In libraries, a part of the library's collection that includes encyclopedias, handbooks, directories, and other publications that are useful in research for finding overviews of information and facts. (**Note:** *Reference* may also indicate a desk or counter where librarians provide assistance to researchers.)

review article   An article that evaluates the published research on a topic. The purpose of a review article is to select the most important publications on the topic, sort them into categories, and comment on them so that a researcher can gain a quick overview of the state of the art in that area.

scholarly journal   A journal that is primarily addressed to scholars, often focusing on a particular discipline. Scholarly journals tend to be refereed publications and for some purposes may be considered more authoritative than magazines. Scholarly journals tend to have articles that are substantial in length, use specialized language, contain footnotes or endnotes, and are written by researchers (whose academic credentials are often provided) rather than by journalists. *See also* **refereed publications**.

search engine   A program that allows users to search for material on the Web or at a specific Web site. Sometimes the search function of a database is called its search engine.

secondary source   A source that comments on or relies on primary sources. An article in a newspaper that reports on a scientific discovery or a book that analyzes a writer's work is a secondary source.

serial   A term used in libraries to encompass all publications that appear in a series: magazines, journals, newspapers, and books that are published in a regular series such as annual reviews.

server   A host computer that is linked to other computers over a network. A corporation may have one server through which users have access to the Internet, e-mail, data files, databases, and software. A computer that hosts Web sites is also called a server.

subject heading   A descriptive word or phrase assigned to an item in a database using controlled vocabulary. Most academic library catalogs use *The Library of Congress Subject Headings* to describe the subjects of books in the catalog. Other databases create their own list, or thesaurus, of accepted descriptive terms. In some databases subject headings are called descriptors. Researchers can benefit by examining subject headings as they search a catalog or database. Subject headings provide content information that can help the researcher evaluate whether a book or article is worth further examination. Subject headings also suggest alternative terms or phrases to use in a search.

subscription database   A database that can be accessed or licensed only through a subscription. Libraries provide a wealth of information freely to their patrons, but most of the electronic materials they provide are paid for by the library through a subscription. Often the material provided in a subscription database is more selective and quality controlled than sources that are freely available on the Web. Because databases are often provided through a license agreement, these databases are sometimes referred to as *licensed databases.*

synchronous communication   Communication in which messages are sent, received, and responded to simultaneously. Online chat is a form of synchronous communication.

thesaurus   A list of subject headings or descriptors that are used in a particular catalog or database to describe the subject matter of each item. A thesaurus is useful to researchers because it identifies which term among a variety of available synonyms has been used by the database compilers to describe a subject. Some databases provide a searchable thesaurus that helps researchers choose the most effective search terms before they start searching.

thread   A list of postings in electronic communications that deal with a common topic. A thread is usually used in the context of newsgroups and discussion lists and often contains a common or slowly evolving subject line.

truncation   In online research, a shortened version of a search term. In some search engines and databases, the root of a word plus a wild card symbol (such as an asterisk or a question mark) can be used to search all possible variations of the root. For example, the search term psycholog* will find instances of the terms *psychology, psychologist,* and *psychological.*

URL   (uniform resource locator)   A Web address, such as <http://www.bedfordstmartins.com/hacker/resdoc>. The components of a URL are a protocol type (such as *http* or *telnet*), a host or server name (*www* in this case), a domain name (*bedfordstmartins*), and an extension of letters and/or numbers to identify exact Web pages within the domain.

wild card   A symbol used to substitute any letter or combination of letters in a search word or phrase. A wild card symbol may replace a single letter (as in *wom*n,* to search for *women* or *woman* in one search) or any number of letters (as in psycholog*, to search for *psychology, psychologist,* and *psychological*). Though an asterisk is frequently used as a wild card symbol, some databases use other symbols such as a question mark or an exclamation point. S*ee also* **truncation**.

Authors' names   Reverse the order of all authors' names. Use initials for first and middle names, with no periods or spaces.

Spier RE, Griffiths JB.

When author is an organization or government agency, provide the group's name.

National Vaccine Advisory Committee.

When the author is anonymous, begin with the word *Anonymous* in brackets.

Titles   Capitalize only the first word and proper nouns for books, periodicals, and Web sites. Do not underline, italicize, or place titles in quotation marks. Abbreviate journal titles of more than one word.

* *Book:*

  Biodiversity and conservation.

* *Article in a periodical:*

  Artificial sight. Discover

* *Article from an online periodical or subscription service:*

  A gene that heals. Popular Sci

* *Short work from a Web site:*

  Rhinoviruses [report on the Internet].

Publisher, dates of publication and retrieval

* *Book:* Give the publisher's location, an abbreviated version of its name, and the publication date.

  Harvard Univ Pr; 2001.

* *Article in a periodical:* Follow the periodical title with the publication date.

  Discover 2001 Aug

* *Article in an online periodical:* Follow the periodical title with the phrase *serial on the Internet* (or *Internet*) in brackets. Provide the publication date and the retrieval date (in brackets). End with the URL.

  Jnl of Cell Biol Online [serial on the Internet]. 2001 Aug 6 [cited 2001 Sep 18]; 154(3):478. Available from: http://www.jcb.org/cgi/content/ful/154/3/478

* *Article retrieved from a subscription service:* Follow the periodical title with the publication date and volume, issue, and page numbers. Provide the database title with *database on the Internet* (or *Internet*) in brackets. Give the publisher's location and name and the database copyright date. Include (in brackets) the retrieval date and an estimate of the number of screens or lines. Follow the URL with the accession number.

  Popular Sci 2001 Sep; 259(3):41. In: Health Source: Consumer Ed [database on the Internet]. Ipswich (MA): EBSCO; c1984- [cited 2001 Sep 20]. [about 25 lines]. Available from: http://ehostweb17.epnet.com/ehost.asp?key=204; Accession No.: 4928058.

Page numbers   If *consecutive*, provide the range (e.g., 310–30, 22–4). If *nonconsecutive*, list all pages (e.g., 7, 8–12). If *no page numbers*, estimate the number of screens or lines being cited, in brackets (e.g., [about 10 screens]).

Authors' names   Reverse the order of the first author's name. Use first and last names and middle initials.

Riordon, William, L., and Anne Gund

When the author is an organization or government agency, provide the group's name.

U.S. Department of State

When the author cannot be determined, begin with the work's title.

Titles   Capitalize all major words. Underline or italicize titles of books, periodicals, and Web sites. Place titles of articles or short works from Web sites in quotation marks (followed by the title of the periodical or Web site).

- *Book:*

   A First Draft of History.

- *Article in a periodical:*

   "Radiation in Russia." U.S. News and World Report

- *Article from an online periodical or subscription service:*

   "Democracy Held Hostage." Salon.com.

- *Short work from a Web site:*

   "Historical Background." Garden and Forest.

Publisher, dates of publication and retrieval

- *Book:* Give the publisher's location and full name followed by the date.

   New York: Knopf, 2001.
   New Haven: Yale University Press, 2000.

- *Article in a periodical:* Follow the title or volume number with publication date.

   New Yorker, 24 September 2001
   College English, 72 (2001)

- *Article from an online periodical:* Follow the title of the periodical with the date of publication, the URL, and the retrieval date.

   Salon.com. 29 September 2001. <http://www.salon.com/news/feature/
      2001/09/20/democracy.index.html> (29 October 2001).

- *Article retrieved from a subscription service:* Follow the periodical title with as much information as is available, followed by the name of the database (underlined) and service, and retrieval date.

   Journal of Social History 34, no. 2 (2000): 261. Expanded Academic ASAP,
      InfoTrac (20 March 2001).

Page numbers   If *consecutive*, provide the range of pages (e.g., 210–43; 399–401). If *nonconsecutive*, do not include them in the bibliography. (However, do include nonconsecutive page numbers in any notes.) If no page numbers are given, provide the section heading.

Authors' names   Reverse the order of all authors' names. Use initials for first and middle names. Use an ampersand (&) for *and*.

> Goodglass, H., & Blumstein, S.

When author is an organization or government agency, provide the group's name.

> American Psychiatric Association.

When the author cannot be determined, begin with the work's title.

Titles   Capitalize the first word and proper nouns for books, articles, and other short works. Capitalize all major words for journals. Italicize the titles of books, journals, and short works from Web sites. Do not put article titles in quotation marks.

- *Book:*

  The lost children of Wilder: The epic struggle to change foster care.

- *Article in a periodical:*

  Lead therapy won't help most kids. *Science News*

- *Article from an online periodical or subscription service:*

  Comprehension skills of language-competent apes [Electronic version]. *Language and Communication*

- *Short work from a Web site:*

  Exploring nonverbal communication.

Publisher, dates of publication and retrieval

- *Book:* Follow the author's name with the publication date. Follow the title with the publisher's location and name in brief form. (Spell out *University Press*.)

  Bernstein, N. (2001). *The lost children of Wilder: The epic struggle to change foster care.* New York: Pantheon.

- *Article in a periodical:* Follow the author's name with the year, month, and day of publication. Include the volume number after the article's title, in italics.

  Roloff, J. (2001, May 12). Lead therapy won't help most kids. *Science News, 159,* 292.

- *Article from an online periodical:* For an online article with a print counterpart, no URL is needed; instead, include [Electronic version] following the title. For an online article without a print counterpart, include the retrieval date and the URL.

  Ashe, D. D., & McCutcheon, L. E. (2001, May 4). Shyness, loneliness, and attitude toward celebrities. *Current Research in Social Psychology, 6*(9). Retrieved July 3, 2001, from http://www.uiowa.edu/~grpproc/crisp.htm.

- *Article retrieved from a subscription service:* Include the retrieval date, name of database, and document number (if available).

  Holiday, R. E., & Hayes, B. K. (2001, January). Dissociating automatic and intentional processes in children's eyewitness memory. *Journal of Experimental Child Psychology 75*(1), 1-5. Retrieved February 21, 2001, from Expanded Academic ASAP database (A59317972).

Page numbers   If *consecutive*, provide range (e.g., 310–330). If *nonconsecutive*, list all pages (e.g., 7–10, 210–222). If *no page numbers*, provide paragraph or section numbers.